ON
POLITICAL
WAR

Paul A. Smith, Jr

ON
POLITICAL
WAR

National Defense University Press
Washington DC

National Defense University Press Publications

To increase general knowledge and inform discussion, NDU Press publishes books on subjects relating to US national security.

Each year, the National Defense University, through the Institute for National Strategic Studies, hosts about two dozen Senior Fellows who engage in original research on national security issues. NDU Press publishes the best of this research.

In addition, the Press publishes other especially timely or distinguished writing on national security, as well as new editions of out-of-print defense classics, and books based on University-sponsored conferences concerning national security affairs.

Opinions, conclusions, and recommendations expressed or implied in this volume are solely those of the author and do not necessarily represent the views of the National Defense University, the Department of Defense, or any other government agency.

William A. Palmer Jr., Cheltenham, Maryland, proofread page proofs of this book. Renee Loeffler, System Analytics of Virginia, Inc., Reston, Virginia, prepared the index.

NDU Press publications are sold by the US Government Printing Office. For ordering information, call (202) 783-3238 or write to Superintendent of Documents, US Government Printing Office, Washington DC 20402.

First printing, December 1989.

Library of Congress Cataloging-in-Publication Data

Smith, Paul A., 1925–
    On political war / Paul A. Smith, Jr.
      p. cm.
    Includes bibliographical references.
    1. World politics. 2. War. I. Title.
D32.S65   1989
327'.09'04—dc20   89–13146
                                  CIP

For war consisteth not in battle only, or the act of fighting; but in a tract of time where the will to contend by battle is sufficiently known.

—Thomas Hobbes, *Leviathan*, 1651

CONTENTS

FOREWORD

Warfare is often defined as the employment of military means to advance political ends. So understood, conventional warfare may be seen as one military means to ensure national survival and pursue national advantage. Another, more subtle, means—political warfare—uses images, ideas, speeches, slogans, propaganda, economic pressures, even advertising techniques to influence the political will of an adversary.

Through political warfare, a nation can express its vision of the world as well as its sense of what particular role it intends to play within the international setting. Major political warfare campaigns often target an adversary's populace as a whole. In an effort to isolate an adversary, they may address that adversary's allies and neutral or nonaligned nations as well. And, working through client states, a nation may influence a broad range of events without actually involving itself directly in conventional armed conflict.

In this study of political warfare in the Western world, Paul A. Smith, Jr, traces the development of political warfare since antiquity. His grasp of history, literature, art, politics, and armed conflict comprehensively informs his contention that political warfare is often as crucial to national survival as the massing of great land, sea, and air power. Now that the Soviets' 40-year campaign of aggression, intimidation, and hegemony is in apparent retreat and the world is increasingly beset by low-intensity conflict and struggles for economic domination, political warfare will be at the forefront of our national security agenda.

James A. Baldwin
Vice Admiral, USN
President, National Defense
University

PREFACE

On a slow day in the mid-1970s, an Air Force officer walked into my office in the old US Information Agency building on Pennsylvania Avenue and asked if he could talk to me a bit about communism. Because I happened to be the editor of a magazine called *Problems of Communism*, his request seemed reasonable enough. We chatted, and he eventually asked if I would be willing to give a lecture on Soviet strategic propaganda. Western strategic propaganda, my visitor said, would be discussed on the same day and could I suggest someone to handle that topic? Or would I prefer to do the West as well? I hastily mentioned the name of another scholar, pointing out that his office was merely two blocks away and adding that he was much better positioned than I to say what the West—however defined—might think to be strategic propaganda. The Soviet case, I said, would be quite enough for me.

Over the next decade, I and a series of friends from other agencies lectured regularly to the Air Force Special Operations School and to a number of other service schools, both civilian and military. Soon all concerned saw clearly that I had much the easier task. The Soviets, whatever else one may think of them, have this much to be said about them: they have a theory and they try—however imperfectly—to act in accordance with it. The West at that time seemed to have little will to compete in the area of propaganda, and often seemed convinced that it should not try. The result was an enduring asymmetry that allowed me to describe fairly clearly the Soviet case if only by citing their record of words and deeds, whereas my partner could at best explain what he thought perhaps could be done if the West really took the challenge seriously.

This situation was manifestly unsatisfactory to most of our audience, who, whatever their world outlook (and they varied greatly), were engaged in a profession of arms which involved spending large sums of tax money, and risking their lives, on the premise that there was a threat of some kind. The Soviets, in their usual obliging manner, demonstrated on several occasions, such as in 1979 and 1980 in Afghanistan and Poland, not to mention their strategic arms construction programs and vigorous propaganda campaigns, that the threat was real. My task, at least, continued to be relatively easy—depressingly easy.

Why—I found myself asking after watching a decade of service school faculty and their students rotate through their assignments—why did they always ask the same questions? And why could we not provide better or at least fuller answers? Notable among the questions were these:

- What is propaganda, and why do the Soviets use it so aggressively and persistently?
- What does the West do to defend itself?
- Is the Western posture always and only defensive? Has it ever been otherwise?
- What is the likely outcome if the present asymmetry continues?

Beyond these questions, there is today, as this book goes to press, the issue of Mikhail Gorbachev's reforms, and what they may mean for future patterns of Soviet behavior in the conduct of political war. Gorbachev's program also includes a number of declaratory statements and some personnel changes suggesting an intention to depart from the traditional principles of class hatred embedded in Leninist doctrine and to substitute for them a less aggressively hostile principle on which to base relations with non-Marxist polities and societies. If these changes are followed through to their logical conclusion, they will bring shifts in the foreign and defense policy of the Communist Party of the Soviet Union and the Soviet state, leading to a significant reorientation—and possibly a major abatement—of Soviet political warfare operations against the West.

Whether any government in Moscow will ever completely abandon political warfare is, in my view, doubtful indeed. Nor, to be fair, will any other modern nation. Gorbachev cannot change the past. He cannot, or should not, be allowed to alter our perception of that past as we know it from the historical record, except possibly to reveal details that we inferred but could not fully document. Revisionists of various persuasions may attempt such a reprise, but I do not think they will succeed, over time, in altering much in the basic realities of history. Efforts by Moscow to distort or continue to conceal the truth by refusing free access to party and state archives through which such an assessment can be tested will only make a mockery of the proclaimed principles of openness. As of this writing, we are still far—very far—from seeing any such measure of authentic openness.

If Gorbachev's gamble—and it is a gamble—succeeds, it will be important to have a clear idea of how and why it has been undertaken. For that, we will need to be quite clear about the record. If the gamble misfires, or goes awry in any of several ominous directions, we will need to watch carefully the connections between new Soviet programs of political warfare and past Soviet activities.

There is no way to guarantee a future free of political warfare conducted by other and possibly still more formidable international actors, Russian or otherwise. We will always need accounts of past wars, battles, and campaigns to provide perspective and instruction. This book seeks to provide a background and a conceptual framework for interpreting the record of political warfare in both the Eastern and Western halves of European—including Russian and American—culture, and to do so with as much objectivity and detachment as possible in the face of the changes now being announced, daily, by the Soviet press.

In this book, I seek to offer some answers to the questions posed by the Soviet past as well as those of the present. I do so from a descriptive viewpoint. Most of my students, I found, shared my reluctance to become involved in policy recommendations. As public servants, they and I were quite willing, however we might vote or make known our personal views, to let the Congress and the president decide what *ought* to be done. For our needs, we wanted to be a little more sure that we understood what in fact *was* being done. And to understand that, we needed first to be clear as to what *had* been done, by both the East and the West.

Some historical perspective appeared necessary. On reflection, it seemed that it should be a long perspective. Of all large-scale human activities, politics and war are the most deeply embedded in the cultural patterns of the nations which practice them. To describe the East-West political conflict in the idiom of modern systems analysis seemed to me excessively abstract and divorced from the reality that I knew from personal experience—and that I knew my students would have to face.

Long perspectives, alas, do not fit easily into the curricula and reading time available at service schools. My task was thus one of compression and clarity, but also one of objectivity and accuracy. With that in mind, I chose a series of case studies from periods of history, appropriate, I hope, to the present day, and necessarily in the cultural and political traditions of the two great antagonists now dominating the international scene. Some readers might challenge the result as either too little or too much. What, I can hear it asked, do the rhetoric of Aristotle and the politics of his patron, Alexander of Macedon, have to do with the cut and thrust of political conflict today? The short answer, I submit, is, a great deal. For a longer answer, I suggest this book.

ACKNOWLEDGMENTS

A number of people—as noted below—took time from busy schedules to share their experience and views with me. They cover a spectrum of political opinion, institutional affiliation (noted for identification only), and national background. Their inclusion here in no way implies any responsibility for the conclusions of this study; that responsibility is mine alone. For those with differing perspectives, I can only say that I hope they will take the trouble to express them in print and thus continue the dialogue.

Political war in its most visible and audible form is propaganda, and propaganda is ever present in the channels of international communication. Yet serious study and analysis of it is rare. One of my motivations for attempting this book was the hope that it might help initiate a discourse among the kinds of scholars and practitioners noted here.

I owe a special debt to four of the people with whom I talked about this project for having subsequently taken the time to read the manuscript in its entirety and to offer a number of stimulating suggestions. John Armstrong was kind enough to share with me the perspective and critical encouragement of a senior professional historian; J. T. Kendrick and Michael Duncan offered critiques of both style and substance drawn from their wealth of practical experience; and Gifford Malone suggested a number of helpful correctives from his background as a senior administrator and fellow scholar.

Last—or perhaps foremost—let me express my appreciation for the steady professional judgment and solid support offered during my year as a Senior Fellow at the National Defense University by the editorial group of the NDU Press. Director Fred Kiley, Associate Director Colonel Robert Kvederas, Professor of

Research Joseph Goldberg, my technical editor Tom Gill, and Deputy Director for Production Major Don Anderson were generous in offering useful leads and constructive hints.

The fact that the remaining names appear lumped in a list in no way reflects any less appreciation on my part for these people's contribution:

Waclaw Bninski. Voice of America Correspondent, the Vatican.

James Critchlow. Staff Member, Board for International Broadcasting, Washington DC.

Richard Doty. Curator, National Numismatic Collection, Smithsonian Institution, Washington DC.

Corey Gilliland. Curator, National Numismatic Collection, Smithsonian Institution, Washington DC.

Roy Godson. Editor, *Disinformation Forecast*, Washington DC.

Joseph Gordon. US Defense Intelligence Agency, Washington DC.

Timothy Healy, SJ. Georgetown University, Washington DC.

Paul Henze. Rand Corporation, Washington DC.

Alexander Kazhdan. Senior Fellow, Dumbarton Oaks Center for Byzantine Studies, Washington DC.

David Krause. Library of Congress, Washington DC.

Edward Lansdale. Major General, USAF (ret.), Washington DC.

Carl Linden. George Washington University, Washington DC.

Carnes Lord. National Institute for Public Policy, Fairfax VA.

Alexander Neale. Special Agent (ret.), Federal Bureau of Investigation, Washington DC.

Stephen Olynyk. Colonel, US Army (ret.), Washington, DC.

Alfred Paddock. Colonel, US Army, former Commanding Officer, Fourth Psychological Operations Group, Ft. Bragg NC.

Michael Pinto-Duschinsky. Brunel University, Middlesex, England.

Walter Raymond. Former Staff Member, US National Security Council, Washington DC.

Leonard Reed. Former Chief, World-Wide English, Voice of America, Washington DC.

Eugene Rostow. Distinguished Visiting Professor, US National Defense University, Washington DC.

Michael Schneider. Deputy Associate Director for Programs, US Information Agency, Washington DC.

Paul Seabury. Professor of Government, University of California, Berkeley.

Natalia Teteriatnikova. Curator, Department of Visual Resources, Dumbarton Oaks Center for Byzantine Studies, Washington DC.

Vladimir Toumanoff. Executive Director, National Council for Soviet and East European Research, Washington DC.

Hans Tuch. Former US Public Affairs Officer, Bonn, former Acting Director, Voice of America, Washington DC.

William Wade. Former Chief, Current Affairs, former European Bureau Chief, Voice of America, Washington DC.

Gerhard Wettig. Federal Institute for Eastern and International Studies, Cologne, West Germany.

Gottrik Wewer. Institute for Political Science, University of Hamburg, West Germany.

Frederick Zusy. Journalist, Washington DC.

To all named here, and to anyone whose name belongs here but has, through oversight, been omitted, my sincere thanks.

ON
POLITICAL
WAR

1

THE NATURE OF POLITICAL WAR

Political war is the use of political means to compel an opponent to do one's will, *political* being understood to describe purposeful intercourse between peoples and governments affecting national survival and relative advantage.[1] Political war may be combined with violence, economic pressure, subversion, and diplomacy, but its chief aspect is the use of words, images, and ideas, commonly known, according to context, as propaganda and psychological warfare.

This book presents an overview of the elements making up political war. It includes discussion of war aims; the possible actors in the drama, and the ethics which inform them; the scope available to them in space and time; the resources they must command; and the outcomes they may expect or fear. It seeks to make clear how the elements of political war relate one to another and how, taken together, they fit within the larger context of wars which may or may not include physical violence.

Propaganda—that is, political advocacy aimed abroad with hostile intent—is usually but not always deployed in conjunction with some form of political organization. The organizational weapon, often clandestine in some measure, is essentially hostile to the constitutional structure of the existing state in the target area. It has been defined, in twentieth century practice, as

> organizations and organizational practices . . . used by a power-seeking elite *in a manner unrestrained by the constitutional order of the arena within which the contest takes place*. In this usage, "weapon" is not meant to denote *any* political tool, but one torn from its normal context and unacceptable to the community as a legitimate mode of action.

Thus the partisan practices used in an election campaign—insofar as they adhere to the written and unwritten rules of the contest—are not weapons in this sense. On the other hand, when members who join an organization in apparent good faith are in fact the agents of an outside elite, then routine affiliation becomes "infiltration."[2]

Various periods of history—Eastern and Western—have witnessed the deployment of organizational weapons, as later chapters describe. Both Catholics and Protestants used organizational weapons during the wars of the seventeenth century, usually in the guise or with the accompaniment of religious conflict. Napoleon I benefited from the disruptive activities of political movements inspired by the ideals of the French Revolution. Both the Soviet Union and Nazi Germany vigorously deployed clandestine political movements in the 1930s based upon both socialist and nationalist ideologies. Moscow retains a powerful capability to this day. During the Cold War, Britain and America launched a program of political organization when they sought to shape an organized democratic political opposition to Soviet power in Eastern Europe and the USSR. In all of these cases, as we shall see, several elements, or arms, of political warfare were involved.

Paramilitary operations are such another coordinate arm of political war. As the term suggests, paramilitary activity is transitional in nature, leading from relatively small-scale use of violence with primitive organizational structures, through a series of stages, to full-scale conventional war. A classic ladder of escalation rises from infiltration and subversion to small armed-band operations, to insurrection at regional and national levels, and finally to all-out civil war.[3] In the earlier stages, paramilitary operations may be indistinguishable from sabotage.

All arms of political war involve subversion in one sense or another, with the choice of degree of openness or clandestinity depending on the tactical requirements of the situation. It is important to remember that clandestinity is a *mode* of political war, not its defining characteristic. Counterpropaganda and counterinsurgency commanders who attempt to define political war and its various arms solely in terms of clandestinity will often find themselves in difficulties. Legislators, particularly in democratic polities, who fall into this trap make their societies vulnerable to the many and ingenious techniques of legal maneuver which suggest themselves.

The propaganda arm, by its nature, is an overt activity. But the *origin* of propaganda, and the *agenda* which informs its practitioners, may or may not be overt. Paramilitary operations in early stages may be completely covert, as in the case of a surreptitious assassination masked as an accident. In later stages, paramilitary force is usually noisy, indeed explosively obvious to all. Classic subversion, as in converting a high government official to function as an agent of influence, remains (it is hoped) completely clandestine.

The creation, deployment, and commitment to battle of these arms of political war are a function of statecraft and of high command. Unlike conventional military force, these arms often involve civilian or at least out-of-uniform personnel. All may involve high percentages of volunteers, who usually bring with them a level of disciplinary and command and control problems unknown to modern military commands. The constitutional framework, particularly in democratic societies, may be unknown to the broader public and unclear to the legislative bodies which must provide the funding for war or preparation for war. Some states, as we will see, maintain ongoing capabilities for political war, others develop them ad hoc; many claim to have nothing to do with political war, and some few actually mean it. All states, *in extremis*, revert to political warfare in one form or another. Those who practice it most frequently usually conduct it most effectively.

As in the establishments devoted to conventional war, the allocation of priorities among service arms often creates difficulties. Confusion in the popular mind regarding the various roles and missions of ideology, propaganda, organizational weapons, subversion, sabotage, and paramilitary forces may lead to confusion in legislative and executive branches of government. Debate over the ethical principles of this and other forms of war, and doubts as to the efficacy of any or all of them in advancing a nation's national security, may often be heated and misinformed. Policy may frequently be vulnerable to manipulation in one form or another on either practical or ideological grounds.

I do not intend in this book to establish any necessary priority among the arms of political war. As in all forms of conflict, the situation and the context are paramount; and in any engagement among forces of comparable strength the judgment of statesmen and commanders and the quality of forces, equipment, and training will probably be decisive. As a general rule, those states with forces in being are likely to have a marked advantage over those which must start from scratch. Commanders should at least consider principles of strategy and tactics applicable to conventional war before deploying political warfare forces, whether defensive or offensive. The art is not totally intuitive, but it is an art, not a science. As in all arts, experience may be a better guide than reason.

I have chosen in this book to look first and foremost at the propaganda weapon. It is the least understood, at least in the West, although it is often the arm most actively deployed by our adversaries in direct attacks on Western societies.[4] It is fashionable at the moment among Western statesmen and political leaders to deny that propaganda is in any way part of the Western armory. It is also fashionable to discount hostile propaganda aimed at the West by other powers and political movements as largely irrelevant or at worst a minor nuisance. Western foreign and defense analysts are likely to see propaganda, whatever its efficacy, as intellectually dubious and best ignored in serious writing. Like sex in the Victorian age, the more it is experienced, the more it is ignored in polite discourse. As the Victorians eventually learned, ignoring vital areas of life—whether one practices them or not—can have lamentable results.

The basic skill needed to conduct propaganda is the classic art of rhetoric—an art perhaps best described as the "systematization of natural eloquence."[5] All art, remember, is in itself neutral—like fire, it can be used constructively, as in a blast furnace, or destructively, as in the blast of an artillery shell. A judgment of moral worth depends upon the intent of the user, not the nature of the instrument.

Rhetoric, as persuasive communication, has in some periods carried a burden of unwarranted opprobrium arising from a strand in Western philosophy, dating back to Plato, that associates it with empty posturing, insincerity, and distorted meaning. Rhetoric, in this critical view, not only is immoral but also corrupts the process by which men search—or should search—for objective truth. The denunciation is inherently elitist, assuming that some philosopher-king or body of learned men is capable of achieving ultimate truth by dispassionate reflection, and of dispensing it without prejudice or favor to the rest of mankind. We should note, though, that those—like Plato—who were most insistent in denouncing rhetoric usually employed the same techniques of rhetoric to do so. Aristotle, who was Plato's pupil but was by no means intimidated by him, provided a better assessment of rhetoric, affirming its utility as a means, within argumentation, for working toward the truth, and as a resource of defense for those who are under attack.[6] As such, rhetoric should rightly be seen as practically useful as well as morally neutral.

Modern discourse on propaganda suffers from contradictory definitions in academic writing and addiction to catchy neologisms in journalism. To clear the ground, let me state briefly how I shall use three terms. They are related, but distinguished according to context.

Propaganda is political warfare conducted by civilians in the service of national, including ideological, objectives. It is mostly aimed at mass audiences, usually civilian. It may or may not be truthful, as determined by those who deploy it.[7]

Psychological operations is political warfare conducted by military personnel for strategic and tactical military objectives. Its target is usually hostile military personnel, but may also be neutrals and civilians.[8]

Public diplomacy is a form of international political advocacy directed openly by civilians to a broad spectrum of audiences, but usually in support of negotiations through diplomatic channels. It is aimed at civilians and is confined in the main to forms of advocacy acceptable to host governments. It seeks to elicit popular support for solutions of mutual benefit and avoids threats, compulsion, or intimidation. It is not a form of political warfare, although it may be used in combination with political warfare.[9]

Propaganda has many aspects, two of which require notice at this point: namely, propaganda of the word and propaganda of the deed. *Words* as used here includes a range of channels by which thoughts and emotions can be conveyed from one mind into another. Language in all forms, from comic strips to religious catechisms, can be propaganda *if it has a hostile political purpose.*

Commercial advertising and authentic devotional services are not propaganda, although they may be used as such for cover. Cultural life and the creative talent of a society may be used for propaganda purposes, but they are not propaganda per se. *Deeds* means acts intended to elicit a political response—a response, let it be noted, which depends upon the target's interpretation of the act. Foreign policy slogans announced at a Soviet Party Congress are propaganda of the word. Relocation of a military unit, or an increase in subsidies to a foreign communist party, may be propaganda of the deed (in addition to serving other ends). Embassy information and cultural bulletins circulated in a host country with the permission of the authorities usually purports to be public diplomacy.

War throughout history has taken many forms. Let us note here that its essence is fighting, but that not all fighting involves physical violence, at least not at all stages. The threat of violence can be an act of war. Indeed, the absence of violence, as in the case of a state failing to act within its own jurisdiction against terrorists attacking citizens and property of another state, can be an act of war. Gifts concealing violence, such as the Trojan Horse, are clearly acts of war. Gifts innocuous in themselves, when offered with hostile intent, are commonly described as acts of war. To limit the concept of war to acts of physical violence conducted within a framework of formal military organization may be bureaucratically satisfying, but it is analytically weak and is a poor guide to the policymaker. *War is power applied with hostile intent.* Now and throughout history, war has been pursued through channels intended to conceal or blunt that simple fact. Concealment of that fact is one aspect of political war.

European nation states, born of the Renaissance, gradually articulated rules which enable them to say—if they find the statement expedient—that they are or are not in a state of war. Attacks on military forces, persons, and property; territorial incursion; and formal declarations of bellicose intent are some of the more obvious criteria. But the record has been less than clear in most cases. The student of the extended conflict between England and Spain may find distinctly different conclusions warranted as to whether

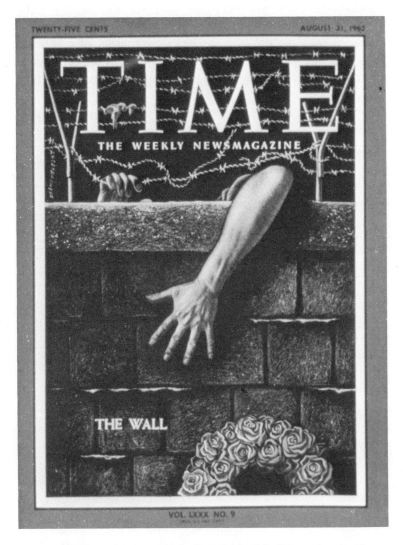

"Berlin Wall," cover painting by Artzybasheff for Time, *August 31, 1962. Political war is the use—or suppression— of words, images, and ideas to impose one's will on the enemy.*

a state of war existed depending upon his sources. A reading of the diplomatic record may give one impression, the records of merchants yet another, and the logbooks of Drake or Morgan still a third.

A simple solution to such confusion would be to limit one's judgment to conclusions supportable by the formal diplomatic record: when the participating governments said in state documents that they were at war, then they were at war; and when they jointly announced by treaty that they were at peace, they were at peace. Very tidy—and very wrong. War depended upon the political will of the actors, both governments and broad sectors of society included. When they were intent on conducting war, there was war by whatever means; when they tired of it and sought to use the instruments of policy for mutual advantage, there was peace. At times, they did both concurrently. Seldom did either side consider itself limited to purely military means in the conduct of operations.

States and political movements wage wars on the basis—one would like to think—of internal consensus reflected and expressed in some recognized form as a national goal. The reality may often be a projection, sometimes coherent, more often contradictory, of a loose and shifting alliance of political forces serving particularist ends. National policymakers find such conditions messy and intolerable. In seeking to impose order upon circumstances which are inherently disorderly, they may deceive themselves, thus becoming more prone to miscalculation than if working under more modest assumptions. In such circumstances, it may well be (as it is today) that the actors in the international arena have quite different perceptions as to whether they are or are not at war. Such misperceptions, or more accurately, difference of perceptions, may be acknowledged, or denied, or recognized and purposefully manipulated. In any event, the conditions are conducive to the conduct of political warfare.

Some people may argue that there is little utility in acknowledging the existence of these anomalies, much less in accepting them as a basis for policy. Those interested in conducting aggressive political warfare will find their activities facilitated by popular ignorance or uncertainty regarding their operations. Those intent on moving international discourse out of the ways of conflict and along the paths of peace will argue on hopeful grounds that any negotiation is desirable as an example of good intent, whereas any attention to what are regarded as forms of international political pathology is simply not helpful. Professional military establishments, rightfully sensitive to the complication politics usually introduces into their lives, will argue for a clear separation between war and politics in both policy and operations.

The observer who contemplates such a scene of confusion, cross-purposes, and contradictory signals may well ask, if one cannot rely upon law as expressed in treaties, then what basis for order, short of Hobbesian autocracy on a global scale, is to be found in international life? This survey of political—as distinguished from purely conventional—war in Western culture offers several clues. Among those clues might be the value of striving for law as a basis for order while recognizing its limitations, and of avoiding the pursuit of diplomacy and its legal instruments to the point of self-deception.

Those states that have prospered and attained a modicum of international security seem to have kept firmly in mind that many international actors did not see negotiation within a framework of law and enshrined custom as a end in itself. Most resorted overtly, and covertly, to other instruments of policy, instruments that lay outside the realm of law and that had to be dealt with on their own terms. Those terms included a different conceptual framework than that underlying the precepts of international law and practice. Political war is that different concept. Its essence lies in the political will of those who practice it.

Political will is at the heart of all serious forms of conflict. Often obscure, usually complex in origin, always sensitive to investigation, political will can nevertheless be reduced to two elements: a vision of the world, and a set of assumptions as to the actor's role in it. Put differently, political will involves a statement of national objectives and a formulation of policies to achieve them. Either or both may be articulated in programmatic documents, declared in speeches and state papers, or conveyed less formally by interviews and personal utterances of leaders. They also may be conveyed in various art forms pitched at widely differing levels of subtlety. All such visions must be fleshed out—if they are to have any substance—in some more or less systematic way for both domestic and foreign audiences. Political movements of lesser magnitude than the nation state, such as extremist groups and insurgencies, may tend to be long on vision and relatively short on programmatic specifics, even to the point of adopting great literary works or national epics in place of constitutions and legal acts as the central points in their political life.

For nation states, acting in isolation from alliances, a constitution usually defines the terms on which war will be conducted; and the terms, even in autocracies, usually set some limits on the will of the executive power. A constitution that provides for complex checks and balances offers a dilemma in the conduct of war, most especially political war. The dilemma has been resolved in various ways, some of which are noted in later chapters. Suffice it here to note that the dilemma exists and that much grief can be avoided by facing and resolving it rather than attempting to avoid it or deny its existence. Also note that a constitutionally based nation state thus will be likely to conduct political war in ways quite different from those of a totalitarian—as distinct from a merely authoritarian—power.

Alliances must rely for the projection of political will on diplomatic agreements and joint appeals by leaders, neither of which elicit much solid support. Nor are they likely to be of much use in supplying a framework for policy. An alliance is most effective in political war when its members share some basis, and the will to evoke it, in national or cultural traditions. Alliances of pure policy or intimidation are weak instruments in war: they have inherent disadvantages that can be mitigated by defensive political warfare; they offer little or no basis for assertive political warfare. Diplomatists conclude them, soldiers mistrust them, propagandists regard them (rightly) as points of vulnerability.

Empires tend to perform most effectively in political warfare when driven by a militant, messianic ideology that complements and transcends the rational-legalistic framework of the nation states within them. Such combinations of ideological and statist elements in an empire can create problems, indeed very serious problems, when an inherent tension between the ideology and the state arises at the core of the imperial political vision. The outcome can be divisive, particularly for multinational empires. Such problems are not unmanageable, though; some empires have survived for extended periods while riven with ethnic and social contradictions. And yet a strong political warfare strategy against such empires may be spectacularly successful, as Anglo-American strategy was against Austria-Hungary in 1918. On balance, a large multinational empire still seems to require some form of potent ideological adhesive to hold it together. To dissolve that adhesive is a task of political warfare.

For all kinds of actors, there appears to be a fundamental difference—sometimes obvious, more often latent—between the statements of political will needed to rally internal support and the idiom in which the same political vision is made known to the world at large. Nazi Germany was a prime example, one in which the internal dynamic provided both the drive to conquest and a serious barrier to the conduct of any form of political warfare short of the crudest forms of intimidation. Goebbels, as we shall see later, recognized and sought to diminish this destructive tension. He failed. Early Nazi successes in the 1930s were spectacular, deriving mainly from a threatened unleashing of widespread violence. This posture matched well the inner dynamic of the regime, even though it exceeded by far Germany's actual military capacity. Once decisively confronted by other nations, the German posture of intimidation became strongly counterproductive.

Status quo powers, and powers whose political vision reflects mainly mercantile interests, seem to have more success than expansionist and ideological powers in defusing these internal-external tensions. Few nations have expressed the mercantile ethos as strikingly as the English. "Upon the whole," wrote Daniel Defoe in 1728,

> Trade is the Wealth of the World; Trade makes the Difference
> as to Rich and Poor, between one Nation and another; Trade
> nourishes Industry, Industry begets Trade; Trade dispenses the
> natural Wealth of the World, and Trade raises new Species of
> Wealth, which Nature knew nothing of; Trade has two Daughters, whose fruitful Progeny in Arts may be said to employ
> Mankind; namely Manufacture and Navigation.[10]

Alexander Pope, another noteworthy publicist of the period, added a philosophical and humanist dimension to the mercantile ethos when he wrote,

> The time shall come, when free as seas or wind,
> Unbounded Thames shall flow for all mankind,
> Whole nations enter with each swelling tide,
> And seas but join the regions they divide; . . .
> O stretch thy reign, fair peace! from shore to shore,
> Till conquest cease, and slavery be no more;[11]

Forms of political advocacy most appropriate to this classic mercantile approach would be described today as public diplomacy. They can be alternated or combined with more aggressive forms of advocacy merging into outright political warfare as well as conventional military force. Observers of political warfare may deplore but should not ignore the conclusion that the mixture has been a highly effective political warfare strategy in some periods of history.

For extremist political groups and insurgencies, political warfare is a natural means of expression and self-assertion. Lacking diplomatic status, the internal-external conflict is often minimal. Because their prime objective at the outset is often to gain attention at any price, these movements place a premium on stridency. Most such groups aspire eventually to diplomatic recognition as a symbol of success and a legitimation of status. But few are willing to surrender their political warfare operations to achieve it. Thus a paradox arises: as they move toward enhanced awareness, they generate increased resistance to recognition. In general, the more specific the core political vision—national identity, for example— the easier will be the transition away from political warfare strategies. Conversely, the more millenarian the vision, whether religious or secular, the more likely a group is to remain committed to the use of political warfare.

All practitioners of political warfare need an acute sense of *Zeitgeist*, or Spirit of the Times. *Zeitgeist* may be rational or romantic, radical or conservative, or some mixture of all. Historically, tides in popular attitudes have tended to move with a certain measure of regularity. They are, alas, best perceived in retrospect, but some measure of their force and direction has long been felt to be an essential quality of the statesman. Historical

determinists, such as Marxist-Leninists, claim legitimacy based upon the predictive power of their world view. Non-Marxists may express "faith in the future," but are usually inclined to be more cautious in tying specific policies to any system of beliefs. Both remain under an existential compulsion to make judgments and to act upon them.

The historical examples reviewed in this book tend to indicate that the most successful practitioners have been those who avoided predictions, instead focusing their analytical skills on accurately assessing short-term trends in popular attitudes and acting accordingly. They may have missed some flood tides, but they were less likely to find themselves stranded at the ebb.

Political warfare among millenarian expansionist powers may be clear-cut and explicit (which does not mean that subversion and deception are not used): both actors are committed to conflict, and the battle is joined. The nature of the combatants indicates that either one or the other is likely to win, usually decisively, within a calculable period. Because both sides know this, the conflict is doubly envenomed by the ideological aspirations of the contestants and by the justifiable fear of the consequences of defeat. The outcome, barring intervention by third parties or fate, may involve scenarios reminiscent of Greek tragedy in the Homeric age.

Political warfare between an expansionist power and an evenly matched status quo power is much less clear-cut. The outcomes are less easily predicted, and the consequences may be less stark. The duration may be much longer, indeed the contest may be open-ended. Victory, if attained by the expansionist power, will no doubt be a historic event, whatever its consequences for the defeated. Victory, if such is the right term, by a status quo power amounts to little more than a cessation of external threat at best, and a monumental new set of occupation worries at worst. The conflict, in principle, would seem less likely to erupt militarily. It is also inherently more susceptible to the sustained but sporadic use of political warfare conducted along parallel but dissimilar lines. Such is the condition of the world today.

Let us turn now to the ethics of political war. Western culture since the days of Saint Thomas Aquinas has had a conception of the principles of just war. However much scholars and statesmen might disagree on their application, they usually agreed on the principles as providing valid norms for international behavior. The advent of totalitarian regimes in the early twentieth century brought a major threat to the continuity of this tradition. The totalitarian position on war, peace, and neutrality has much to do with historical patterns of political warfare. We will look more closely at its consequences later. But first, let us recapitulate the Western principles of Just and Limited War.

A modern scholar, writing in the Catholic tradition, has stated them thus:

> The *jus ad bellum* [recourse to war] lays down conditions that must be met in order to have permissible recourse to armed coercion. They are conditions that should be viewed in the light of the fundamental tenet of just-war doctrine: the presumption is always against war. The taking of human life is not permitted to man unless there are exceptional justifications. Just-war doctrine provides those justifications, but they are in the nature of special pleadings to overcome the presumption against killing. The decision to invoke the exceptional rights of war must be based on the following criteria: there must be competent authority to order the war for a public purpose; there must be a just cause (it may be self-defense or the protection of rights by offensive war) and the means must be proportionate to the just cause and all peaceful alternatives must have been exhausted; and there must be right intention on the part of the just belligerent.[12]

To this statement of principles governing recourse *to* war (*jus ad bellum*) must be added principles concerning conduct *of* war (*jus in bello*), for which the single underlying requirement is that such a war must be limited:

> This basic principle means at least two things. First, a belligerent never has the open-ended right to use all means at his disposal and/or to use any means that will injure the enemy irrespective of their conformity to the rules of the *jus in bello*. Second, permissible armed coercion must be limited, that is to say, controlled. Means that tend to escape the control of the belligerent are prohibited.[13]

Because political war does not involve a direct and immediate attempt to kill, it could be said that it is not war and therefore not subject to the principles of Just and Limited War. Such a view might be argued by those who see no distinction among various forms of advocacy, lumping commercial promotion, religious proselytizing, and milder forms of political advocacy together with propaganda and psychological war under the general rubric of persuasion. In abstract, such a grouping is perfectly valid, just as it is logically valid to consider gunfire between victims and criminals as acts of violence on both sides. Practically, it is of little legal, moral, or policy value to base international behavior on such an extreme level of abstraction.

The essential element in war is not killing per se, but rather the compelling of an opponent to do one's will. Killing may or may not be involved; indeed, under limited war principles it should be minimized if possible. The essence is a contest of political will, whose means may involve varying forms and degrees of compulsion. In all forms, let us note, loss of life is accepted as a necessary concomitant.

Such is also the case with psychological warfare and indeed with propaganda. Inducing troops to shoot their leaders is clearly a part of psychological warfare. Inducing popular uprisings against governments, which usually are accompanied by some degree of killing, has long been one of the objects of propaganda. In totalitarian practice, the killing involves officially stimulated and conducted mass extermination derived from unlimited incitement to class or race hatred. Western governments that choose to employ propaganda as an instrument of political war have tended to do so in more restrained forms consonant with their traditions of Just and Limited War. They have not regarded revolution, including varying degrees of violence, as illegal, immoral, or impractical. But they have sought to confine its consequences to sane and limited ends.

Propaganda as an instrument of war thus carries with it a presumption that life and property may—on the decision of the policymakers and commanders—be put at hazard for either *raison de guerre* or *raison d'etat*. For the West, revolutionary propaganda should be considered legitimated by and bound under the rules of Just and Limited War.

The East holds a quite different vision, one rooted deeply in Imperial Russian culture and tradition but transformed and deformed by the totalitarian imperatives of late nineteenth and early twentieth century Europe. The practical consequences of these differing traditions and attitudes are explored in later chapters. But we should at this point establish that they exist and say why.

The collapse of the European system of world order—for such it was, however turbulent and imperfect—after World War I brought actors onto the stage with uncompromising views of the world, their roles in it, and the ethical system that should regulate it. Best summed up as totalitarian, this new force took root in the defeated and fragmented empires of Germany and Russia, and in the emerging nation state of Italy. The German and Italian variants were smashed by superior external force in World War II. The third, now the Soviet Union, remains and provides today the geographic basis for one of the two superpowers. The nature of this remaining totalitarian state—also a multinational empire—is significant for students of political warfare. In the words of one close observer,

> Its power is based, above all, on thought control. Communist leaders realized that force alone cannot impose and sustain social cohesion. For that reason [they] have placed enormous emphasis on political propaganda . . . [because] in the age of mass literacy, control over access to the mind is the point of departure for control over political behavior.[14]

This concern with ideas and propaganda as instruments of power applies not only domestically, where a communist party is in power, but also externally, to the concepts of war and international relations. Documentation on this score is voluminous, and I cite some of it in later chapters. Let us simply note here the entry on War in the current edition of the *Great Soviet Encyclopedia*, which (predictably) cites Lenin:

> "The main thesis of dialectic is that war is simply the continuation of politics by other (that is, violent) means. Such is the formula of Clausewitz . . . and it was always the standpoint of Marx and Engels, who regarded any war as the continuation of the politics of the concerned powers—and the various classes within those countries in a definite period." In war, armed force, as well as economic, diplomatic, ideological, and

other means of struggle are used as the chief and decisive means of achieving political goals.[15]

Lenin's position (recorded elsewhere) was quite clear on the political object of war: "The character of the war (whether reactionary or revolutionary) is not determined by who the aggressor was, or whose territory the enemy has occupied, it is determined by the class that is waging the war, and the policies of which this war is a continuation."[16] The dominating, intrusive aim of this political vision was equally clear:

> The art of politics (and the communist's correct understanding of his task) lies in correctly gauging the conditions and the moment when the vanguard of the proletariat can successfully seize power, when it will be able, during and after this seizure of power, to obtain adequate support from sufficiently broad strata of the working class and the non-proletarian working masses, and when, thereafter, it will be able to maintain, consolidate, and extend its rule.[17]

Morality, as it informs the Western position on Just and Limited War, was brusquely dismissed by Lenin: "Our morality is entirely subordinated to the interests of the class struggle of the proletariat . . . we do not believe in eternal morality."[18] Lenin's position on ethics in international affairs is found variously throughout his works, but the thrust is usually consistent and emphatic: "Morals is that which serves to destroy the old, exploiting society and to unite all toilers behind the proletariat."[19]

Anyone who doubts the extent to which Lenin's views shape the decisionmaking of present-day Soviet political and military elites, and suffuses the political culture of at least the Russian elites of the Soviet population, may wish to review a year's file of, say, *Pravda* and *Red Star*, as well as the programmatic statements of the current Soviet leaders.[20] Soviet tactical positions may be cautious or not in any given circumstance, but the strategic thrust on the record of words and deeds remains firmly rooted in the Manichaean, self-righteous political ethos of Lenin.

We need to highlight here two points about this stark difference between Eastern and Western notions of war and morality, and about the political postures that accompany them. The first is simply that they exist and guide policymaking on both sides. The second is that they have profound historical and cultural roots,

roots that cannot be removed or ignored in the search for treaties and agreements negotiated at the diplomatic level. This asymmetry in ethos is one of the features of the current international scene, one on which leaders in Moscow insist and which leaders in the West tend to explain away or ignore.

The question of "truth" is one on which ethical differences among the opposing forces can be seen in sharpest relief. Each side, of course, asserts a monopoly on truth, deriving its claim from the philosophical principles at the core of its political vision. Because both the principles and the visions are in key areas mutually exclusive, the basis is laid for each side to charge its opponent with falsehood. And each in pursuit of its mutually exclusive vision can usually succeed in making a plausible case against its opponent and on behalf of its own rectitude. The essential philosophical difference today lies in the Eastern commitment to truth as an expression of orthodoxy, and the Western view of truth as an expression of individual conscience.[21]

This distinction between Western and Soviet perceptions emerged clearly during that part of World War II in which the Anglo-Saxon powers and the USSR were allied in the conflict against Hitler's Reich. During a visit to London in September 1943, Politburo member Shvernik warned Anthony Eden that Soviet cultural programming, which the British expressed a willingness to receive, would be "propagandistic." "Nonsense," Eden responded. "There is no propaganda between allies."[22] By Western standards Eden was right. Political communication among Western nations should rightly be judged on both ethical and practical grounds as subject to laws of evidence and philosophical truth based on an appeal to individual conscience. As such it is not propaganda and not political warfare. The distinction was not one that Shvernik could accept.

Political communication addressed by a Western government to home audiences should not be termed propaganda unless it is involved in civil war. Despite terminological confusion, the principle of separate, organizationally distinct capabilities for external propaganda and for political mobilization of home audiences has tended to be the rule in the West. Attempts to combine the wartime functions of external and internal programming, as in the US Office of War Information, worked poorly, if at all, and resulted in confusion until a de facto division of labor was worked out with other agencies. In Soviet practice, the term *propaganda* applies to communication to both internal and external audiences, as is appropriate to the fortress mentality of any ruling communist party towards its population.

Today in Soviet-American relations, a pattern seems to have emerged of mixed and alternating use of political warfare and Western alliance style public diplomacy. American practice seems to move toward the political warfare end of the spectrum in times of tension and perceived threat, and toward the public diplomacy format when relations are seen as improving. Such shifts appear also to be motivated by attempted tactical "signaling" to the Soviet authorities in a pattern of diplomatic maneuver. With the exception of a period in the late Truman and early Eisenhower administrations, there is little record of sustained and coherent US planning for either instrument. Soviet reactions to this pattern over the years seem to include acts of opportunism with occasional signs of puzzlement. The Soviets' own commitment to political warfare on classic totalitarian lines remains strong.

In areas which lie outside the formal alliance structures of the superpowers, such as the Middle East, one may observe political warfare practiced by smaller national entities. Some of these entities are in transition from insurgency or extremist political grouping to something approaching statehood. There are also examples of regional powers that employ political as well as conventional warfare in pursuit of both state interests and the visionary goals of a messianic religious belief.

Political movements tend to overuse political warfare, possibly because it is a weapon most easily grasped and wielded by such unsubstantial entities. I am speaking here of extremist movements—both right and left—which lack the territory and apparatus of a nation state, and which often possess little more in the way of resources than their canonical books and the allegiance of zealots. In its purest form, a political party of radical bent is simply a political warfare capability looking for a permanent geographic home. Only through success can it achieve the other attributes of sovereignty, seeking to create and deploy military force, wield economic resources, and extend diplomatic connections. Most fail, some succeed, usually at great human cost. As practitioners of political warfare, they are themselves most vulnerable to it when it is conducted against them.

Resources are required for political warfare as such and should not be confused with the resources allocated for other forms of war. Propaganda resources can be considered under broad common categories, such as ideas, manpower, materiel, intelligence, physical plant and facilities, and technology. Many of the human skills needed can be found in related walks of life, both private and public. Nations can conduct political war with capabilities thrown together in haste from such sources. Anglo-Saxons, with their penchant for the gifted amateur and their essentially mercantile social structure, are much given to this solution. Russians, with their long reliance on centralized imperial government, mobilized society, and command economy, tend to do things differently.

Let us leave aside the question of which approach is better (better for what?) and simply note that the patterns of organization, recruitment, supply, and deployment of resources are usually rooted in the history and traditions of the state which maintains and uses a political warfare capability. This pattern, in turn, tends to create a kind of national—or imperial—style; an organizational momentum at the operational level develops, and a reliance on particular strengths and an avoidance of some organizational weaknesses results. Political warfare commanders may benefit from studying such differences, or pay penalties for ignoring them.

Ideas are the first resource of political warfare, and the most difficult to marshal in its service. Controlled on a national scale and crystallized into dogma, as in the empires of the East, ideas become state ideologies. What is gained in consistency and predictability, making easier the linkages to other instruments of policy, is lost in originality and spontaneity. Radical political movements usually operate on ideational programs linked in some way to one or another of the prevailing secular or religious faiths

22

of the age. At the secular end this usually means some variant of Trotskyism or Marxism-Leninism; at the religious end, some fundamentalist variant of one of the world religious movements. The secular and religious aspects are logically in opposition; in practice, they often combine in potent forms of mysticism.

In all cases, the central political vision becomes the touchstone for propaganda policy. The policy must in turn be translated into guidelines for programmers—writers, broadcasters, artists—who relate the guidelines to events in ways appealing to their respective audiences.

Serious practitioners of political warfare usually have sought to distinguish between two main levels of action: one for elites and people who are themselves influential propagators of ideas, and another for the common man at the end of the chain of influence. The distinction has more than merely practical significance, at least among totalitarians. Most totalitarian ideologies are gnostic in some degree; that is, they see their central visions as involving esoteric truths which only the initiated can understand and interpret for the masses. This esoteric truth can be founded in religious revelation, asserted by a charismatic leader, or attributed to superior scientific wisdom. There is often an accompanying claim of historical inevitability leading in some distant future to apocalyptic resolution. Pending such resolution or final days, the world is seen as divided along Manichaean lines into good and evil, usually represented in some way by forces of light and powers of darkness.

From these concepts emerges a key principle of totalitarian political warfare: the distinction between propaganda and agitation. As put by Lenin, propaganda is many ideas for a few, whereas agitation is a few simple ideas for the many. The Russian terms *propaganda* and *agitatsiya* have quite specific political, legal, and administrative content unknown in Western languages. The English terms *education* and *publicity* convey, to a limited degree, some measure of equivalence.

Political warfare practiced in the Western tradition is less likely to insist upon or even take note of this distinction, no doubt because the tradition lacks (Calvinist principles of predestination notwithstanding) any strong gnostic element in its prevailing political vision or visions. Theoretical writing on Western psychological warfare has sought to focus attention on the utility of two-step communications theory, in which some degree of trickle-down or recycling of messages through influential hearers to mass audiences is intended. And Western commercial advertising is not ignorant of the concept of "influentials." In both cases, though, the thrust and effect associated with a gnostic political vision is lacking. Perhaps both East and West have derived their practices from an awareness of Aristotelian concepts of esoteric and exoteric rhetorical schools. If so, we see an interesting example of historical divergence in East and West from common philosophical sources.

Note that behind these concepts rests a distinction between a central political vision which lies at the core of a nation's or movement's political will, and the unfolding of that vision into ideas, guidelines, and media products for political warfare purposes. The unfolding process is complex, and an understanding of its patterns is essential to coherent and purposeful political warfare, both defensive and offensive. Note also that the process is dynamic; even in the most rigidly structured and strictly disciplined nations it can change with lightning rapidity. It may also be subject to slow, glacial movement, discernible only by extended trend-line analysis but still meaningful in cumulative effect. Recent history includes instructive cases of political warfare conducted either in ignorance of such forces or, more disastrously, on the basis of oversophisticated and schematic perceptions of them.

Research is usually deemed to be a resource of critical importance to adequate understanding and use of the propaganda and agitation patterns inherent in political warfare activity. The research must be sustained, specialized in political war, effectively funded and staffed, and properly subordinated within the command structure. Its uses (and abuses) must be known to commanders and its products available to programmers. It should be linked to, but kept organizationally separate from, the research and analysis support for other arms and services, including the military and diplomatic.

Its intellectual integrity must be carefully buffered from ideological distortion and political forces. Such appear to be the desiderata for research capabilities contemplated by serious political warfare practitioners, at least in the West. Eastern practice appears to be similar, notwithstanding the commitment to ideological orthodoxy at the agitational end. On both sides, actual practice often falls short of the ideal.

After ideas, manpower can be the single most critical factor for any state or movement bent on conducting political warfare. Questions of motivation, allegiance, functional skills, languages, terms of employment, and talent have been solved in various ways throughout history. Empires with long traditions of sustained activity in political warfare have tended to develop recruitment and staffing patterns along bureaucratic organizational lines, usually with an added measure of orthodox ideology and associated social structures.

Western staffs, notably those of the Anglo-Saxon powers, have tended toward a mix of civil service and private sector media in recruitment, organization, and ethos. I know of no research on which to base conclusions about patterns among smaller nation states. There seems, oddly enough, to be more evidence available about the manpower used by radical political groups, where high levels of voluntarism and self-selection prevail.

Material resources needed for political warfare range from the simplest and cheapest tools, such as paper and pencil or a soap box in Hyde Park, through widely available, small-scale technology such as videocassettes,[23] to the costly and complex machinery of printing plants and broadcasting facilities deployed by major actors. Smaller actors appear more likely than their larger opponents to devote high proportions of their foreign affairs budgets to creating, maintaining, staffing, and deploying political warfare capabilities. Although it is by no means guaranteed to succeed, political warfare is a form of conflict which offers, or appears to offer, the small participant a disproportionally large payoff under certain conditions. Piggybacking on the activities of larger allies also offers possibilities. Moreover, extremist political leaders, as individuals, often tend to be personally knowledgeable and experienced in the operations of propaganda. The temptation is great to gamble large percentages of a limited warfare budget on political war.

General magnitudes of cost for superpower political warfare operations appear to be relatively small percentages of overall foreign operations budgets. Western observers in 1980 estimated the Soviet annual expenditure at the $3 billion level, which is small compared to annual outlays for military and foreign aid.[24] For various reasons, including highly partisan legislative attitudes, it is difficult to say whether the United States has any activities funded by appropriations which qualify as political warfare. Depending upon the definitional categories, one might argue that US expenditures on public diplomacy run around $2 billion annually.

Geographic location, including considerations of airwaves and space as well as the obvious need for on-site access to key target areas, presents problems for political warfare operations analogous to those presented by terrain for the military planner. Radio transmitters, comparable in potential to a ground army or a major naval unit, have distinct propagation characteristics that must be related to audience targeting, physical security, and international agreements before they can become operational. Lead times for such units can run up to ten years.

New technologies unknown today, as well as existing possibilities such as Direct Satellite Broadcasting (DSB), must be taken into account in net assessments.[25] Printing plant location, regional and national systems of newspaper and book distribution, and a large variety of local regulations and rulings need continuing attention by competent and sustained research. We might hypothesize (subject to further research) that the smaller actors with the most specific kinds of national objectives are likely to be the most efficient in their use of material resources.

Some evidence suggests that the superpowers, particularly the Soviet Union, can be wasteful in their use of major categories of plant and equipment, relying on mass and momentum to carry them through. Smaller powers, though, with more sharply defined objectives, often use their resources more efficiently through a combination of sharply focused objectives and precise targeting.

Any practitioner must study the advantages and pitfalls of collocation of plant and facilities, and control of common-user items, among various categories of political warfare operations—

overt and covert. Such issues are seldom amenable to resolution on purely budgetary grounds (as often happens in parliamentary democracies) or on bureaucratic power principles (as seems to occur in totalitarian states). Regardless of the setting, there is a clear need for careful coordination among propaganda, military, diplomatic, and economic operations in the deployment of resources.

A sound and practical solution to such problems of coordination often provides a distinct advantage for those who can manage it; failure to achieve such a solution can leave a gaping vulnerability. Popular discourse tends to hold that totalitarian and authoritarian powers do better here than democracies. The historical record tends to discount this notion and to point instead to sheer quality of leadership (as in the case of Lloyd George in Britain) or possibly deeper patterns in bureaucratic culture (which may influence the Soviet Union's modern practice more than its totalitarian principles). More than in conventional war, sound judgment in high command seems to be critical to success or failure in all aspects of political war.

What outcomes can a commander contemplate when launching a political warfare campaign? How can strategic and tactical objectives be defined? How can success be exploited for larger ends, and what must be done to guard against and minimize the damage attendant upon defeat? The following chapters offer historical perspective on these points. Let us note here that, historically, political warfare commanders, like their conventional warfare colleagues, tend to have a bias toward victory, or at least toward tactical success. The bias is understandable. All leadership requires confidence, and, "It is essential," in Field Marshal Montgomery's words, "to understand that battles are won primarily in the hearts of men."[26] Nowhere in war is this more the case than in political war.

It is fashionable today in the West (but not in the East) to decry or ignore the very idea of victory as incompatible with the dangers of the nuclear age.[27] And yet, as suggested earlier, it remains likely (if lamentable) that varying levels of political and military conflict

will continue as they have throughout history. Under these circumstances, it seems wise to assume that national leaders of all
kinds, political and military, will feel compelled to fight wars with
every intention of winning them. One should ask not whether
leaders seek victory, but rather, how they define victory and defeat.
The question is paramount in political war.

One may seek an answer to such questions in abstract terms,
or one may ask how they have tended to be answered on various
occasions in the past. One of the premises of this study is
that history is a better guide than pure theory in matters of war
and peace. With that in mind, let us turn to some examples from
the past.

2

ANTIQUITY

E uropean political culture—which today appears in several distinct forms from the Urals to the Atlantic and westward to the American areas of the Pacific—is still strongly influenced by classical thought. How the peoples in this vast expanse conflict and communicate among themselves still depends upon the ideas and symbols first defined in classical periods of Hebrew, Greek, and Roman history. Let us look at some of those cultures' ideas regarding politics, rhetoric, and war.

Although Joshua's conquest of Canaan, following the Mosaic exodus from Egypt, occurred in 1100 BC, it still resonates in the political lexicon of modern times. As an archetype of revolutionary action, rebellion against exploitation and oppression, assertion of national and religious autonomy, and sheer combative spirit, its lessons structure the rhetoric and inspire the action of people of many nations. The subsequent conquest of territory under Joshua and the Hebrew kings offers a core rationale for one recently established political entity, and has been seen as an inspiration of great force and continuity by a number of earlier nations. Our record of the period, in the form of the Bible, is at the core of several world religions. The biblical accounts of the battles of Joshua helped to carry these archetypal ideas forward and stamped them with the mark of physical power in pursuit of divine and popular will. In the words of one modern scholar,

> This combination of divine wilfulness and popular choice,
> providence and covenant, determinism and freedom is char-
> acteristic of Exodus politics and of all later versions of radical
> and revolutionary politics. We can see it most clearly among
> the Puritans, where covenant theology, modeled on Exodus,

is hardly consistent with the theology of Predestination: and yet, the two coexisted over a long period of time. The idea of divine election (or historical inevitability) provides, perhaps, a necessary background for radical politics.[1]

The rhetoric of Moses and Joshua rings down through the ages as a powerful weapon of political warfare. In addition to its essential religious message, it has inspired, guided, and rallied warriors of all kinds with more vigor and persistence than any other writing.[2] Curiously, it seems to have lost little in vividness and vitality as it was translated into other tongues.

Foremost has been its splendid power to concentrate men's minds on the simple fact of combat as a means of survival. How many leaders throughout history have cited the Book of Judges (III:27-28):

And Ehud . . . blew a trumpet in the mountain of Ephraim, and the children of Israel went down the mount, and he before them. And he said unto them, follow me; for the Lord God hath delivered your enemies the Moabites into your hand.

Or recall Winston Churchill's call to action in 1941, in the language of Maccabees (1 Macc. III: 58–60):

Arm yourselves, and be ye men of valor, and be in readiness for conflict: for it is better for us to perish in battle than to look upon the outrage of our nation and our altar.

These passages, as cited through the centuries, have been directed mainly to internal audiences, intended to inspire confidence and determination essential for survival and to tie the mass of the nation to its leaders by reminding them of the nation's unique vision of the world and its part in it. Mainly, but not entirely. Another object, possibly the most important in some situations, was to warn opponents and encourage potential allies by a striking assertion of unity and implacable determination based upon a transcendent source of legitimacy and will. Here, at a seminal stage in the patterns of war rhetoric, we see an important feature emerge—the interaction of internal confidence-building and external defiance. Here we see it in a mutually supportive mode. We shall see later examples in which it became strongly contradictory.

War, rhetoric, and the arts in Canaanite Palestine: An ivory tablet, found at Megiddo (Armageddon), 12th century BC. Note the juxtaposition of armed soldiers, prisoners of war, a court bard (with lyre), and the crowned leader before the throne, much as they appeared to Joshua during his Canaanite campaign.

The radical content of the Mosaic message is also noteworthy for its resonances in later periods. Karl Marx, reflecting upon the failures of radical movements, in 1848 proclaimed,

> The revolution, which finds here not its end, but its organizational beginning, is no short-lived revolution. The present generation is like the Jews whom Moses led through the wilderness. It has not only a new world to conquer, it must go under in order to make room for men who are able to cope with a new world.[3]

Yet another element retained from antiquity in the pattern of modern political war is the principle of a vanguard or elite element to receive, interpret, and apply to the times those eternal truths deemed necessary for the salvation of the nation. In the Mosaic text, this concept took the form of a Great Legislator, in the person of Moses and later Joshua, responsible for articulating and prosecuting war aims as well as defining the internal order of society.

A similar concept appears in Greek and Roman practices, as we shall see later, under the form of gnosticism.[4] The gnostic ethos and a more specific later form, Manichaeanism,[5] had as their essential features an assertion of superior wisdom and an adamant conviction that the universe was separable into the realm of the good and the realm of the evil. One of the political manifestations of this ethos has tended to be an authoritarian and rigid posture toward all nonbelievers. The ethos has had a persistent role throughout European culture, at times expressed in forms of national assertion, including war and revolution[6] (on which, more later).

Finally, let us note the consistent attention, in the war posture of ancient Israel, to psychological weapons in battle. However one may explain it, Joshua's blast of trumpets at the taking of Jericho appears as a successful act of psychological warfare with both tactical and strategic consequences; Israelite practice in communicating with and maneuvering among the more numerous tribes of Canaan, yet more so. (It was this flexibility which did much to diminish the contradictory aspects of Israel's external and internal ethos).

At the outset of the Davidic empire, David's propaganda of the deed in successfully confronting Goliath before the assembled armies of the two sides played a major role in the battle that

Joshua, from wall frescoes in the Dura-Europas Synagogue on the Euphrates, painted ca. AD 214. The frescoes are significant for the importance of Joshua in Jewish representational art more than a thousand years after his conquest of Canaan. Note also the early Byzantine influence in form: the frontality of the figure (which is arranged in a symmetrical setting with other patriarchs) and the calculated disregard of perspective and depth, techniques of visual art that Justinian used three hundred years later on a larger scale for imperial propaganda.

followed as well as in the later Davidic legend on which the empire rested. The central location of Jerusalem as the site for the seat of the empire had strong political as well as trade route and strategic significance.[7] The ancient Israelites did not go into battle quietly, or without regard to the power of images and ideas in gaining and consolidating victory, defined in terms of survival for their nation and their altar.

Ancient Greece gave further impetus to some of these Israelite concepts of political war and added yet others. Deceptive communication, known today as disinformation, was not unknown in the Homeric age. The case of the Trojan Horse needs no recounting. It sometimes is forgotten that the key to getting the men, concealed within the wooden horse, inside the walls of Troy was the false report of the horse's purpose, supposedly an offering to the gods. Another case from the period appears in the account of a forged letter purporting to come from Priam, King of Troy, offering gold to Palamides, a rival of Odysseus in the Greek forces. The forgery, and some gold, were secreted by Odysseus' men in the tent of Palamides, who was subsequently put to death by the other Greek commanders, who feared his defection to Troy.[8]

For several centuries after the death of Alexander in 323 BC, the Hellenistic world revolved around the city of Alexandria in present-day Egypt. These centuries sowed the seed of a profound split between East and West, one leading to the later division of Imperial Rome into rival empires of East and West. More will be said on this split later; but first let us look at some points of style which European culture—East and West—derived from the heritage of pre-Hellenistic classical Greece.

Rhetoric and its sister muse, theater, are *par excellence* the arts of the Classical Greeks. We will see later, in examining the Reformation, something of the influence of theater on European styles of political war. Here, we will look at the use of rhetoric. The Greeks did not invent it, but they clearly cultivated it at a level of skill and effect unknown previously and possibly not equaled since. Their use of it in politics and war, their dependence upon it for the formulation of philosophic concepts, and their sheer beauty of expression echo in our ways of thought and patterns of action today. It is worth noting the categories into which they classified rhetoric, for those same categories are part of the arsenal used by any modern propagandist in the European tradition, East or West.

Aristotle, both as the leader of a major school at Athens and as the tutor and political agent of Alexander of Macedon, did much to define the role and forms of rhetoric as a tool of politics and war. Aristotle distinguished between lectures given in the morning to his own students, which he termed esoteric—that is, for the educated and the initiated—and those given in the afternoons, pitched to a much simpler audience of ordinary Athenians, involving simpler concepts expressed in plain language, later termed exoteric—"external" lectures for the masses. The key point here lies in the notion that some preparation is required before an esoteric teaching can be presented to the uninitiated, who might otherwise misunderstand or misuse it.

Aristotle's concept (without the name) later emerged in Lenin's theories of propaganda as many ideas for a few close followers, and agitation as a few simple ideas for the masses. This basic concept is important to an understanding of all modern political advocacy, although for various reasons it has crystallized into formal procedures in the Eastern style and become more diffuse in that of the West.

Aristotle and other rhetoricians, Roman as well as Greek, drew other distinctions in rhetoric according to purpose. To advance the speaker's personal credibility, to stir the emotions on a topic, or to persuade by the force of reason, was one early formulation of categories. Others, after Aristotle, included declamatory speech, suitable to state occasions, heavy and formal in tone; forensic speech, using a mixture of subtle and dense argument with emotion as suited to law courts; and various specialized forms, such as erotic and cunning (deceptive) persuasion. From all of these practices and distinctions emerged a tradition of speech as an instrument of political power, perhaps best characterized by the *Orestia* plays of Aeschylus, which show the use of words as superior to brute force in settling disputes or compelling acquiescence.[9]

The expansion of Macedonia under Philip and the conquest by his son, Alexander, of the known world in the fourth century BC had momentous consequences of several kinds, not least among them being the spread of Greek forms of rule and of warfare across an arc stretching from western India and central Asia to the shores of the western Mediterranean. It may be instructive to recount an incident in Philip's rise to power, showing how the arts of persuasion were deployed in combination with armed force and diplomacy by him and his allies. The account is rendered by Demosthenes in a work entitled *The False Embassy*. Written circa 343 BC, it gives an account of contacts both diplomatic and rhetorical between Philip and the Athenian state which continued to resist his aggression.

The terms of a temporary peace agreed upon between Athens and Macedon provided that each should retain the territories in its possession at the time the peace was concluded. As Philip was constantly engaged in fresh conquests, it was urgent, once Athens had accepted the peace terms, that a second diplomatic mission proceed with all speed to obtain Philip's ratification by oath of the terms worked out by the negotiations. In spite of the remonstrances of Demosthenes, who spoke for the party in Athens opposing concessions to Philip, the negotiators delayed, and Philip delayed further. By the time peace was ratified, Thrace had been subdued by Macedon. Moreover, on the negotiators' return to Athens, one of them, Aeschines, gave so flattering an account of Philip's intentions regarding Athenian interests that the legislators of Athens voted the extension of the treaty to Philip's descendants, allowing Philip to occupy strategically placed sites such as Thermopylae. In so doing, the Athenians abandoned a major ally, the Phocians, to their fate.

Later in the year, when Philip's aggressive policy had roused public feeling at Athens, Demosthenes was able to impeach Aeschines on the grounds of the injury done to Athens as a consequence of his delay as a negotiator, and of his false reports; and Demosthenes suggested that bribery was the cause of Aeschines' pro-Macedonian policy. Aeschines' reply secured a decision in his favor by 30 votes. Demosthenes then publicly charged in his speech "On the Chersonese" that Philip, though pretending to be at peace, was in fact at war with Athens, and all his operations were designed ultimately to encompass the ruin of Athens; the longer his actions were tolerated, the more difficult he would be to overcome.[10]

The interplay of war and diplomacy with rhetoric—or propaganda, as we term it—offers a useful perspective and necessary reminder for those inclined to separate such tools of policy into neat and mutually exclusive categories. Philip obviously knew how to combine them, and to use appropriate talent in pursuing them. In him, and in his son Alexander, the offices of strategist and political leader were closely merged. Athens was accustomed to distinguishing the two functions—the *Ecclesia* (legislature) appointed the *Strategos* (military commander), of whose prerogatives the Athenians were obsessively jealous—and when Athens was wisely ruled, its citizens were able to protect their freedoms as well as cultivate them. They failed in the end to solve the dilemma posed by the determined and ruthlessly ambitious dynasty that arose in their sister state of Macedon.

Money as propaganda was an aspect of conquest introduced by the Macedonians, or at least applied by them at an unprecedented scale. Alexander's domination of vast new territories and peoples created problems of immense proportions for his successors. Among them were the basic issues of how to organize the newly subject peoples' economic life and how to legitimize the decisions taken by local authorities. An instrument was needed that cut across language and cultural differences, was easily comprehended by all classes, and yet was amenable to centralized control. Coinage was such a tool. The "Alexander Tetradrachm," a silver coin with Alexander's portrait on one side and a Greek deity, Zeus, on the other served the purpose admirably. It was standardized as to weight and format, and minted at authorized sites throughout the occupied areas. Once in circulation, the new coinage provided ubiquitous visual evidence to all inhabitants of the Hellenistic world that Greek power prevailed.[11]

Philip's triumph brought an end to the brilliant and diverse culture of the Greek *polis* (city) and initiated a style of rhetoric and political thought characterized by formalism, artificiality, and imperial pomp. This style, termed Asianism, took root and expanded in the later Roman Empire's Eastern half. Much of its essence came from the influence of Persian models informally

*Alexander the Great. The "Alexander Tetradrachm" was one of the
first universal coins, used by the Macedonians to bind the nations
conquered by Alexander into a viable empire. A ruler's image on
currency was and still is one of the most effective symbols of
legitimacy and an important tool of political warfare, particularly in
occupied areas. The coin shown was probably minted in Odessa.
Similar coinage continued to be minted for nearly two centuries after
Alexander's death.*

adopted after Alexander's conquest of the Persian Empire, an influence resisted in vain by Alexander's former tutor and political adviser, Aristotle.[12]

Roman contribution to the art and practice of political warfare traced a trajectory similar to that of classical Greece: moving from a Republican period, as represented by Cicero, through the rhetorically gifted and ruthlessly purposeful early emperors such as Caesar and Octavian, into patterns of formality, imperial adulation, and religious mysticism under Constantine I and later Justinian I. The process covered a span of nearly six hundred years, and it was marked by irregularities, exceptions, and reversals. But the trend was clear—a skeptical, secular, and politically pluralist polity under the Republic giving way before a centralized, rigidly controlled administration under a divinely anointed God-emperor.

The scope, duration, and diversity of the Roman experience can make written generalizations seem both difficult and suspect. A visual comparison of the dry realism of statues and coinage portraying the emperors of the West (see portrait of Vespasian, p. 40) with the idealized mosaics of the Byzantine emperors in the East (Justinian, p. 49) points up the contrast between two basic propaganda styles, a contrast which kept its relevance well into modern times. Note for example the wartime portrait of Churchill, as contrasted to those of Hitler (pp. 183, 143 and 152).

Externally, the Roman Republic conducted its affairs— whether peaceful or bellicose—as one state acting within a system of states. The Empire acted on the premise of imperial dominance over the subject client states or dependent nationalities whose status sank to that of ethnic minorities within a multinational empire. The Roman historian Tacitus left a vivid account of these trends.[13]

This imperial system of the eastern half of the Empire, with its capital at Constantinople, was not—however intolerable it may appear to modern minds—either weak or unworthy in the eyes of many of its subjects. It lasted in one form or another for nearly a thousand years, and its philosophy and practices provided an alluring (but unattainable) model for many of the ambitious rulers of Renaissance Europe. It was consciously and explicitly adopted

This contemporary bust of Vespasian (Roman emperor, AD 69-79), deliberately presenting him as an unpretentious middle-class Italian, shows the spirit of dry realism customary in portraits of Republican and early Imperial Rome. The contrast to the hieratic, idealized portraits of later Byzantine emperors reveals much about the social and cultural differences that placed their stamp on propaganda in the western and eastern halves of the Empire. Also compare this representation to the portraiture shown later of Churchill and Hitler in World War II.

as a symbol and model under Ivan IV and his successor tsars of late medieval Muscovy, and later by twentieth century ideologues using quite different symbols but animated by the same spirit.[14]

Students of political warfare should note the works of at least two emperors in this proud and ominous tradition: one, Constantine I, for his successful use of mass religious fervor as an instrument of imperial conquest and rule; the other, Justinian I, for his consolidation of these principles and their spectacularly brilliant expression in art, law, and architecture.

Constantine I, called the Great, ruled the still-united empire of the Romans from AD 312 until his death in 337. He was the first emperor to adopt Christianity as his personal creed and to acknowledge it as a major influence in the Empire. His reasons for doing so are instructive to students of political war. According to his official historian, Eusebius, Constantine asserted that in the course of his march on Rome to evict a rival to the throne, he had seen a vision: a cross athwart the sun, and beneath it the words, "In this sign conquer." Before the walls of Rome, he saw a further vision bidding him place the Christian monogram Chi Rho on the shields of his soldiers. This was done and his troops were victorious.

Under Constantine, previous limited edicts of toleration of the Christians, persecuted sporadically for centuries under earlier emperors for their stiff-necked refusal to worship the emperor, were confirmed and more rigorously enforced. In AD 330, Constantine transferred his official residence from Rome to Byzantium and launched an extensive building program at the new site; thus divinely legitimated, the center of political gravity gradually shifted from West to East.

Constantine died having been, according to Eusebius, baptized a Christian (albeit in the heretical Arian manner) shortly before his death. Although some scholars argue that Constantine had long before identified himself personally with the Christian church and creed, others dispute the conversion. It does seem clear, though, that he thought the prosperity of the Roman state bound up with the unity of the Catholic church, and that he worked seriously to strengthen the church through influencing episcopal appointments, encouraging church councils such as that of Nicea in 325, and building new basilicas. Regarding Constantine—and

Chi Rho, a Greek anagram for Christ. One of the most successful symbols in history of imperial majesty and divine authority. Adopted by Constantine the Great and continued by his successors for over a thousand years. This version is seen on a large bronze coin struck in a provincial capital, Amiens, ca. AD 350. The Greek letters Alpha and Omega, flanking the Chi Rho, symbolize the beginning and end of the universe, affirming the universalist claims—secular as well as religious—of the Byzantine empire.

his modern emulators—a major question remains: How much must a charismatic ruler's professed faith arise from an inner vision, and how much may it reflect a calculated appraisal of political realities and propaganda strategy?[15]

Constantine was neither the first nor the last to link religious commitment with imperial ambition, but he was arguably one of the most successful. The Empire as he reshaped it was the most enduring of its kind in European political culture, East or West. Several features of his rule deserve special note.

First, the context was highly conducive to such a blend of religion and imperialism. Late Imperial Rome had continued to decline in moral force, as the elites were in many cases corrupt and opportunistic, and the circumstances of everyday life for the ordinary citizen were increasingly turbulent and onerous. A movement like Christianity, arising from genuine mass enthusiasm and reflecting authentic piety, had much to recommend it to both rulers and ruled. Constantine, striving to establish some form of political unity in a multinational empire, may well have acted from a sober political calculation that the most dynamic of the empire's many creeds was the best on which to base his rule at home and efforts to elicit support among the population of his adversaries. The adoption of the faith produced a new element of popular participation across a broad spectrum of society. Note, though, that it also brought an element of doctrinally based sectarian violence into the political and economic rivalries among bishops seated in major regional capitals.

Second, and possibly most important, Constantine appears to have succeeded, whatever his personal belief, in creating a sustainable image of divine legitimation for his principles of governance, while permitting individuals of diverse ethnic origin to rise to the highest levels of power, both secular and ecclesiastic. Although favoring one religion, he continued to offer scope for others, including, for example, the Jews, who like the Christians had been subject to sporadic repression and intimidation under previous emperors. As a prototype for later rulers of totalitarian bent, Constantine offers a powerful but mixed example. It was possibly this inconsistency, if it be such, which enabled him to succeed where his later imitators—such as Hitler or Mussolini—came to grief.

Fel Temp Reparatio *(Happy Days Are Here Again), Redeemer and Defender theme. The legend and accompanying image of a Roman infantryman defeating a raiding barbarian cavalryman appear on a bronze coin struck in Antioch, a regional capital of the Byzantine Empire, ca. AD 350. The guarantee of stability and order was a strong point of imperial propaganda, particularly for anyone with wealth. Coinage offered a highly effective, self-targeting medium through which to convey it.*

Finally, the content of Constantine's version of Christianity contained significant elements of compatibility, if not identity, with previously strong ideological tendencies in Roman life—those of the Stoic school of Athens, adopted in essence by patricians as diverse in outlook as Julius Caesar, Seneca, and Virgil. In early Christianity, these links had been rejected. But under the influence of second century theologians such as Clement of Alexandria and Origen, the idea had grown up that ancient culture was still valuable and not necessarily incompatible with the new religion.

Constantine's espousal of a monotheistic creed was also useful at the symbolic level so important to his military mobilizational needs. By blending the symbol of the cross with the symbol of the Sun god, Constantine linked two symbols that had proven particularly effective among military units. Constantine's conversion thus offered a bridge to the past as well as a vision of the future at several levels.

These points may appear at first to apply in the main to the conditions within the Empire, leaving the question of what relevance they may have to foreign wars. The reality of late Imperial Rome, though, was that in an empire of such scale and tenacity, the distinction between domestic and foreign matters was often unclear; many nations existed within the Empire, and few organized states contiguous to it were capable of interacting on any more than a client-dependency basis analogous to the relationships with nationalities inside the Empire. The Goths, Huns, Vandals, Slavs, and other barbarian tribes pressing down from the north and east were dealt with by the Roman emperors at a variety of levels, including occasional embassies. But the relationship was usually a fluid and relatively porous one in which the barbarians tended to be incorporated into and rose within the Empire as constituent elements, both individually and as groups. Political and religious proselytizing by Roman officials and clerics was an influential part of this rather turbulent process. Conversion as well as conquest was part of the Imperial style of war.

In the centuries after Constantine's death, the Roman world began to polarize into a stronger Eastern and a weaker Western half, with

Roman Occupation Coinage: Head of Constantius II, minted AD 337-361 in Alexandria, then capital of Roman-occupied Egypt. Reveals a significant evolution in the imperial leader image on currency, begun nearly seven centuries earlier by Alexander of Macedon. Compared to the earlier Macedonian image, which was robustly assertive in style, the Constantius image is characteristic of the ascetic, exalted theocratic ethos of the Byzantine court. The image is, however, supplemented on the reverse by the quite practical Redeemer and Defender message often used in the same century by Rome to elicit support among the population of occupied areas, in both Europe and Asia, against barbarian invaders.

incursions from the barbarians most pronounced in the West. By the middle of the fifth century, the Italian peninsula and most of North Africa had succumbed to barbarian rulers who in many cases adopted the (Latin) religious and administrative patterns of their Roman subjects. Conflict was endemic both among the barbarian tribes and between them and the remaining center of Imperial power in Constantinople, as Byzantium's capital was now known.

The rule of Justinian in the East (AD 527-565), and his efforts through a military commander of outstanding genius to bring the religiously vigorous but militarily disorganized Western empire to heel, marks a further progression in the Eastern tradition of political warfare. As military history, the campaigns of the Eastern commander, Belisarius, and his successor, Narses, have been carefully studied by later generations of military leaders.

A brilliant and vigorous tactician, wrongly suspected by Justinian of harboring aspirations to rule, Belisarius first reconquered North Africa and then occupied the Italian peninsula, allowing Justinian's viceroys to impose temporarily the Eastern, Byzantine vision of ecclesiastical polity and civil rule throughout the West. How they did so, it is now clear, involved not only a distinctive military style but also the deployment of liturgical, theological, and artistic talent on a magisterial scale. It was in this unprecedented deployment and concentration of military style, ideational concepts, and visual images that Justinian made a decisive and enduring contribution to the art and practice of political warfare.

The imperial style of conflict adopted by Justinian with the help of his marshals and bishops, and his stage-wise wife, amounted to more in its totality than the sum of its parts. At the military level, Belisarius and Narses consciously exploited the superior discipline and engineering skill of their troops by inculcating a sense of qualitative superiority and confidence in the face of the frequent numerical superiority of the barbarian Western forces. Belisarius was decisively victorious on numerous occasions through his use of the tactical defensive. Watching the barbarian inclination to attack with heavy cavalry, he adopted a tactical defense designed to lure them into precipitate attack that exposed them to counterattack and defeat by his better-coordinated forces. His strategy was thus more psychological than logistical, building an image of his forces' invincibility in the minds of the barbarian commanders and troops, an image that led his enemies to take self-defeating actions.[16]

This carefully cultivated spirit of tactical superiority and confidence was reflected and amplified at the strategic level by Justinian and his Court into an image of imperial invincibility. The cumulative effect of such a posture went well beyond the outcome of a single campaign. The imperial ethos, with resonance for a number of later empires, was emerging and establishing firm cultural roots. In the Byzantine case, it did much to sustain the Empire for centuries to come. Later imitators have been less successful.

Large-scale political warfare requires, above all, a great capacity for simplification. Justinian and his entourage did not invent but brilliantly used one of the most impressive and enduring forms of simplified mass communication—the large-scale visual image expressing transcendent political and religious principles in concrete and easily grasped forms. The times clearly required such an instrument: the Eastern half of the Empire was predominantly Greek-speaking, at least among its elites; the Western half, Latin-speaking. In both halves, a turbulent and fluid array of emerging tribes and nations groped their way toward a sense of national identity that eventually crystallized a half-millennium later in the nation states of Eastern and Western Europe.

Religious and related ethical concepts needed to bind and animate the imperial administration were often expressed in complex and tortuous theological debates, which worked their way into the minds of provincial administrators and then descended into the consciousness of the masses. Justinian sought to simplify these procedures by bold and sweeping acts, of which his code of laws and his art forms were of enduring worth. Leaving aside the laws, let us look more closely at the art. We will see it adopted in startling verisimilitude by the totalitarian regimes of the twentieth century, used for the same purpose that animated Justinian.

As one may see from the Ravenna mosaics, installed following Belisarius' occupation of the West, Byzantine art was an uncompromising totalist assertion of divine mandate to rule. Justinian is presented larger than life, crowned with the halo of sanctity, flanked on his right by his marshals in full armor and on the left by his ideologists, the bishops and the patriarch. The pose

Justinian I with bishops and marshals. This sixth century (AD) portrayal of unbending imperial will, with the divinely anointed emperor flanked by the might of the military and the power of the word, raised visual imagery as an instrument of conquest to new heights. The creative artistry apparent in these life-size mosaics has seldom been surpassed in totalitarian political propaganda. These were installed in Ravenna, the Byzantine regional capital in Italy, following Belisarius' subjugation of the Italian peninsula.

is uncompromisingly frontal, hierarchical, and pervaded by a sense of absolute, unbending finality. It is, moreover, charged with a beauty and power of artistic expression difficult to explain for those in the Western tradition, who are accustomed to identifying creativity with a system of political diversity based upon freedom of religious and political expression. The Irish poet William Butler Yeats, hardly a conformist, contemplated these forms of totalitarian art in his *Sailing to Byzantium* and rightly termed them artifices of eternity. Modern totalitarian art, although clearly inferior in execution, is still animated by essentially similar views of the world.

Political warfare conducted by and against people steeped in such traditions must take into account and properly assess these traditions. Their art has profoundly deep religious and cultural roots; it is, moreover, capable of eliciting mass support and cohesion even in its presently degraded form. A political warfare campaign against opponents whose use of such art forms corresponds to the traditions and culture of peoples in the Eastern ecumene has a formidable task. It would be a grave mistake to ignore or dismiss such a task. Poor as the present Soviet art and literature may be today, it retains a tremendous potential for future political warfare use among populations imbued with these cultural traditions.

3

THE REFORMATION

W e now turn to a period of major transformation in the West, a transformation so profound and so broad that it created a wide gulf between the Eastern and Western halves of Judeo-Christian political and religious aspirations. In essence, the emerging nations of the West rejected the imperial ethos and returned to the conflictual, chaotic, and diversely brilliant models of Greek city states and Roman republican days. The transforming event was the Renaissance and its following political manifestation, the conflict between the Protestant (or Reformation) states of northern Europe and the Counter-Reformation Holy Roman Empire of southern Europe. At its most intense the conflict had ramifications spreading into the Mediterranean and across the Atlantic to the Americas.

Out of this north-south split in the West emerged a diverse, pluralist culture that, after several centuries of warfare, amounted to an affirmation of the Reformed ethos. No such reformation took place in the East, which continues to this day to function on principles strikingly similar to the imperial models of latter day Rome. Later chapters look more closely at these East-West differences. Here, we will explore the consequences of the Reformation for political war in the nations of Western Europe, especially Tudor and Stuart England. The consequences were profound, and are instructive for modern commanders.

The conflict between England and Spain, lasting from the mid-1500s to the end of the 1600s, presents a remarkable case of limited versus unlimited strategic objectives pursued through political war including propaganda, covert action, use of conventional arms, and economic interaction. Modern historiography focuses on the naval war, specifically the defeat of the Armada. Contemporary English strategists thought of that conflict mostly in trade terms: "The hurt that our state should seek to do him," wrote the Earl of Essex of the King of Spain, "is to intercept his treasures, whereby we shall cut his sinews and make war on him with his own money."[1] But the use of trade weapons and of military force was intermittent on both sides, sometimes sanctioned by diplomacy, often not. Only the propaganda struggle was sustained and intense on both sides. It was usually, but not entirely, conducted on religious and cultural grounds.

The religious differences were more apparent than real. But in political conflict, appearances attain a dynamic of their own; and when amplified by the power of literature and the arts, they attain massive proportions. This force was particularly marked in England and Spain. To grasp its significance for the conduct of political war, we need to look not only at the theology of the age, but also at its theater, painting, poetry, and architecture, much of which was conceived in the spirit of conflict and was quite consciously used in the struggle by rulers of the day.

Making a case for the value of actors on patriotic as well as social grounds, a contemporary of Shakespeare's proclaimed, "So bewitching a thing is lively and well-spirited [stage] action as it hath power to new-mold the hearts of the spectators and fashion them to the shape of any noble and notable attempt."[2] The Elizabethan theater was most emphatically a political arena.

Elizabeth I directly, and more especially through her Lord Chamberlain, Hunsdon, and military leaders like Essex and Raleigh, protected and subsidized artists, actors, and above all playwrights. Shakespeare, through Hunsdon, and through Essex's client Southampton, was a principal beneficiary, a status he also enjoyed—with possibly more direct support—under James I. Staging a Court play in the time of Elizabeth I has been estimated to have cost around four hundred pounds in the money of the day. The Court often paid much of the initial expense.[3] Shakespeare's company acted regularly at Court, and was listed in the Court accounts as receiving payment for the performances.[4] Under Elizabeth, command performances averaged around three a year; under James I they numbered about thirteen a year, more than those of all other companies combined. And James doubled the remuneration.[5]

It is natural for the student of propaganda to ask how much of Shakespeare's work was written on direct instruction from the Court, how much was less directly inspired or influenced, and how much was created purely on the playwright's own initiative. First, it seems clear, at least to me, that William Shakespeare was the author of the plays and poetry published under his name. Neither courtiers like the Earl of Oxford, high officials like Lord Chancellor Bacon, nor anyone else wrote these works. It also seems clear that the author was neither a committee nor a bureaucrat. At the risk of stating the obvious, it should be emphasized that William Shakespeare was a creative writer of original and inspired genius who possessed as well an acute sense of both domestic and international politics.

Shakespeare did not need detailed guidance or censorship to know what to think or write about the events of the era. He was, from time to time, leaned upon by this or that high official or faction at Court, usually for reasons of personality or power rather than high policy. He usually responded, on his own terms. In short, William Shakespeare gave to the Crown more than the Crown gave to Shakespeare. He was no less powerful a propagandist for all that.

Although the documentary evidence is sparse, it seems probable that Shakespeare did receive direct instruction from the Queen in some cases. Her insistence that he write a play—the *Merry Wives of Windsor*—devoted to the further adventures of Falstaff is perhaps best known. The play serves no obvious foreign policy purpose, as do the great historical dramas, but the incident demonstrates the sovereign's intimate interest in Shakespeare. And the play did lend a note of earthy humanity and wit to the popular image of Court life, a public relations objective by no means foreign to the governing style of Elizabeth Tudor.

Throughout the Elizabethan period of his professional life, Shakespeare appears to have been personally beholden to the youthful and ambitious Earl of Southampton rather than to the Queen directly. Southampton, in turn, was a client of the brilliant but erratic Earl of Essex, Elizabeth's last (and disastrous) military leader and Court favorite. Essex and Southampton overplayed their hand in 1601, failing in a bid for power against the chief minister, Cecil. Essex was beheaded and Southampton went to prison;

Shakespeare never publicly denounced his former patron, South-ampton, though he apparently had serious misgivings. (*Hamlet*, written in 1601, probably reflects much of this ambivalence about the Earl's political judgment.) While continuing to write and per-form for the Court's—and England's—benefit, Shakespeare was silent with regard to the person of Elizabeth.

I have discovered no evidence of direct influence by foreign governments on Shakespeare, although I find it hard to believe that in the atmosphere of the time none made the effort. On at least one occasion, under James I in 1608, the French Ambassador at London protested against a scene in a play, not written by Shakespeare but staged at the Blackfriars, of which he was part owner. The Ambassador—with some justice—regarded the scene as derogatory of his sovereign, the French Henry IV.[6] The scene was deleted, and the theater closed for a period.

Shakespeare, to our knowledge, never served in the army. But he lived through a period of constant warfare, and he acted and wrote plays for men (and women) who were much involved in it. His two theaters, of which he was part owner, appealed to fighting men from the camp as well as the Court. How he portrayed these men to each other and to allied audiences powerfully affected their sense of identity and purpose, as well as their fighting spirit. He had no desire to foster illusions about war, or about the lottery of battle. He often portrayed both with grim and disillusioned realism. But he did so in ways that make us, even today, sensible of the need for combat as a means of survival and national as-sertion. Two of his rhetorical methods[7] to this end stand out and deserve notice by any propagandist today: caricature, both positive and negative, and poetic amplification.

The Welsh captain, Fluellen, in *Henry V*, is one of the classic caricatures in English. Both as an ethnic type and as a fighting man, he speaks to us convincingly as he debates tactics with his commanders before the battle of Agincourt. His Welsh burr, his love of the Welsh national emblem, the leek, and his cocky fighting spirit put Welshmen as fellow fighting men firmly into the minds of his English, Scottish, and Irish comrades in the Tudor ranks.

The English armed forces during Shakespeare's day were still distinctly multinational. (The House of Tudor, itself, was of Welsh origin.) Welding these violent and volatile soldiers into a single force was essential to victory in a very direct and immediate way. Plays like Shakespeare's—as popular in their day as television is today—did the job by forging images based on caricatures which shaped men's opinions of each other and the way they acted together in battle. Shakespeare produced many such caricatures, some ethnic, some social; some, like Prince Hal, were protagonists, others, like Fluellen, supporting cast. All were subtle and many-sided, but nonetheless vivid and effective.[8] Some were negative, some positive, with the negative types usually opposed to the national purpose, the positive types, with all their foibles and weaknesses as well as strengths, supportive of it.

Poetic amplification in Shakespeare's work was worthy of the classical models of Greece and Rome which it drew upon in part for inspiration and form. In the prologue to his dramatic portrayal of the life of Henry V, the playwright calls,

Oh for a Muse of fire, that would ascend

The brightest heaven of invention,

A kingdom for a stage, princes to act,

And monarchs to behold the swelling scene!

Then should the warlike Harry, like himself,

Assume the port of Mars; and at his heels,

Leash'd in like hounds, should famine, sword and fire

Crouch for employment. . . .

Referring then to his Globe theater, where the play was a roaring success, Shakespeare asks,

Can this cockpit hold

The vasty fields of France? Or may we cram

Within this wooden O the very casques

That did affright the air at Agincourt?

Shakespeare's genius in lifting his audience's view from their everyday parochial concerns onto the stage of international events did much to enhance the English vision of the world throughout the era of the anti-Spanish alliance of northern Europe.

Shakespeare was part owner, actor, and playwright for two London theaters. One, called Blackfriars, staged controlled-access productions favored by the nobility and gentry of the Court; the other, the Globe, was open to all sorts and conditions of men (and women), including numerous foreigners living and working in London both at Court and in private life.

"All the foreigners who came to London at the turn of the century were struck by the London theaters, their gorgeous show, the quality of the acting, and the large resort to them." The modern scholar who offers this appraisal adds, "Nothing quite like them had been known in Europe since the days of the Roman Empire, and not for more than another two hundred years was there any other city which could show so many permanent theaters at one time."[9]

Embassy personnel, including Ambassadors and their wives, were frequent theatergoers in Elizabethan London, as were visiting heads of government, particularly those from the numerous small German principalities (whose alignment was important in the balance of power on the continent). The French and Spanish Ambassadors regularly reported on theatrical productions and entertained the players. Foscarini, the Ambassador from Venice, who represented an important (but unpredictable) maritime power, was well known for his enthusiastic behavior in the theater; he was often ridiculed for his conduct by wits in the rival Florentine Embassy.[10] An Embassy public affairs officer today, coping with media and cultural life in a major world capital, would recognize the scene; so would a modern disinformation officer.

The Globe's repertoire consciously played to this sophisticated, international audience, offering plays focused not only on English history, but also on events in France, Italy, Scandinavia, the Balkans, Egypt, and the new world of the Atlantic islands like Bermuda. It was not unusual for characters—such as French commanders portrayed in *Henry V*—to speak French, or for actors to portray foreign personalities and rulers in historical and contemporary settings.

Shakespeare belonged to a circle of intellectuals grouped around the Earl of Southampton. The group included a gifted Anglo-Italian translator and swordsman, John Florio, and a sultry young Italian musician, Emilia Bassano, who performed with her father at Court. Emilia was for a while the mistress of the Lord Chamberlain, Hunsdon, and later became the shared mistress of Southampton and Shakespeare. She is immortalized as the "dark lady" of Shakespeare's sonnets. Emilia, herself a prolific poet, was an articulate and defiant feminist. She seems, from Shakespeare's rueful portrayal in his later sonnets, to have been a shattering personality.[11]

The modern manager of public diplomacy and propaganda operations, faced with stringent personnel and security requirements for programmers, should bear in mind that the creative artists required for effective operations often lead disorderly personal lives, and that they can become involved unpredictably with powerful political figures. This knowledge may be small consolation to those faced with lurid revelations in tomorrow's headlines; it may, however, suggest ways to put the problem into context.

Elizabeth and her staff used the resources of the London theater quite freely and deliberately for what we would today call public diplomacy as well as for propaganda. On March 6, 1600, for example, Lord Hunsdon, as Elizabeth's Chamberlain, summoned Shakespeare's theatrical company—known as The Lord Chamberlain's Men—to present a command performance at Court for the edification of an allied state's envoy, the Dutch Ambassador.[12] The play chosen was *Henry IV Part 1*, the first part of a series dramatizing the exploits of one of the most popular of English heroes, Henry V. The drama of Prince Hal, who as Henry V in 1415 had reconquered the English Crown's possessions on the mainland of France, presented an instructive statement on the sustained dynastic commitment of the Tudor rulers to a role in the affairs of continental Europe.

The character of Prince Hal, portrayed in the first parts of the series as a loose-living, riotous young man and later as a much-reformed King, may have had additional interest to the Dutch and to other English allies, who were conscious of Elizabeth's advancing age and infirmities, and concerned about the continuity of English policy during a succession. The message, for allies and opponents alike, was that English policy had staying power that was not merely the result of a particular sovereign's transitory whims. This point was an important one to convey, with all the vivid and evocative power possible, to England's suspicious allies in the embattled Netherlands. The London stage, above all Shakespeare's, drove it home with eloquence and wit.

The newly independent Protestant Republic of the Northern Netherlands had come under renewed attack from Spain in 1599; in 1600 the Dutch counterattacked with 10,000 men. After mixed results in the field, the Dutch fought on for several years in alliance with England, until, in 1604, their fears were realized; James I, the new ruler of England who had succeeded Elizabeth in 1603, signed a nominal peace with Spain. In 1606, the Dutch succeeded in extracting recognition and a peace treaty from Philip III of Spain. Since 1572, when the wars in the Netherlands began, the ground and sea conflict had sputtered on, punctuated by occasional truces. But the actual combat always took place against the backdrop of a continued ideological and propaganda struggle among the political elites of all contestants. Although the truce of 1606 was temporary and unsatisfactory (it lasted for twelve years), it did mark a new stage in the breakup of Spanish hegemony on the continent and the emergence into full nationhood of the Dutch.[13]

We can hardly assess, at this remove, the role of English and Dutch propaganda, in comparison to that of military force, in achieving this outcome. But, clearly, the political weapon was deployed, with vigor and skill, throughout the conflict. Given the indecisive nature of the military conflict, it is arguable that public diplomacy within the Anglo-Dutch alliance and propaganda between the warring Protestants and Catholics in the Netherlands and elsewhere in Europe were major factors. One need only read Shakespeare's plays with the political and military events of the time in mind to feel the intimate involvement of English theater with the course of the war.

Shakespeare's great historical plays, covering Roman and British history, were above all works of art; but they were also Tudor and Stuart propaganda with a powerful message for Englishmen, as well as for visitors to London from Protestant Europe. One of their strongest appeals is to a combative spirit: "O God of battles, steel my soldiers' hearts,/Possess them not with fear," reflects the King, in *Henry V* (act 4, scene 2), in the cold dawn before the climactic

*David Killing Goliath, by Rembrandt. One of a series of illustrations
for a book, in Spanish, by Rabbi Manasseh ben Israel, leader of the
Sephardic community in Amsterdam and founder—through
connections with Cromwell and Milton—of the modern Jewish
community in England. Line drawings are a powerful tool of political
advocacy, and many modern cartoonists use techniques developed by
Rembrandt.*

struggle against the French at Agincourt. Characteristically, Shakespeare linked lines like this with others, put in the mouth of a soldier, evoking a ruler's responsibility to his people in committing them to battle: "But if the cause be not good, the King himself hath a heavy reckoning to make. . . . Now if these men do not die well, it will be a black matter for the King that led them to it" (act 4, scene 1).

Shakespeare's portrayal of power as he saw it in the English monarchs, and as he attributes it to the Roman emperors, is illuminating. The emperors were semi-divine, their rule based on an image of themselves standing above and outside of the fates governing ordinary mortals. A Tudor monarch, however authoritative, was ultimately a man or woman like others, subject to the law and endowed with an individual religious conscience.

This spirit, in essence one of popular sovereignty, was still rudimentary, but it existed and its expression in the literature and theater of the day did much to strengthen the English and their Protestant allies in their struggle. Tied to a sense of growing national identity and pride, it made a formidable basis for the conduct of political war. Note, in a later play, *Henry VI Part 3*, its influence:

Hastings: Why, knows not Montague, that of itself
England is safe, if true within itself?
Montague: Yes, but the safer when tis backed with France.
Hastings: Tis better using France than trusting France:
Let us be backed with God and with the seas,
Which He hath given for fence impregnable,
And with their help only defend ourselves.

(act 4, scene 1)

Shakespeare's use of the stage to bolster understanding for a continued English wariness in the face of diplomatic maneuver by France and Spain appears also in the Introduction to *Henry IV Part 2*. Writing in 1598, shortly after conclusion of a peace treaty between France and Spain, Shakespeare says, in obvious reference to the duplicity of both, "I speak of peace, while covert enmity/ Under the smile of safety, wounds the world." The allusion was clear to English and Dutch officials who saw the hopes of peace at the diplomatic level undermined by massive Spanish assistance in men, arms, and subsidies to the Irish rebellion against English rule, a rebellion which forced Elizabeth to divert scarce military forces from assisting the Dutch.

Elizabeth and her staff had no inhibitions about giving as good as they got. Political warfare, including the use of emigres and the calculated choice of weapons—both the word and the sword—were part of the Tudor style. Consider the story of the emigre Roman general Coriolanus, who defected to the hostile Volscians, led them to conquer Rome, and then, torn by divided loyalties, failed to impose a peace satisfactory to the Volscian leaders, who killed him. The translation of Plutarch's *Lives*, from which this comes, exerted a powerful influence on Elizabethan prose, and on Elizabeth herself, who knighted the translator, Sir Thomas North, in 1591.

Shakespeare's stage version of *Coriolanus* dramatized the potential and complexity of the strategic use of emigre leaders. It also contained some passages offering trenchant operational advice:

Now this no more dishonors you at all
Than to take in a town with gentle words,
Which else would put you to your fortune and
To hazard of much blood.
I would dissemble with my nature where
My fortune and my friends at stake required
I should do so in honor.

(act 3, scene 2)

Shakespeare's sensitivity to the importance of popular sovereignty did not blind him to the problems of fickle public opinion. Listen to the deposed King in part three of *Henry VI*:

Ah, simple men, you know not what you swear!
Look, as I blow this feather from my face,
And as the air blows it to me again,
Obeying with my wind when I do blow,
And yielding to another when it blows,
Commanded always by the greater gust;
Such is the lightness of your common men.

(act 3, scene 1)

This awareness of basic principles to be observed in shaping opinions finds expression elsewhere in Shakespeare's work, as for example in *Love's Labour's Lost*:

A jest's prosperity lies in the ear
Of him that hears it, never in the tongue
Of him that makes it.

(act 5, scene 2)

How many professional propagandists have tried, in vain, to make this simple principle apply in the face of contrary political compulsions from their masters?

Shakespeare was by no means the only voice available to Elizabeth. Edmund Spenser's adulatory epic on Elizabeth, *The Faerie Queen*, was a spectacularly successful response to her Papal excommunication, earning its author the title throughout Europe of "the English Dante." Elizabeth rewarded him with an estate in Ireland and a generous annual pension (which she later reduced when she thought his work fell off). The King James Bible, so named because it was translated by a Royal Commission, gave linguistic as well as theological shape to the English Protestant vision, and brought that vision within the reach of any person who spoke English. The force and scope of this cultural renaissance was possibly the most powerful element in the English armory against Spain, a country with four times the English resources and a much superior military and naval force.[14]

Two aspects of this English use of literature and the arts are especially significant for an understanding of its role in national assertion. The first is its sheer brilliance and the confidence of a leader like Elizabeth in fostering and developing it for her purposes. The second is the spirit with which talented people in her realm responded. Much of what they accomplished represented individual initiative as much as, or more than, royal command. It also responded to popular attitudes, and it was often crassly commercial as well; Shakespeare, among others, died a wealthy man. Perhaps the genius of Elizabeth was, more than anything else, that she knew how to harness individual initiative and her nation's strong mercantile instincts to the purposes of national policy.

Elizabeth I of England, the "Rainbow Portrait" painted by Marcus Gheeraearts ca. 1600. One of a number of portraits, rich in political symbolism, commissioned by Elizabeth and members of her Court, often using Dutch and German artists. This portrait portrays the Queen in a setting of good fortune, with the rainbow in her hand, and royal authority in foreign affairs, symbolized by the pattern—evocative of her intelligence services—of eyes and ears woven into her cloak and the serpent of wisdom and guile embroidered on her sleeve.

Much of the Elizabethan genius for political warfare arose from this remarkable woman's personal style of governance. Note, for example, a contemporary account of her conduct of affairs:

> She would keep Burghley till late at night discussing the gravest issues; they usually agreed, but she would sometimes submit her judgment to his. Then she would call Walsingham in private for his views. On the morrow everyone did come forth in her presence and discourse at large. If any had dissembled with her, or stood not well to his advisings before, she did not let it go unheeded, and sometimes not unpunished.[15]

Sir John Harington, who wrote this account, supervised Elizabeth's Court staff and her personal servants; Burghley was her principal minister, and Walsingham headed her intelligence service. They were a formidable set of personalities who often disagreed among themselves over power and on personal grounds as well as on policy. Burghley tended to favor a search for accommodation with Spain and a negotiated settlement; Walsingham was stiffly opposed, and regarded the Spanish as irreconcilable.[16] Harington, who was himself a writer of considerable facility, spent much effort in lightening the atmosphere at Court with his wit and personal charm.

Elizabethan political style, as embodied in literature and the arts, derived from a deeper theological and constitutional ethos. One of Elizabeth's influential bishops, Richard Hooker (1554–1600), expressed as well as any thinker of the day the English vision. His seminal work, *The Laws of Ecclesiastical Polity*, written in 1593 and never fully published until the reign of James I, had a profound influence during his lifetime in establishing a favorable environment for learning, scholarship, and political tolerance. Following Hooker's lead, Anglican controversialists tended to show a lack of dogmatism, disclaiming infallibility and exclusive rights to salvation, thus softening the Calvinist rigidity strong among English Puritans.[17]

In Hooker's work lies one of the classic statements in English of the Western principle that individual conscience rather than official orthodoxy is the proper source for standards of human conduct. The preface to *The Laws of Ecclesiastical Polity* makes this quite clear:

The first mean whereby Nature teacheth men to judge good from evil, as well in laws as in other things, is the force of their own discretion. Hereunto therefore Saint Paul referreth oftentimes his own speech to be considered by them that heard him. "I speak as to them which have understanding; judge ye what I say" (*1 Corinthians* X:15). Saint Paul's rule therefore generally is: "Let everyman in his own mind be fully persuaded of that thing which he either alloweth or doth" (*1 Corinthians* XI:13).[18]

The vision animating Spain and Counter-Reformation Europe was quite different: "You may assure his Holiness," wrote Philip II in 1556 to his envoy at Rome,

that rather than suffer the least damage to religion and the service of God, I would lose all my estates and a hundred lives if I had them; for I do not purpose nor desire to be the ruler of heretics.[19]

This spirit informed the institutions and men of the Counter-Reformation—or, depending upon one's view, the Catholic Revival. It had inspired the formation of several militant religious orders, of which the Jesuits as educators and propagandists and the Capuchins as diplomatists are best known. And it brought the papacy in 1622 to create the Congregatio de Propaganda Fide, a Committee of Cardinals to oversee foreign missions, who have had their name (rightly or wrongly) taken to designate any association, scheme, or concerted movement for the propagation of a doctrine or practice.

The Spirit of the Times in late sixteenth and early seventeenth century Spain was one of flaming religious fanaticism. To accomplish the task they thought God had set them, Philip and his advisers and successors for several generations felt bound to use their secular power to the point of ruthless political tyranny. They pressed their ideological goals with zeal in the Netherlands, and would have done the same in England had they succeeded through naval power, assassination, and extensive political subversion in destroying England's national independence.

The respective roles of imperial ambition and religious conviction are extremely difficult to untangle in this period, as indeed they are in later periods of European history. In fairness to the papacy, it should be recalled that even the popes of the day found it sometimes difficult—and disconcerting—to try to distinguish between Philip's view of God's will and the interests of the House of Hapsburg. Pope Sixtus V, for example, observed, "The preservation of the Catholic religion which is the principal aim of the Pope is only a pretext for his Majesty, whose principal aim is the security and aggrandizement of his dominions."[20]

The Spanish Hapsburgs were not only highly organized at the center for the conduct of political warfare; they also deployed a diverse and spirited following of intellectuals and religious believers to work among English Catholics, many of whom were torn between religious conviction and national loyalty.[21]

One of the most formidable organizers among the English Catholic emigres working for Spain was Father Robert Parsons, SJ, alias Dollman. Born in 1546 to the family of a Protestant blacksmith, he was educated on scholarship at Oxford (Balliol), where he developed strongly Catholic views. In 1576 he emigrated to Louvain, where he was ordained. After training in the English College at Rome, he was sent with Father Campion as co-head of the Jesuit clandestine mission to England. He established a secret printing press and supervised the work of an extensive network of influence agents and intelligence collectors. His base of operations on the continent estimated that recruits to the Catholic cause, as measured by conversions, amounted to 20,000 converts in one year. Based on this and other evidence of response, the mission to England asked for, and received, an annual subsidy from Philip II and the Vatican of 2,000 crowns, and a promise of an 8,000-man invasion force to be staged from the Spanish Netherlands. This force was formed in 1584, recruited mainly from English emigres and commanded by an English Catholic peer, the Earl of Westmorland.

Parsons was a prolific and compelling polemicist. Like most of his order, he was devout, rigorously trained in rhetoric and theology, and adept in the uses of political power. During his stay in England he urged Mary Queen of Scots to marry the Duke of Parma, then the Spanish commander in the Netherlands, to provide a political basis for a post-invasion English government. He drafted a manifesto charging Elizabeth I with illegitimacy, thus sustaining the claim that her subjects were free to switch their allegiance to Mary. Following the failure of the invasion and the Armada in 1588, Parsons returned to Spain and, under the patronage of Philip II, established an English college (still extant) at Valladolid. He continued to advocate alternative rulers to Elizabeth, who had executed Mary for treason, producing a tract under his pseudonym, Dollman, titled *Conference About Succession to the Crown of England*.

Parsons (or Dollman) is memorable in the history of political warfare for his application of the principle of "equivocation." The principle, as elaborated and followed by operators on both sides (and numerous others since), has been described as follows:

> A moral problem arises when one is forced to answer a question but is obliged not to reveal the truth. Theologians on both sides taught that a lie was always evil: hence the development of theories which would justify an answer by which one was not obliged to convict oneself or others. Equivocation is the generic term, which is divided into verbal equivocation and mental reservation. Verbal equivocation requires that the words used be capable of bearing two meanings. . . . Mental reservation involves the suppression of part of a statement or proposition.[22]

These principles have been much denounced; an awareness of them still exists in modern legal procedure. They remain, in essence, part of the standard polemical armory for most international propaganda and of clandestine operating procedure, as they were in Parsons' day. The political point of the conflict, then as now, lay in the divergent requirements of political allegiance and the individual conscience. Anglican propagandists like John Donne (of whom, more later) struggled for several decades in seeking to unravel the dilemma.[23]

Elizabeth's intelligence service sent agents to penetrate the centers of English Catholic emigres on the continent, both for information and for counterpropaganda. A recent survey of Sir Francis Walsingham's combined security and intelligence services estimates their annual costs at about three or four thousand pounds, including in 1580 four agents in Spain, twelve in France, nine in Germany, four in Italy, three in the Low Countries, and three in

Algiers, Tripoli, and Morocco. They were not lavishly paid, but they were clearly a respectable capability for the time.[24]

The talent employed was often spectacularly gifted. In the 1580s Christopher Marlowe, then a young Cambridge scholar and poet, was recruited and sent to France by Walsingham's agents. Marlowe continued his involvement with intelligence and propaganda for the rest of his brief and turbulent life. His theater pieces reveal intimate personal knowledge of the Machiavellian politics of the day, as well as access to information which could only have come from intelligence sources. Marlowe's death during a brawl in an obscure portside tavern at the end of a dispute with some of Walsingham's other men raises still unresolved questions. It also suggests an early example of the innate tension between intelligence collection and political warfare operations.[25]

We have other examples of talented writers working as laymen on the Catholic side, some with direct involvement of the Spanish head of state. The career of a Catholic scholar from Oxford named Richard Verstegen, alias Rowlands (1565–1620), is characteristic. Denied his degree for religious reasons, he emigrated to Antwerp, dropped his English name, and adopted that of his Flemish grandfather. Equipped with a printing press, he acted as an agent for the transmission of Catholic literature to England. In 1587 (the year of heavy propaganda preparation for the Armada and its associated invasion force) he was living in Paris, where the English Ambassador pressured the French authorities to imprison him for publishing a book against Elizabeth's treatment of Catholics. In 1595 he had an interview with Philip II in Madrid.[26]

These and other cases offer a clear picture of sustained, strategically coordinated propaganda operations, including personal guidance by heads of state, involving diplomatic pressure, and linked to major naval and land force deployments like the Armada invasion of 1588. The scope, intensity, and targeting varied over time, and was often influenced by internal political considerations on both sides. The most intensive preparations, or at least those for which evidence is still available today, were in the period just before major engagements. The invasion forces assembled under the Duke of Parma in Flanders before the Armada sailed included not only large troop formations but also intelligence collection and propaganda teams, and diversionary units usually

Sir Francis Drake, English naval commander and commerce raider against Spain. Contemporary broadsheet showing Drake supervising loading of naval munitions. Accompanying anti-Spanish text in Latin and German indicates intended use among European audiences.

employing emigre manpower trained by the English Jesuits. Penetration and disruption of these units, in Flanders and after their arrival in England, was a primary task of Walsingham's organization.

Dealing with the internal security implications of these challenges within the context of England's social and constitutional structure raised a number of issues still relevant today. A large proportion of the English population, possibly a majority, considered themselves Catholic, as they chose to define it; sorting out their loyalties presented challenges for all concerned.[27] As between Elizabeth and Philip, it was clearly Philip who made the most serious miscalculation. Elizabeth succeeded in untangling, one way or another, the questions of religious faith and political allegiance. To Philip they were one and the same.[28]

I would argue that Philip's obsessive linking of propaganda and political subversion, indeed his holistic style of political warfare, was massively counterproductive; that it was at the root of his failure to achieve his goal of subjugating England and Holland and returning them to the community of Catholic Europe. He was led into this failure by his own narrow-minded fanaticism and by the disciplined fervor of his instruments, both political and military. "The typical English Catholic," in the words of one modern observer,

> who desired only to be allowed to follow his worship in peace, was obscured by the missionary activity of the Jesuits whose purpose was avowedly to win back England to their faith. Their method was the assertion of popular rights against the monarchy, and the doctrines of Bellarmine and Suarez, which were given in English version by writers like Dollman [pseudonym of Robert Parsons], arguing in 1583 against the legitimacy of the excommunicated Elizabeth seemed to have perilous affinities with the politics of the ultra-protestants. The consequence was a wide and profound hatred of Rome.[29]

A clear example of this consequence is the conversion of the poet John Donne, raised as a devout Catholic in a family with Jesuit connections, to a position of strongly Anglican persuasion.

Donne was employed by Elizabeth's successor, James I, as a diplomat and cleric as well as a very effective life-long propagandist. A prolific and brilliant essayist, Donne's sermons and pamphlets were much better known in Jacobean life than was his poetry.

Donne worked under explicit royal direction. A contemporary account is noteworthy for what it tells us of the way in which propaganda guidance was formulated and conveyed:

> About this time, there grew many disputes that concerned the *Oath of Supremacy and Allegiance,* in which the King had appeared, and engaged himself by his public writings now extant; and, his Majesty discoursing with Mr. Donne, concerning many of the reasons which are usually urged against the taking of these Oaths; apprehended, such a validity and clearness in his stating the Questions, and his answers to them, that his Majesty commanded him to bestow some time in drawing the Arguments into a Method and then to write his Answers to them: and having done that, not to send, but to be his own messenger and bring them to him. To this he presently and diligently applied himself, and, within six weeks brought them to him under his own handwriting, as they now be printed; the Book bearing the name *Pseudo-Martyr*, printed anno 1610.[30]

Donne produced two major propaganda works, *Pseudo-Martyr* and *Ignatius: His Conclave*, for James I at this time, as well as a rich collection of sermons, essays, and other writings. Of the two, it is more likely, in the view of at least one modern scholar, that the work on Ignatius was the subject of James' guidance in 1610, if only because it was shorter and more likely to have been produced in six weeks than the more densely argued and longer work *Pseudo-Martyr*.[31]

Donne's propaganda was clearly intended for use abroad as well as in England. *Ignatius*, for example, was drafted in Latin, then the *lingua franca* of elites throughout both Protestant and Catholic Europe, and later translated into English. At least one of the English-language versions was printed abroad, probably in Germany. Of the different versions, the Latin is the more elegantly styled.[32]

Some aspects of Donne's rhetorical method merit attention from any propagandist working in the English idiom. He was, for example, adept at combining conciliatory and polemic approaches. He had a sure sense for transforming a personality, such as St. Ignatius, into a symbol for a group or class of people, such as the Jesuit order. He could mount a slashing attack on a personality without descending to personal invective and abuse, and he developed to a fine point the art of allowing his target to condemn himself by his own purported statements. His work was usually well researched and documented. Above all, his vivid and compressed style lent itself to a devastating form of mockery, often enhanced by a mixture of self-mockery.

As a propagandist, Donne was concerned mainly with the protection of English sovereignty and the legitimacy of royal authority. But he also showed a continued streak of independence in speaking for freedom of conscience and personal integrity, even when these principles conflicted with strict obedience to political control. For these as well as personal reasons, his relationship with his political patrons was frequently strained. But his style proved influential in his day, and was still attractive to modern writers such as T. S. Eliot and Ernest Hemingway. Donne was tolerated and used by James I, who eventually made him Dean of St. Paul's in London.[33] Philip would have burnt him at the stake.

Philip II was a suspicious, sincerely devout, withdrawn man who had little talent for popular rhetoric, lacking contact with his own people and heavily dependent upon his agents for his understanding—such as it was—of popular sentiment at home and abroad. His view of English politics should have been better, given the skilled diplomatic agents he employed and the extensive network of emigres and other informants who served him. Appearing to have suffered from a weakness for believing most those with whom he most fervently agreed, Philip seems never to have understood the extent to which he was misinformed by English emigres regarding the nature of English Catholic opinion. Many English, possibly a majority of the population, accepted the principles of

Philip II of Spain, by Titian, with symbols of imperial majesty and power. Philip's rigid political style did not blunt his taste in painting, which was the source of one of the greatest art collections in Europe, still largely intact in his palace, the Escurial.

the Catholic faith; they did not, however, accept Philip's interpretation of those principles, nor the political conclusions he drew
from them. Philip is one of the most striking cases in modern
history of a decisionmaker misled by public opinion statistics.[34]

The English, in using emigres to interpret political sentiment
in an enemy country, appear to have been more discriminating
and more realistic than the Spanish. An English commander, reporting on an interrogation after the successful raid on the key
Spanish naval base of Cadiz in 1596, wrote,

> from Her Majesty's good ship the Mary Rose: the wiser sort
> of Spaniards that are prisoners with us do confess in one voice
> that a greater grievance could not have been done him [Philip]
> inasmuch as they are of opinion that his people with their
> clamor will enforce him to seek peace.

The English commander, however, goes on to report evidence
of Spanish financial losses resulting from the raid, losses which
his superiors in London knew were having a significant impact on
the financial standing of Philip's Italian bankers. "The Spaniards
themselves said," in the words of a modern scholar reflecting on
the Cadiz raid, "that reasonable Anglo-Dutch opinion had peace
with Spain in view; it was the King who would not make peace
with heretics. One sees the division between Philip and his subjects
transpiring discreetly."[35]

Philip's style of political warfare was intransigent. He meant
it to be seen as such by his own people and by those he sought
to bring into his ecumenical world. Recantation was open (in
theory) to heretics, but no other basis for reconciliation was
given—which is not to say, though, that Philip's diplomatic efforts
at the state-to-state level rejected truces when tactically necessary
or advantageous. But given the scope and majesty of the combined
imperial and religious effort on which the Counter-Reformation
had embarked, Philip probably could not have acted otherwise
than he did. His vision and policies had attained a momentum of
their own.[36]

Elizabeth's style was quite different: much more limited in scope
and aim, more flexible in implementation, much more sensitive

to issues of freedom of conscience for her own and allied peoples, and much better attuned to the utility of political communication with her opponents when she thought it possible to reach them in such ways. In short, the real problem for Elizabeth, as noted by one of her biographers, "as always in politics, was to assess the relative weights of the opposing forces, the length to which wills would go."[37] Political will for the English was relative; for the Spanish it was absolute. The student of political warfare should note that, notwithstanding the extensive use of armed force, the conflict was essentially political; and that the politics were markedly asymmetrical and rooted in national cultures.

Elizabeth's own words provide vivid confirmation of her political warfare style. Two examples can be cited both for their tactical sense and for the resonance across four hundred years of a strikingly effective rhetorical voice.

In 1585 Elizabeth spoke on the causes which moved her to send English troops and money to help Holland resist Spanish dominion. The language used toward Philip was respectful. In reply to a malicious slander propagated by Spanish agents, that she had plotted to assassinate the Duke of Parma, then Spanish Viceroy in the Netherlands, she ends with a notable and generous tribute to the enemy commander,

[Parma] . . . of whom We have ever had an honorable conceit,
in respect of those singular rare parts we have always noted
in him.

The statement, her biographer notes, was characteristically Elizabeth, for she admired greatness in a man, even her adversary; it was generous and at the same time astute. Elizabeth clearly intended to stir Philip's suspicion of Parma's loyalty, and by the same stroke to set a standard of decency and good conscience for European opinion. In 1584 Philip's agents had assassinated the highly popular Dutch resistance leader William the Silent, and it was politic for Elizabeth to remind her European allies and potential allies that political assassination was a weapon approved by Catholic powers and rejected by Protestants.[38] (In 1580, the papal nuncio in Madrid queried the Vatican as to whether English Catholic exiles would incur sin if they assassinated Elizabeth. The papal Secretary of State replied, "Whosoever sends her out of this world with the pious intention of doing God's service not only does not sin but gains merit."[39])

Elizabeth's posture was consistently directed to a peaceful settlement if it could be had on terms reasonably close to England's strategic interests: freedom of conscience, the practical autonomy of the neighboring Netherlands, and an open door for commerce with America and the East. Nothing—not the papal excommunication, the plots against her life by Spanish agents, Philip's support for Mary Stuart's claim to her throne, the adamant prohibition of trade with America, or the execution of English traders as heretics—deterred her from these limited goals. It was her practice to make them known to the world and to her own people in declarations, speeches from the throne, and state papers.

But flexibility notwithstanding, Elizabeth could use the rhetoric of war with compelling effect. Listen to her speak to the English troops and fleet on her appearance among them in 1588, with Philip's Armada off the Channel coast, and Parma poised in Flanders for an invasion:

> I have come to live or die amongst you all, to lay down for
> my God and for my Kingdom and for my people, my honor
> and my blood, even in the dust. I know I have the body of a
> weak and feeble woman, but I have the heart and stomach of
> a King, and a King of England too. And I think foul scorn
> that Parma or Spain or any Prince of Europe should dare to
> invade the borders of my realm.[40]

It is doubtful that Philip, who never left his monkish cell in the Escurial, got this message. But Elizabeth's people did, and so did her allies, the Dutch, and the rest of Europe. Drake and the Channel storms took care of the Armada, Parma's troops remained in Flanders, and the balance of power shifted from the Mediterranean to the Atlantic.

It is easy—and wrong—for an observer in the English-speaking world to be scornful of the Spanish style in political war during the Reformation. Philip II, like the later English King Charles I, was a tragic figure. We need to see the Spanish style of the period in historical context, particularly in terms of the challenges it faced from Arab occupation and, later, from the Ottoman invasion of Europe. Neither power was accustomed to dealing with opposition on any but the most imperious terms. The Spanish response was

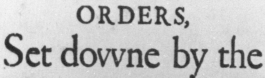

ORDERS,
Set dovvne by the
Duke of Medina, Lord general
of the Kings Fleet, to be obferued in
the voyage toward England.

Tranflated out of Spanifh into Englifh by T.P.

Imprinted at London by Thomas Orwin for Thomas Gilbert, dwelling in Fleetftreete neere to
the figne of the Caftle. 1588.

English elite propaganda against the Spanish Armada of 1588. Title page of a book published in London in 1588, shortly after the Armada sailed from Lisbon, containing in English translation the instructions issued by the Commander of the Armada. Similar translations appeared in other European capitals, substantiating English warnings of the Spanish threat to Protestant Europe. The original document apparently came from an intelligence source.

English political agitation, for mass audiences, in the form of playing cards with anti-Armada themes. The Jack of Spades reproduced here shows a Jesuit as the Jack, with several members of the Order hanging from a gallows. An example of ingenuity in developing mass appeal items capable of bridging language gaps.

appropriate and successful. Had it not been so, Europe would today be Muslim, and probably fragmented on the model of the nineteenth century Balkans.[41]

Remember also that the great Catholic revival produced art forms, spiritual and philosophical values, and architectural innovations that are still among the high points of Western culture. Baroque architecture, spread by the Jesuits from Manila to Vienna, is a magnificent expression of the ability to combine in building a spirit of material and human unity. The tragedy of Philip and of his people was that the style of warfare developed for dealing with the Eastern threats was largely irrelevant in coping with a rising maritime, ideationally pluralist, Western power. Context and culture were controlling factors in this case, and Philip's Spain ignored them, to its cost.

Ideational pluralism and its essential corollaries, freedom of conscience and freedom of expression, were further developed and explicitly asserted as aspects of the English style in political warfare during the English Civil War of 1641-49. The Cromwellian period also offers an interesting field for study of the conduct of political warfare, with strongly developed propaganda operations, in a civil war occurring in an English-speaking country.

Fighting a political contest as well as a military one to assert Parliamentary rights against Royal prerogative, Oliver Cromwell and his chief propagandist, John Milton, soon realized that the fanatics within their ranks were as disruptive to their larger aims as were the fanatics fighting for the Royalists. Given a taste of power, the extremist Puritans—Levellers and Fifth Monarchy Men—were eager to suppress all contrary opinion by censorship backed with brutal force. They were, in fact, more eager in many ways than their Cavalier opponents. The consequence of such fanaticism was a further polarization of society. Cromwell, who instinctively sought to build on the middle ground, rightly saw this outcome as ruinous for the future of England, whatever its form of governance. Milton, then Secretary of State, and John Thurloe, his chief of counter-intelligence, viewed the rapidly growing print media of their day as critical tools in warfare. But they

*Charles I of England, painting by Anthony Van Dyck ca. 1635.
Completed on royal commission by one of Charles' preferred
portraitists, this picture conveys powerfully the royalist ethos of
effortless superiority on which the dynasty relied. Within less than a
decade, Charles had lost his head and his dynasty had been replaced
by a military dictatorship under Oliver Cromwell.*

saw these tools in a quite new context of freedom for all. Thurloe, in the words of a Restoration Parliamentarian, "carried the secrets of all Princes of Europe at his girdle." So did many spymasters of the day. What matters for the art of political warfare is that Thurloe and Milton promptly published many of those secrets to serve their strategic ends.[42]

Milton saw clearly, and expressed in memorable prose, a value in asserting and guaranteeing "the liberty to know, to utter, and to argue fully according to conscience above all liberty."[43] His position was utilitarian, stressing the social evil of censorship and the social utility of liberty. His concern, shared with Cromwell, was to build a social consensus on which to base the maintenance of a sustained, professional military, and to deprive his opponents of the legitimacy which they claimed by right divine rather than popular will. The Parliamentary side had good reason to know and respect the force of political action. Effective use of Parliamentary debate, pamphlets, literary works, and publicized official documents had done much to keep their cause alive. The Royalists, too, used these means vigorously, often with marked tactical success.[44]

After a major battle at Naseby in 1645, Cromwell's propagandists published a series of documents captured from the Royalist camp. Detailing King Charles' correspondence with his French Catholic wife, they disclosed his attempts to bring an Irish Catholic army to England and the favors he had promised to extremist English Catholics. The publication convinced the peace partisans in Parliament that a binding agreement with the King was impossible, and it equally strengthened the hand of the war party that sought to end the fighting by completely defeating the Royalists.[45]

Other instances of propaganda charge, refutation, and countercharge abound, ranging in style from the prose of Milton to the barracks room ballads of military units. All show a rapid development of technical skill in readiness, if not quality, of printing and circulation. Captured, doctored, forged, and fraudulent documents circulated widely. Both sides used with much originality poetry, essays, and visual arts from paintings to placards to rally support and weaken or divert opposition.

Oliver Cromwell, miniature painted by Samuel Cooper ca. 1650, after Cromwell had moved into formal and lasting control of the national political as well as military affairs of England. The mood is characteristically natural.

Cheap and ready printing, which markedly enhanced the problems of an effective censorship, spurred freedom of the press. Milton, recognizing this fact, derived practical advantage from it as he also asserted it in principle. His view, as amplified and extended by John Locke, John Stuart Mill, Edmund Burke, and others, has remained a core element in the English-speaking style of both political war and governance. No modern commander coming from this tradition can conduct political warfare for long in defiance of this principle, and most commanders who learn how to apply it can benefit greatly.

Note, however, that a commitment—and it was a genuine one—to freedom of the press did not prevent Cromwell and his Secretary of State from using vigorous pressure tactics to choke off public opposition abroad. On October 24, 1655, Cromwell signed the Treaty of Westminster with France, which covered the preliminaries to England's official renewal of war against Spain. In form, the treaty was only a commercial agreement. But a secret clause provided for the expulsion of English Royalists from France, where they had been producing pro-Royalist and anti-Parliament propaganda for use in England as well as on the European continent.[46] Cromwell also worked vigorously to control extremists at home, both Catholic and Protestant.

Both the Royalists and the Parliamentarian parties paid considerable attention to assassination, terrorism, and associated propaganda exploitation. An example of Royalist propaganda produced abroad and circulated in Commonwealth England, is a proclamation issued in 1654 over the name of the emigre Charles II, offering a knighthood and an annual pension of five hundred pounds sterling to the slayer of "a certain base mechanic fellow called Oliver Cromwell." It was accompanied by a pamphlet titled *Killing No Murder*, of which at least two of Charles' senior officers appear to have had personal knowledge.[47] This pamphlet clearly established the Royalist position on the issue of political assassination, and it did so in the context not of plausible denial but of overt propaganda.

Cromwell personally seems to have regarded assassination with contempt. He could, however, be ruthless in ordering executions, such as the beheading of Charles I, and summary killings in battle to strike fear into his opponents or to suppress rebellion

THE
SOULDIERS
CATECHISME:
Compofed for
The Parliaments Army:

Confifting of two Parts : wherein
are chiefly taught:

1 *The Iuftification*
2 *The Qualification* } *of our Souldiers.*

Written for the Incouragement and In-
ftruction of all that have taken up Armes in
this Caufe of God and his People; efpe-
cially the common Souldiers.

2 *Sam.* 10.12. *Be of good courage, and let us
play the men for our people, and for the Cities of our God, and the Lord do that which
feemeth him good.*

Deut. 23.9. *When the Hoft goeth forth againft
thine enemies, then keepe thee from every
wicked thing.*

Imprimatur. JA. CRANFORD.

Printed for J. Wright *in the Old-Baily.* 1644

The Souldiers Catechisme, *title page of a tract used in recruiting for
and maintaining military morale in Cromwell's New Model Army,
published in London, 1644. The no-nonsense instruction, combined
with citation from the Bible, is typical of the best of Parliamentary
propaganda.*

in his own New Model Army. There was a strain in him of the Roman stoic or the stern Israelite of Joshua's stamp. Advising Parliament in 1649 to deal summarily with a fanatic Puritan element in the army, he said crisply, "You have no other way to deal with these men but to break them, or they will break you."[48]

Following the battle of Drogheda, when his control of conquered Ireland was still shaky, Cromwell was adamant in granting no quarter to the defeated Catholic and Royalist defenders:

> It [death] was the righteous judgment of God on the barbarous wretches. . . . It will tend to prevent the effusion of blood for the future, which are the satisfactory grounds for such actions, which otherwise cannot but work remorse and regret. . . . The enemy were filled upon this with much terror.[49]

After later battles in the Irish campaign, Cromwell granted easy terms to the surrendered enemy forces, whom he sought to win over by reasoned discourse and mercy to the Parliamentary cause.

Civil wars are seldom merciful, least of all those in the seventeenth century. In the English Civil War, adequate discipline was rare and lines of command, particularly among the Royalists, were often diffuse; drunkenness and debauchery afflicted the Royalists; the Parliamentary army was often accused of sanctimonious brutality. Ammunition for political warfare abounded. Of the two sides, the Parliamentarians seem to have wielded the propaganda weapon, alone and in combination with the power of the sword, to more profit and purpose. Reading the prose (and poetry) of the two sides today, we can conclude that part of the Parliamentarians' propaganda success stemmed from their facility in defining terms to suit themselves. Milton was a master of the art.

Modern strategists may make of these campaigns what they will. Assassination, in the form of direct and lethal assault, without due process in an open trial, on a head of state or lesser official, has remained a vexed issue for the English-speaking world. Most totalitarian regimes practice it, sometimes covertly, sometimes openly. Extremist political movements celebrate their use of it in full propaganda exploitation. Modern statesmen may or may not choose to use such methods; they must always, however, allow for the likelihood that the weapon will be used against them in one form or another. In any event, if used, the propaganda exploitation and counter-exploitation of the deed, as Cromwell and

THE TENURE OF

KINGS

AND

MAGISTRATES:

PROVING,

That it is Lawfull, and hath been held fo through all Ages, for any, who have the Power, to call to account a Tyrant, or wicked KING, and after due conviction, to depofe, and put him to death; if the ordinary MAGISTRATE have neglected, or deny'd to doe it.

And that they, who of late, fo much blame Depofing, are the Men that did it themfelves.

The Author, J. M.(ilton)

LONDON,

Printed by Matthew Simmons, at the Gilded Lyon in Alderfgate Street, 1649.

Title page to John Milton's justification of Charles I's trial and execution. Published in London in 1649, two weeks after the execution, the work reveals an ability of Milton and his propaganda apparatus to respond rapidly to political events. It has also become a classic rationale for tyrannicide.

86

Milton clearly recognized, are usually more weighty than the act itself.

A review of Renaissance political warfare inevitably raises questions of broad cultural import for the modern statesman: What produced such talent? Is eloquence and wit of comparable worth available today? Questions of motivation and political will aside, where are the writers, artists, producers, and performers with the ability to stir allied audiences and confound those of an opponent with the force and acuity of Shakespeare, Marlowe, and Milton? If they exist, could the commander of today be relied upon (as Elizabeth and her staff relied on their commanders) to identify, support, and deploy them effectively for strategic ends?

One answer among many stands out: The rebirth of classical learning in early modern Europe, both Protestant and Catholic, accorded a high place to the classical Greek and Roman forms of rhetoric. Indeed, the practice of rhetoric was so admired by statesmen and military commanders that it shaped a universe of discourse beginning in the schoolroom, continuing through university life, and flowering in an unprecedented range of verbal, visual, and literary forms.

Elizabeth Tudor received rigorous training in rhetoric beginning in her early childhood. She did not need to be told when she saw and heard the productions of an upstart London playwright from the backwoods of Warwickshire that the man was a natural genius. She knew and felt it herself, not only because she had an instinctive feel for talent, but also because the same classical models in which she had been trained—those of Aristotle, Cicero, Seneca, and Quintilian—had been drilled into Shakespeare in Stratford Grammar School. Elizabeth's senior commanders, Raleigh, Essex, and Hunsdon, knew and respected—and used—these same forms. So did other leaders, including field commanders like Sir Philip Sidney, whose conduct of campaigns in Flanders, where he was killed in action, was matched by his reputation as a Court poet. This skill in the use of words for the purposes of war (and peace) was rooted in the Spirit of the Times and woven into the

Mercurius Rusticus, *a broadsheet published in 1685 after the restoration of royal authority, portrays "the sad events of the late unparalleld rebellion." The events depicted include the plundering of universities and manor houses, the humiliation of clergy, and pitched battles such as the one at Edgehill.* Mercurius *had been one of the Royalist newspapers published during the war.*

entire structure of society beginning with the primary education system. For Renaissance states, England above all, humanist learning was a primary resource for national assertion and survival.

4

THE NAPOLEONIC ERA

For the next stage in our review of political war we advance to the leaders of Revolutionary France. They and their era saw new impetus given to the techniques of mass propaganda, intense and directed use of the printed word, use of visual images for massed crowds, and combination of propaganda with various forms of political organization, subversion, diplomacy, economic pressure, and military menace in pursuit of unlimited aggressive aims.

Carl von Clausewitz grappled with the problems of revolution, aggression, and war throughout his long service in several armies. He understood the dilemma of political aims in conflict with military imperatives, but he never resolved it. Obsession with his famous dictum, "war is a continuation of political activity by other means,"[1] has often obscured the deeper ambivalence in his thought. Consider, instead, another passage from his writings:

> An aggressor often decides on war before the innocent defender
> does, and if he continues to keep his preparations sufficiently
> secret, he may well take the victim unawares. Yet such surprise
> has nothing to do with war itself, and should not be possible.
> War serves the purpose of defense more than that of the ag-
> gressor. It is only aggression that calls forth defense, and war
> along with it. The aggressor is always peace-loving (as Bo-
> naparte always claimed to be); he would prefer to take over
> our country unopposed. To prevent his doing so one must be
> willing to make war and be prepared for it. In other words, it
> is the weak, those likely to need defense, who should always
> be armed in order not to be overwhelmed. Thus decrees the
> art of war.[2]

In short, Clausewitz seems to be saying here, political war may be effective, but it is not war. (Unlike later people of tidy and legalistic proclivities, though, Clausewitz was willing to advocate military response to an activity he sought to exclude from the category of war.) Napoleon, by contrast, seems to have understood and acted upon the principle that war was any action that moved him toward victory; political weapons no less than cannon were a means to victory, a means, moreover, that could be used with compelling effect in times not formally designated as war.

An English contemporary of Clausewitz, Edmund Burke, urged an alarmed Europe to resist the political as well as the military expansion of Napoleonic France. Burke warned Parliament, "France, on her new system, means to form a universal empire, by producing a universal revolution."[3] The distinction, as he had earlier explained in a series of essays, between particular national revolutions and universal revolution is a critical one.[4] This distinction is central to the way a nation defines victory and defeat, and has much to do with how it will conduct political war.

Modern strategic thought, both Eastern and Western, is tied in many ways to Clausewitzian perceptions. But Eastern strategists have tended to emphasize the political content while the Western schools have tended to exclude it. The difference forms part of a larger asymmetry between East and West. Its strongest roots lie in late Roman times, but it was powerfully reinforced by the forces let loose in Revolutionary and, more especially, Napoleonic France. In all forms of war, and most of all in revolutionary war, it is crucial to determine whether the intentions of an opponent are limited or unlimited, whether the object of policy is pragmatic or millenarian.

Another feature of Revolutionary France having much to do with modern concepts of political war was the conscious use of terror. We have seen how English revolutionaries, of whom Cromwell was illustrative, tended to ambivalence regarding terror. Political factions arising from extreme Puritanism often revelled in terrorizing their Anglican and Catholic opponents, whom they regarded as idolaters. But they seldom succeeded in gaining more than a limited following in England, and when their leaders sought by subversion and political maneuver to capture control of the state, they were firmly put down by men like Cromwell. Not so in Revolutionary France. Robespierre, the archetypal Jacobin, set the tone in a classic statement:

> The attribute of popular government in revolution is at one and the same time virtue and terror, virtue without which terror is fatal, terror without which virtue is impotent. The terror is nothing but justice; prompt, severe, inflexible: it is thus an emanation of virtue.[5]

Robespierre never seems to have contemplated the possibility that those who must administer justice may at times be less than totally virtuous, or may simply disagree among themselves. In 1794 Robespierre lost control of his party, and himself fell victim to the guillotine.

After several turbulent and murderous years, a military dictator—Bonaparte—emerged to curb the excesses of a revolution gone out of control. Napoleon succeeded in channeling the revolutionary zeal of the Jacobins to coincide with his own imperial ambitions, thus imbuing his style of warfare with a millenarian political content. In this merger, terror became subordinate to structured military and civil power, and it was eventually dispensed with as counterproductive. But the spirit of terrorism survived in the political warfare concepts of most nineteenth and twentieth century revolutionaries, including, above all, the followers of Marx, Engels, and Lenin. It is still very much alive in the extremist movements of Europe and the Third World. Modern Soviet protestations that they have renounced or never really advocated the use of terror should, to say the least, be treated with caution.

A third element in the modern French contribution to the art of political warfare is the renewed obsession with centralization of power. That centralization was founded upon the manipulation of people *en masse*, using ideas and images as well as military organization. Napoleon's rejection of the trappings of monarchy and his reversion to the titles and images of Imperial Rome have more than superficial import. The symbolism, the Spirit of the Times, and the unique qualities of the man combined to create a formidable force. Principles and practices of this kind would have been seen rightfully as megalomania when advocated by men of lesser genius. Embraced by Napoleon I, they proved a framework for the economic, social, and administrative transformation of Europe. Mention of Bonaparte's name today most likely brings to mind the Code Napoleon, the metric system, and much of modern administrative practice in continental states. Behind it all and driving it was the Napoleonic legend.

The key to these aspects of Revolutionary France lay in an awareness of the capacity of a brilliant, purposeful, and charismatic ruler for stirring and manipulating masses of people through propaganda. The France of a later Bonaparte—Louis Napoleon—provided a cultural bridge to modern Europe for this Napoleonic imperial ethos. The pages of conventional histories, replete with dates and battles won or lost, can only faintly convey the raw force of this volcanic popular upsurge. Only in literature and the arts can one perhaps get a hint of what it meant to the millions from many nations of Europe who marched and died under the hypnotic symbol of the Imperial Eagle. Stendhal in his novels and in his own life, Beethoven in his *Eroica* Symphony and Emperor Concerto, and Jacques Louis David in his powerful visual images can still summon up something of the resonance.

Not all of Napoleon's contemporaries were attracted or intimidated by the Napoleonic mythos, but the most perceptive among them were conscious of its force and scope. Clausewitz, for example, in his accounts of service as a volunteer in the Russian forces during the campaigns of 1812, respected Napoleon as a gifted strategist, though he was by no means under his opponent's spell.

Among the English, Sir Arthur Wellesley (later Duke of Wellington) held a similar view. On landing in Spain in 1808 with a British expeditionary force, he observed,

> if what I hear of their system of maneuver be true, I think it
> is a false one against steady troops. I suspect that all the
> Continental armies were more than half beaten before the battle
> was begun. I, at least, will not be frightened before hand.[6]

The key to Wellesley's assessment lies, I would submit, in the words "steady troops" as much as in the cool eye of the Iron Duke. The people of Britain, and the forces drawn from them, had never succumbed to the imperial vision as had much of the population that contributed forces to Napoleon's continental opponents. One can speculate on the reasons why (insular location, traditions, long hostility toward France, religious differences, and political institutions) without losing sight of the central point— British troops were simply not as vulnerable as their continental counterparts to the political warfare appeal of Revolutionary France. Nor, it might be added, were their American cousins, who refused to enter the war against Britain and emphatically rejected the propaganda and diplomatic pressure applied by French agents like "Citizen Genet."

Gustave Le Bon, a French sociologist reared in the France of Louis Napoleon but writing after his fall, had this to say on mass persuasion and the Bonapartes:

> All the world's masters . . . have always been unconscious psychologists, possessed of an instinctive and often very sure knowledge of the character of crowds, and it is their accurate knowledge of this character that has enabled them so easily to establish this mastery. Napoleon had a marvelous insight into the psychology of the masses of the country over which he reigned, but he, at times, completely misunderstood the psychology of crowds belonging to other races and it is because he misunderstood it that he engaged Spain, and notably Russia, in conflicts in which his power received blows which were within a brief space of time to ruin it.[7]

The Peninsular War between Napoleon's occupation forces and indigenous Spanish insurgents, backed by the English expeditionary army of Wellington, gave rise to a new concept in war and a new term to describe it: *guerrilla*, or "little war." Its essence lies in the individual political convictions of the insurgents, as well as in the imperial ethos of the occupiers. It was a form of war fought with ideological zeal and blind ferocity on both sides, as we may see today from the drawings of an artist who lived through it, Francisco de Goya.

Most of the great totalitarian propagandists, including Hitler, Goebbels, and Lenin, read and were influenced by Le Bon's writing on mass psychology and how to apply it on an imperial scale.

*"No Other Way," Plate 15 from the "Horrors of War" engravings by
Francisco de Goya. The execution in 1810 of Spanish resistance
fighters by French troops portrays the confrontation that has given us
the term* guerrilla. *Goya, having experienced much of the war,
recorded it in works of art that still carry a powerful message of
political resistance to armed force.*

(They did not, it might be added, always follow his cautionary
admonitions about the importance of national culture.) The contrast is striking between the views of Le Bon and those of one of
England's Victorian statesmen, Lord Palmerston, regarding public
opinion:

> It is by comparing opinions—by a collision of opinions—by
> rubbing one man's views against those of another, and seeing
> which are the hardest and will bear the friction best—that
> men, in or out of office, can most justly arrive at a knowledge
> of what is most advantageous to the interests of the whole
> community.[8]

Palmerston was quite clear regarding England's desire to see
its liberal principles applied in the conduct of its foreign relations.

"Nadar Elevating Photography," lithograph by Honore Daumier of his friend Nadar's public relations stunt, shooting the first air photos of Paris from a balloon in 1857. The event illustrates three major innovations of the period in mass agitational media: photography, the use of balloons, and the mass-circulation press which Daumier's lithographs did much to make vividly comprehensible to the common man.

"Peace, an Idyll," lithograph by Daumier, published in March 1871 after the fall of Napoleon III, ridiculing the military ambitions of the deposed Emperor. Daumier gave a new impetus and meaning to the political cartoon for mass audiences.

Speaking in 1841 on England's position regarding a new constitution for modern Greece, he announced, "Her Majesty's Government do not happen to recollect any country in which a Constitutional system of government has been established that has not on the whole been better off in consequence of that system than it had been before."[9]

The English liberal ethos, evident in Palmerston's statement above on public opinion, was firmly grounded in the political primacy of the individual conscience and the conscious individual.

Le Bon—and his disciples—saw matters differently:

Organized crowds have always played an important part in the life of peoples, but this part has never been of such moment as at present. The substitution of the unconscious action of crowds for the conscious activity of individuals is one of the principle characteristics of the present age.[10] . . .

So far as the majority of their acts are considered, crowds display a singularly inferior mentality; yet there are other acts in which they appear to be guided by those mysterious forces which the ancients denominated destiny, nature or providence, which we call the voices of the dead, and whose power it is impossible to overlook, although we ignore [do not understand] their essence.[11]

As his translator Merton observes, Le Bon spotted fundamental facts of group psychology in the "intensification of emotions" and the "inhibition of the intellect" when men are merged into a mass.

This concept of political mass, as distinct from political consensus, required a new medium for its expression. That medium was the mass circulation press made possible by new techniques for unprecedented volume and speed of printing, and employing techniques of illustration—press lithography and photography—as vivid and simplistic as the new journalistic style of writing that developed to meet the new technology. Telegraphy gave an immediacy to news reporting. And mass production of newsprint brought the end product, a daily paper, within reach of the masses. The France of Napoleon III led the way in these techniques.[12]

These concepts and techniques became a part of the larger Western and Eastern cultural, economic, and social scenes as the world moved toward the twentieth century. In the collapse of Europe after World War I, they became the midwives of a new political force—the totalitarians.

5
WORLD WAR I

E arly in the twentieth century it was, for a brief moment in 1918, British—not French, German, or even Russian—propaganda which had the greatest impact on events. The reasons for the British success were several. Most important, British wartime propaganda was based upon a massive commitment of talent and resources at a critical moment. But it succeeded also because it was rooted in the vigorous intellectual traditions of liberal political institutions, because it was guided by an inspired political leader, David Lloyd George, and possibly because Britain, thanks to Lords Northcliffe and Beaverbrook, had surpassed other powers in the growth of mass circulation dailies responsive to popular interests. The talent was available, the necessary institutions were brought into existence, the need was clear and immediate. And the constitutionally appointed leader of the nation supplied the political will to use the available resources for the specific and critical purpose of national survival.

The leaders of wartime Germany were appalled by this unexpected Anglo-Saxon resort to what might have been regarded as a weapon more in the Napoleonic tradition of continental Europe: "This [English propaganda] was a new weapon, or rather a weapon which had never been employed on such a scale and so ruthlessly in the past," announced Marshal Paul von Hindenburg in retrospect.[1] Germany's War Minister von Stein had been even more explicit in public statements made during the conflict: "In propaganda the enemy is undoubtedly our superior," was his bald assessment.[2] Although probably wrongheaded, the German leaders' understanding of propaganda was far from simplistic: "Good propaganda," Quartermaster General Erich Ludendorf noted, "must keep well ahead of events. It must act as a pacemaker to policy and mold public opinion without appearing to do so."[3]

British scholars' views of their World War I propaganda, expressed in retrospect, are mixed. At least one eminent historian, reflecting on the unsuccessful Allied effort later in the century to undermine World War II German morale, ascribed the failure to "a grotesque overestimate" of the contribution Allied propaganda had made in 1917-18.[4] Such observations are moot. Most of the works on the subject by those who were involved tend to be similar to those of the Germans. A 1920s report, for example, regarding British home front morale states,

> Propaganda is the task of creating and directing public opinion.
> In other wars this work has not been the function of govern-
> ment . . . but [in this conflict] which was not of armies but
> of nations, and which tended to affect every people on the
> globe, this aloofness could not be maintained. Since strength,
> for the purpose of war was the total strength of each belligerent
> nation, public opinion was as significant as fleets or armies.[5]

A definitive judgment on the contribution of different arms to victory is notoriously difficult. Before attempting one here, let us look at what the British said they wished to achieve, what strategies they adopted toward that end, what problems they faced, and what specific outcomes resulted.

Sir Campbell Stuart, a Canadian who served as Deputy Director of Britain's foreign propaganda agency, known simply as Crewe House, defined the propaganda program's goals in a postwar memoir drawn from the directives of the agency:

> Propaganda means the education of the enemy to a knowledge
> of what kind of world the Allies meant to create, and of the
> place reserved in it for enemy peoples according as they as-
> sisted in, or continued to resist, its creation. It implied also
> the dissemination of this knowledge among the Allied peoples,
> so that there might be full popular support for Allied policy
> and no tendency at the critical moment of peace to sacrifice
> any essential features of the settlement because its importance
> might not have been explained or understood in time.[6]

Stuart also insisted that propaganda should be truthful, although it did not necessarily have to be overt, that is, fully identified as to original source.[7]

In other words, propaganda should be based on a national policy, it should encompass allies and adversaries, and it should always remain cognizant of long-term objectives. Most of these principles were broken more than they were observed earlier in the war, and some of them were less than perfectly carried out after the Lloyd George reorganization of early 1918. As we shall see below, the communication to allies was kept separate from that to enemies, and organizational measures were adopted to see that this was so.

Some of the other deviations were less explicit but also noteworthy. Policy toward Germany, in the hands of H. G. Wells, appears to have driven grand strategy rather than following it for a critical period in 1918. But the message of hope in Wells' concept of a League of Nations for which there would be an honorable place reserved for a peaceful postwar Germany, and in the disavowal of any intent to impose a punitive economic regime on Germany, was lost from view at the Peace Conference. Wartime propaganda emphasized independence for the nations that wished to leave the Austro-Hungarian Empire. But even though the Allies did adhere to this principle at the Peace Conference, the propaganda message had been less solidly based on agreement within the British Cabinet than Crewe House programmers made it appear in 1918. There was confusion and conflict over policy toward Italy, again with more promised by Crewe House than the Allied governments were probably prepared to deliver. These differences, though, appear to have arisen more from the inherent complexity of the situation than from conscious Anglo-American duplicity.

Nevertheless, the basic propaganda concept was reasonably clear and consistent. And those responsible for projecting propaganda abroad understood and supported the concept, at least for the critical period in 1918 when the war's outcome hung in the balance.

British assessments of their experience with propaganda in 1918 were widely read and translated in the 1930s. There were, for example, several German editions of the Stuart memoir, one with an extended introduction that offers an insight into Nazi plans for use of propaganda.[8] A Japanese translation, too, was produced in 1937 (not, alas, accessible to me). One cannot help wondering whether Mao or Ho Chi Minh ever saw a Chinese edition.

The best source, though, on what Britain intended to accomplish with strategic propaganda is probably David Lloyd George, who became Prime Minister in 1916. In his war memoirs, he gave a circumscribed but apparently forthright account of its place in the conflict.[9] Several points stand out. First is his assessment of the shifting psychological balance between his own side and that of the enemy: "The German Army was thus melting away, while the Allies were being reinforced by the steadily rising flood of American troops. . . . The collapse of morale on the German [civilian] side was yet more disastrous." This situation, he notes later, had not applied earlier in the struggle when the Germans still believed themselves invincible. As always in politics, Lloyd George thought first of context and timing. Second, he thought the "deadliest quality in [British] propaganda was its truth," the more so because the German authorities sought to conceal vital information, such as US troop buildups and German submarine losses, from their own population. Third, the British used innovative means to deliver propaganda against both civilian and military targets. And fourth, Lloyd George judged, "such propaganda would have been a vain flutter in the air if the blockade were broken," or if there had been "a certainty of approaching triumph to sustain the hearts of the German people." Propaganda, as Lloyd George saw its role in World War I, was a complement to economic and military pressure rather than the primary arm.

This Welsh politician, steeped in his own brand of radical politics and ever sensitive to the social dimension of radicalism, discounted in retrospect the alleged destructive impact of Bolshevik agitation in German war industries and military formations. "We had these in our country," he notes dryly; social agitation by "pacifist agitators and Bolshevik emissaries" was not responsible for the revulsion against the war that swept Germany in 1918.[10] The true cause was simply a profound sense of defeat and wasted effort. Allied propaganda, using truth, reinforced this mood at a critical juncture.

The Germans made no comparable effort against the British war effort, although many British officials feared they would.

Nervous politicians often prodded Scotland Yard's Special Branch and the War Department's counterintelligence unit, MI-5, to look for evidence of German-financed agitators, particularly Bolshevists, thought to have instigated several major strikes in war industries.[11] The chiefs of both organizations tended to share the politicians' suspicion—or at least said they did—but neither reported much hard evidence of foreign involvement, financial or ideological. Scotland Yard (but not MI-5) had police powers, and used them sporadically throughout the war to disrupt or discredit pacifist groups. The chief of the Special Branch, Sir Basil Thomson, reported that workers' morale rose and pacifism declined as victory came in sight. But he warned against a sharp rise in radicalism after the war, which he predicted (rightly) would include strong indigenous and foreign radical influences.[12]

Organizationally, British World War I propaganda seems to have required much bureaucratic groping and conflict through the early years of war. Lloyd George, giving the subject his personal attention as Prime Minister, acted to bring order to the bureaucracy. In February 1918, despite opposition within his cabinet, Lloyd George installed high-level talent in the persons of the British Empire's paramount press lords: Lord Beaverbrook became Minister of Information, and Lord Northcliffe was appointed as head of foreign propaganda at Crewe House, nominally under Beaverbrook but reporting directly to the Prime Minister. Both were imperious figures, fully confident in their control of mass media and in their ability to shape popular attitudes through manipulation of images and ideas. Both—like their chief, Lloyd George—were self-made men.

The division of labor among these new offices is noteworthy. Northcliffe mounted a propaganda attack against enemy powers only: he had no responsibilities for Allied or domestic audiences. Beaverbrook conducted "popular diplomacy," as he termed it, among the peoples of allied countries, including the dominions. Mobilization of opinion within Britain remained the responsibility of a national war aims committee set up in 1917; composed of representatives of the three political parties, the war aims committee was solely concerned with combating pacifism. The work of Beaverbrook's quite active Ministry apparently was well received, particularly among dominion audiences, including their expeditionary forces. Where most successful, it reflected an extension of similar work Beaverbrook had done earlier in the war in Canada, producing newsreels and exhibitions of war paintings, and maintaining a well-staffed oversea press center for correspondents covering the war from London.

The Foreign Office, viewing Beaverbrook's activities with alarm and suspicion, sought with mixed success to dominate and limit his operations, resulting in continued conflict at Cabinet level. The dispute resulted in a number of acerbic memoranda, and several inconclusive confrontations between Beaverbrook and Foreign Secretary Balfour. One of Beaverbrook's memos, drafted on May 29, 1918, contains a prescient statement of Britain's need for (as we would call it) a public diplomacy capability:

> We [Ministry of Information] have a diplomacy of our own to conduct, a popular diplomacy. . . . Our agents will work not through Chancellories and Courts, but through channels through which no diplomat could safely or usefully venture.[13]

Talent abounded at Crewe House under Northcliffe. At the working levels, in addition to novelist H. G. Wells heading operations against Germany, senior journalist Wickham Steed was in charge of operations throughout Austria-Hungary, aided for the Balkans by academic R. W. Seton-Watson. Wickham Steed had direct experience as Foreign Editor and reporter for the *Times* covering Vienna; Seton-Watson was to author several definitive historical studies of the Balkans. As an organization, Crewe House offered a rich mix of media management skills, direct language and area experience, and library research ability.

Technical support personnel came from a variety of backgrounds including—but not limited to—the military. Distribution to military targets was carried out by the War Office; civilian audiences were heavily targeted by an innovative special section stressing third-country infiltration, mainly in Switzerland and Holland, as well as balloon drops. Leaflets were delivered by balloon, using Royal Army units, the Royal Air Force having refused the job as unsuited for aircraft. By the end of 1918 the Army was putting five million leaflets a month on target and eliciting a lively response in German media.[14]

The Crewe House staff conceived and debated numerous strategies, with proposals then funneled to the political leadership. Among the political leaders, those proposals became the subject of conflicts for personality as well as policy reasons. President Wilson and his aides became increasingly involved toward the end of the war, both through inter-Allied liaison officers and through presidential speeches and statements. Clearly, whatever the outcome, Allied propaganda policy did not suffer from lack of high-level attention, as Wilson's Fourteen Points speech clearly indicates.

Some of the policy disputes are relevant to any political warfare involving a multinational empire. In World War I, British policy toward Austria-Hungary fluctuated for some time between appealing to the Hapsburg elites to abandon their Hohenzollern ally, or stirring up anti-German sentiment among the non-German nationalities of the Empire. It settled firmly in 1918 on a strategy of incitement to national liberation,[15] which soon succeeded in disrupting the Hapsburg military contribution to the war.

British policy toward Austria-Hungary had two aspects, one constructive—liberation—the other destructive—military defeatism. Both required inter-Allied consultation, mainly with Italy, on fostering political activism among emigres. In April 1918, Northcliffe convened a Rome Congress of Oppressed Hapsburg Nationalities, providing a political basis for the appeal to non-German military units fighting on the Italian front. Defections rose, including some by units, and Vienna—also suffering from food shortages—sued for peace. Whether the subsequent collapse of the Austro-Hungarian Empire was in the larger interests of Europe is still a topic for debate, but it did help the Allies win a war that still hung in the balance.

One of the most aggressive propaganda and psychological warfare operations of World War I was conducted by the Italians. Operating against military formations in the field and, through infiltration and airdrops, against the civilian population of the

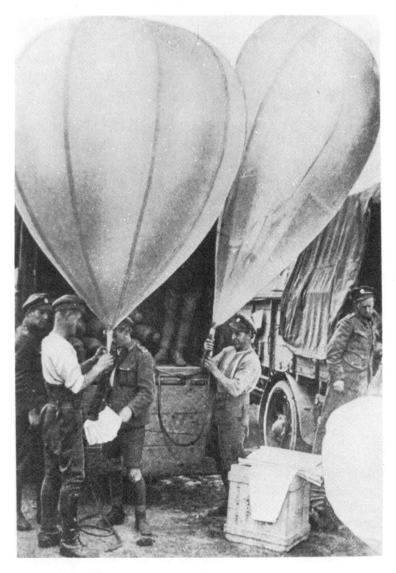

Balloon delivery of print media. A British Army field unit attaching leaflets to hydrogen balloons on the Western Front in 1918. Length of the slow-burn suspension cord was adjusted to provide scatter distribution according to wind speed and direction.

Hapsburg empire, the Italians did much to advance their own national interests as well as broader Allied war aims against Austria-Hungary. Policy control and supervision of Italian political warfare operations were vested in a Central Committee for Propaganda to the Enemy, formed by Italy's Prime Minister Orlando in March 1918. The committee was headed by Ugo Ojetti, a talented writer and skilled organizer. His mandate included oversight of operations against both military and civilian targets, and it involved cooperation with corresponding British, French, and American organizations as well as with Czechoslovak, Yugoslav, Polish, and Romanian exiles.[16]

Ojetti's committee developed an extensive, high-volume, multi-media program on very short order. His attack soon produced impressive results. Between May and October 1918, Ojetti distributed over sixty million copies of 643 leaflets in eight languages, and a total of ten million copies of 112 newspapers in four languages. Distribution channels included air drops over Vienna and infiltration by couriers to Ljubljana, Zagreb, and other regional centers.[17] In contrast to the British, who relied mainly on balloon delivery, the Italians deployed fixed-wing aircraft for delivery (see Italian Air Service photo, p. 110).

An Air Force officer, and poet, Gabriele D'Annunzio, wrote the text for the leaflets dropped over Vienna and led one of the major air raids to deliver them.[18] Another person involved in helping to generate popular support for the Italian war effort, and for measures to achieve the liberation of Czechoslovakia and Yugoslavia from Hapsburg rule, was a wounded war veteran and former socialist newspaper editor named Benito Mussolini.[19]

Evidence that the message was reaching target audiences and that the audiences were receptive to it was impressive. During the June 1918 battle of the Piave, 800 of Ojetti's leaflets were found on 350 enemy prisoners in a single day. Before the June 1918 offensive, enemy deserters gave the Italian command detailed information about the place, date, and time of the main attack. On one occasion, 300 Austro-Hungarian troops from a Czech unit crossed the lines in a group, shouting *Viva l'Italia*. A company of 200 Slovaks surrendered; their commander announced that he was a friend of Hambrisak, the Yugoslav emigre representative on Ojetti's committee, whose name appeared on leaflets dropped

Leaflet drop over Vienna. Italian Air Force operation, probably in 1918. The Italian front was heavily exploited by Allied and emigre forces using a wide range of military and civilian delivery systems.

by Italian aircraft. In October, deserters supplied information on deployment and order of battle to Italian interrogators. Just before and during the final Italian offensive in October, whole Austro-Hungarian regiments mutinied, announcing that they were only willing to fight, if at all, for the defense of their home territories. Hungarian units, affected by news of political-social revolution in Budapest, seemed most vulnerable.[20]

The Allied campaign in 1918 against Austria-Hungary is one of the early examples in modern times of organizational weapons used in close coordination with mass-media strategic propaganda against a civilian population, plus tactical psychological warfare against armies in the field.[21] The campaign was, moreover, conducted by an alliance involving large national entities—Britain, France, Italy, and the United States—with often divergent policy objectives, working with a collection of emerging national liberation movements of varying sophistication and abilities.

Poland, Czechoslovakia, and Yugoslavia, the major players among the nascent political movements, did not exist in 1918 as sovereign states. Whatever their histories and traditions, they had no independent national institutions with which the Allied powers could deal on a footing of conventional state-to-state intercourse. The Rome Congress of Oppressed Hapsburg Nationalities, though it did not call the emigre movements into being—most of them had existed as exile groups scattered about Europe for some time—provided a framework within which these movements could interact meaningfully with the established powers. The task of Allied political warfare commanders in the organizational domain was to provide this framework, and to help broker a constructive resolution of their own conflicts in relation to the new states as well as conflicts among the exile political movements from which these states emerged.

The Allied commanders built a coherent, organized, and functioning political framework within which they could interact and deploy strategic civilian propaganda and tactical military psychological operations. This use of the political organizational weapon, under close operational control, with the propaganda forces of modern industrial societies was essential. These were not operations that could be conducted effectively through the channels of conventional diplomacy; nor were they activities in

Poselství prof. Masaryka československému vojsku v Italii. ─────

Prof. *T. G. Masaryk* poslal z Washingtonu prostřednictvím král. italského velvyslanectví československému autonomnímu vojsku v Italii tento vzkaz:

" *Bratři! Rakousko-Uhersko, chtějíc zlomiti ve vlasti oposici československou, tvrdilo, že naše vojsko je sebranka, jež nemá ani politického ani vojenského významu. Vypustilo dokonce lež, že naše vojsko se skládá z Rusů a jiných národností a že nestává vojska československého. Náš národ neuvěřil tomuto klamu a zůstal nesmiřitelným a hrdým na své vojsko. Tehdy Rakousko-Uhersko pokusilo se zasaditi rozhodnou ránu našemu národu tím, že by zničic vás zničilo vojsko jeko. Chtělo zmocniti se naši vlajky odboje a samostatnosti, symbolu víry a aspirací našeho národa.*

" *Bratři! Vaše vůle, váš dalekozírný hled překazily plány nepřítele. Náš prapor vlaje ještě hrdě na posíci svěřené vaši ochraně Náš národ pozná vaše hrdinské činy a všechna srdce se pohnou hlubokou vděčností k vám. Chloubou nad vámi a hrdou vzpomínkou padlých bratrů.*

" *Jako váš vrchní velitel posílám vám svůj nejsrdečnější dík za udatnosť, kterouž jste znova přispěli k vítězství našeho národa, Italie, Spojenců a celého lidstva.*

Nazdar!"

T. G. Masaryk.

Nutkalo nás pochlubiti se vám uznáním našeho milovaného vůdce, jenž nás i národ náš dovede k vítěznému cíli.

Jsme přesvědčeni, že i vy, ve shodě s celým národem, vidíte spásu Vlasti a uskutečnění našich svatých práv jen v rozbití Rakouska.

Až poženou vás, abyste nastavili prsa za proradnou dynastii, k níž národ nemá žádných závazků, najdete jistě příležitost odpovědět vhodně na staleté útisky a zachránit se pro lepší budoucnost!

Nazdar!

Vojáci-dobrovolci československé armády v Italii.

V Italii 2. října 1918.   420.

The Masaryk Manifesto, an appeal to Czechoslovak units in the Austro-Hungarian armed forces, signed by then emigre leader (later President of the Czechoslovak Republic) Tomas Masaryk and by "Volunteer Forces of the Czechoslovak Army in Italy." Emigre operations on which such material was based involved inter-Allied propaganda conferences and a Congress of Subject Peoples convened in Rome during 1918.

which conventionally trained military commanders had skill or experience. They were powerful weapons of political war, wielded on an intercontinental scale in the modern age. The Allied governments, particularly British and Italian, had them.

The Allied political warfare campaign of 1918 involved a number of confused and at times contradictory battles, conducted under great tension and in a very compressed time frame. But they brought victory. They also brought changes to the political map of Europe that far exceeded the expectations or even the understanding of most of the foreign offices, and some of the rulers, of the powers involved.

Like all forms of war, political war conducted on a grand scale often has massive, enduring consequences that those directly involved in the battle, or even those responsible for defining the political goals that lead to battle, may not foresee. And the victors in war are not guaranteed to wisely enjoy the fruits of victory in the following peace. Nonetheless, the campaign of 1918 against Austria-Hungary remains one of the most significant case studies of victory in political war in modern times.[22]

Policy toward Germany, as drafted by Wells, stressed war guilt of the German leaders. It appealed to the German people to escape the consequences of further military losses and to benefit from a postwar "League of Free Nations," which would guarantee Germany access to raw materials and an affluent standard of living. This line was amplified by President Wilson's Fourteen Points, and was heavily played in German-occupied Russia and Ukraine (by accord with Lenin), and, by balloon drops in the West, to German forces in the field. The Allies worked to gain currency for their message among the German civilian population by placement in the neutral press and by infiltration operations, which included floating leaflets down rivers from Switzerland and agitating among transient foreign workers.

The appearance of unity projected by Anglo-Saxon propagandists throughout 1918 was deceptive and began to show cracks as the end neared. Promulgation of Allied peace terms in November 1918 and of Wilson's Manifesto created sharp dissension within the British Cabinet. Northcliffe had mixed views on the question of a severe or soft peace. He had, as well, strong political ambitions. In the event, he advocated publication of official "peace propaganda" which he proceeded to push (without full Cabinet backing) by writing an article, "From War to Peace," and placing it over his own name in press outlets all over the world. Wells had already resigned from his government position and was agitating for his preferred internationalist solution to postwar problems. When the war clearly was won, the French government, never having favored a soft peace, became increasingly assertive in pressing territorial and economic claims against Germany.

As in military affairs, so with propaganda: operations can tend to lead policy, particularly when conducted with serious strategic intent for high stakes, and when policy is not clearly agreed upon within a government or among allies. Obviously, those charged with wielding a political weapon will find their burdens much eased when they can be sure that their masters are in firm accord on policy and can guarantee them priority over other concerns. But such priorities are a matter for judgment at the highest level of statecraft, where conflicts of power, personality, and policy can be resolved (we must hope) by some rational process. The process appears to have broken down in the Anglo-American case in late 1918, but it survived long enough earlier in the year for the propagandists to contribute significantly, perhaps decisively, to victory.

British experience in the climactic stages of World War I showed propaganda to be a powerful strategic weapon. Clearly, propaganda did not win the war, a task that could only be accomplished by military force; but it very likely shortened the war by at least a year, and in doing so it probably saved at least a million lives in one of the bloodiest conflicts of modern history. For that result, much credit must go to the judgment and political perception of Prime Minister Lloyd George and President Wilson, and to the personal commitment of men like Northcliffe and his staff.

Before leaving World War I, we should perhaps reflect for a moment on a larger European political context. Some aspects of that context apparently had much to do with Britain's success in conceiving and employing propaganda as a strategic weapon against Germany and Austria-Hungary. Two dimensions of the prewar situation seem relevant in retrospect: the nature of the European international system, which was based on a balance of power, and the *Zeitgeist*, or Spirit of the Times.

J. A. Spender, in a passage often cited by other historians, summed up the balance of power problem:

> The stage which Europe had reached [in 1914] was that of a semi-internationalism, which organized the nations into two groups but provided no bridge between them. There could scarcely have been worse conditions for either peace or war. The equilibrium was so delicate that a puff of wind might destroy it, and the immense forces on either side were so evenly balanced that a struggle between them was bound to be stupendous. The very success of the balance of power was in this case its nemesis.[23]

This passage stimulates at least two observations for the student of political warfare. First, the greater the levels of social development, the more potential a country offers for political manipulation, for good or bad. Second, the more evenly balanced the forces, the greater may be expected to be the role of instruments that can tip the balance by altering the basic sources of strength in favor of one side or the other. Political war as the British pursued it gave an important addition to the military and economic power they and their allies expended so liberally on the Western Front. It is plausible that, had the Germans used propaganda and done so as vigorously as the British, and had the British failed to use or misused the instrument, the outcome of the war might have been quite different.

By the eve of World War I, it was also apparent that powerful social and ideational currents were stirring most of the peoples of Europe, complicating in dangerous ways the delicately poised international stability of the continent. The polarization of societies between radical and conservative ideas became an important factor for most national leaders, many of whom sought to resolve their dilemmas by adopting varying degrees of strident nationalism or ethnic assertiveness. The rapid expansion of mass media and mass public education aided their efforts.[24]

The presence of these forces in British society stimulated a spate of exaggerated, emotive hate propaganda in the early part of the war. Such propaganda did little to strengthen the already heady charge of patriotic fervor inside Britain. And though it may have initially helped in justifying Britain's role among Allied and neutral populations, it was counterproductive when projected into Germany, where it simply stiffened the resolve of the Germans. When Britain shifted in 1918 to a posture of serious and calculated political warfare with strategic intent, the remnants of the previous hate campaign continued to complicate the picture. World War I hate propaganda remains a classic example of tactical error in use of a political weapon against an enemy population.

The implications for strategic propaganda policy of the radical-conservative issue were perceived and acted upon in the short term, but never finally resolved in the long term by the British Cabinet. In practice, as often happens, policy tended to shift toward the radical side. This shift was stimulated by personal conviction among strong personalities at the working level (Wells is a prime example) and accelerated under the pressure of circumstances as the war progressed and society began to crumble under its blast. American entry into the war, bringing a powerfully renewed impetus of Victorian liberal idealism, on President Wilson's terms, did much to hasten these trends on one side. On the other side, the emergence of a fanatic, millenarian regime amidst the rubble of imperial St. Petersburg tended to frighten the political middle throughout Europe and America.

Out of this welter of power and ideology arose a myth that still tends to influence strategists, namely, that radicalism is strategically superior to conservatism as a motivating ethos in the conduct of political war. The case is by no means clear. At the level of a general abstraction, a radical bias can lead to monumental miscalculation; but in the specific, historical context of World War I Europe, radicalism had a qualified validity. The qualifications deserve a close look.

A review of the forces at work within the Hapsburg empire may help illustrate the point. A modern historian has stated the issue as follows:

> In 1848 the threat of social revolution had rallied the possessing classes to the Hapsburgs; now [1918] it had the opposite effect. Dynastic authority was obviously incapable of mastering the storm; new national states might do so. National revolutions were supported as the substitute for social revolution, particularly as even the most extreme Socialist leaders were, by the very fact of being educated, themselves nationally conscious.[25]

The British and American support for national self-assertion on the part of Czechs and Slovaks, to cite the most obvious case, was superficially "radical." In fact, it was conservative in the sense of offering a hope for broad social stability and economic progress, which had become increasingly unattainable under the decadent Hapsburg aristocracy of privilege. That stability and progress would also, most politically alert Czechs and Slovaks realized, be impossible to attain under the extreme and authentically radical schemes of the Leninists who had come to power in Russia. The Czechoslovak state and society that emerged from the political warfare operations of World War I was an entity clearly founded in the mercantile civic culture of the West. As such, it was not the product of radical (or reactionary) political warfare.

Thus, to say that strategic outcomes in World War I confirm the effectiveness of radicalism as an instrument of political warfare would be an oversimplification. In the East, where the Germans deployed Bolshevism by sending Lenin and other radicals into St. Petersburg, and in the West and South, where the Allied powers deployed national self-determination and liberal democracy against the Hapsburgs, the established order collapsed—and it collapsed *before* the respective military forces were decisively beaten. But the contexts were distinctly different.

In both cases, the national will was eroded or destroyed and a major war was lost. But in the specific Anglo-Saxon case, the Allies used radicalism in the ethnic—and, more cautiously, so-cial—sense in intense efforts to subvert German and Austro-Hungarian war-will by a mixture of intimidation and hope: the hope being particularly strengthened by Wilson's Fourteen Points, the intimidation by stress on the growth of American military power. And the hope offered was, in essence, a conservative hope.

In the East, the conservative hope represented by the February 1917 Revolution was superseded by a radically extremist hope of Leninist inspiration in the October Revolution. The consequences, for Russian national interests in the war and later for peaceful reconstruction, were disastrous. That the more extreme radicalism produces the greater gains in political warfare is by no means clear. Once again, we see illustrated the principle that victory in political war depends upon accurate assessments of context and situation.

The German leaders in 1918 were quite clear about their situation and they attempted, too late, to salvage it by a political strategy of their own. The German leaders voiced the conclusion quite explicitly at a German Crown Council in Spa, after the Allied offensive of August 8, 1918 (an attack preceded by one of Northcliffe's intensified propaganda campaigns):

> We can no longer hope to break the war-will of our enemies
> by military operations . . . [and] the object of our strategy
> must be to paralyze the enemy's war-will gradually by a stra-
> tegic defensive.[26]

As matters turned out, the German war-will, once broken as this statement implies, went with a rush. A strategic defensive was no longer feasible in the face of mounting social instability on the home front, revolt in military units, particularly the navy, and collapse of cobelligerents. At the very least, Northcliffe's propaganda hastened the end; at the most, it made a significant strategic contribution to victory.

So much, at least, concluded a later generation of Germans (and others, including the Bolsheviks in Russia), whose new totalitarian leaders of the 1930s proceeded to put the lesson to the test in achieving and consolidating power, and in expanding their empires. How they did so, and with what catastrophic ultimate consequences, is the subject we turn to next.

6
MARXISM-LENINISM

It has been argued—perhaps most cogently by Hannah Arendt—
that Nazi Germany and Stalinist Russia were both forms of
totalitarianism; that both sought to transform classes into masses;
that both used terror in dealing with their own people; and that
both used propaganda in pursuit of aggressive aims abroad. The
comparison is anathema to present-day Soviet leaders; but it remains logically compelling for anyone willing to look at the
evidence.[1]

Nazi Germany's form of totalitarianism was defeated, more
by massive military power than by propaganda; the Russian form
has been contained, on the whole, by the threat of strategic military
power. In both cases, totalitarians held the initiative in using strategic propaganda; since World War I, English and American propaganda and other forms of political warfare have for the most part
been sporadic in application, limited in conception, and reactive.
Let us look now at Marxism-Leninism, which came first in time,
had deeper historical roots, and was in several ways responsible
for generating its German National Socialist variant.

For better or worse, the links between propaganda and Marxism were deeply rooted in the nineteenth century origins of the
movement: "The Marxist system," in the words of one modern
observer,

> was a propagandist myth, deceptively adorned with scientific
> analysis. Every word and argument of the *Communist Mani-
> festo* was designed to produce an effect. This was even true
> of the title. The document purported to be the manifesto of
> the Communist Party. No such party existed at that time [1848]
> and one object of the Manifesto was to call it into existence.[2]

Extremist movements ever since have sought to emulate this model. Some—like the Nazis—have succeeded; others have had a shorter run; many are still making the attempt. In most such efforts, the ideology comes first, both in time and in preeminence, over other aspects of the movement. Usually, the Leninist model is followed: based on the ideology and the personal commitment of a charismatic leader, the movement builds a cadre with the help of a party newspaper; it creates political fronts; it forms and deploys a military arm; and it eventually bids to capture the governing institutions of a nation state. Contextual and situational aspects are very important; but the inner dynamic of the movement can often remain for some time independent of them.

Lenin will rightly be remembered (for good or evil is beside the point) as the political genius who raised a small, militant cadre of activists to the point where it could seize and wield power in a vast and ethnically diverse empire. True, he did so at a moment of major weakness resulting from the turmoil and disorganization attendant on a massive military setback. But he did it. And what is more, he remained—to his own astonishment—in power and able to bequeath a going operation to his despotic successors.

Lenin's own words may best sum up his success:

The dictatorship of the proletariat was successful because it knew how to combine compulsion with persuasion. . . . We must . . . see to it that the apparatus of compulsion, activised and reinforced, shall be adapted and developed for a new sweep • of persuasion.[3]

Propaganda thus was present at the 1848 inception of the movement and was made even more explicit, as an act of persuasion and intimidation, by Lenin in the early years of its Russian variant.

Those who shaped the institutions of Soviet power were alert to the needs of counterpropaganda policy consistent with their style of governance. We may see evidence of this awareness in formal papers of the state as well as in leaders' speeches and writings. A passage from an early Soviet legal code is characteristic, prescribing exile as punishment for

Title page of the Communist Manifesto, *purporting to represent the views of a then nonexistent emigre political organization. Printed (in German) and circulated in London in 1848. Officially regarded in the USSR today as the founding of the Communist Party.*

Vozhd *(Great Leader) cult of Lenin. An early Soviet propaganda placard establishing the term and iconographic image of Lenin as the* "Vozhd *of the Proletariat." The image and term (translated into Italian as* Duce *and German as* Fuehrer) *were picked up later by the Fascists and the Nazis.*

Propaganda or agitation on behalf of the international bourgeoisie . . . which does not recognize the legitimacy of the coming
change from capitalism to the Communist system of property,
and which longs to overthrow Communism through intervention, blockade, espionage, subversion of the press, and other
methods.[4]

Lenin and his militant followers were thoroughly imbued with
a sense that mass political action was essential for revolution and
rule. Some, like Trotsky, were even more extreme in their expectations for its efficacy in international relations. When asked how
the Bolsheviks intended to run their foreign affairs, Trotsky, newly
appointed as Foreign Minister, replied with his usual brio, "We
will issue some proclamations and close the place down."[5]

Trotsky soon switched portfolios and, as Minister of War,
founded the Red Army. Although he was politically defeated,
denounced, and exiled by Stalin in 1927, much of Trotsky's radicalism remained in the outlook and organizational style of Soviet
use of military power and political warfare. The Soviets never did
dispense with diplomacy, which they quickly learned to use with
tactical skill. But their strategic emphasis remained on political
warfare over diplomacy, as the resources and manpower devoted
to creation of the Communist International and associated Front
Organizations demonstrated.[6]

The Soviets devoted an agitational apparatus of even greater
scope in media, personnel, and physical plant to the task of consolidating Muscovite rule over the numerous nations of the former
Romanov Empire. In essence similar to the aspirations and methods of Justinian's Rome, these policies and programs were broadly
conceived as didactic attempts to reeducate entire nations along
prescribed ideological lines. Such social engineering on an imperial scale appears to correspond with the deepest cultural roots
of the dominant East Slav—specifically Russian—mentality. It
also benefited from a tidal movement in the Spirit of the Times,
favoring massive societal transformation, economic development,
and imperial ambition.

Nicholas Berdyaev, a distinguished Russian philosopher writing in Paris in 1937, described this transformation of Imperial
Russia as

Agitprop train, 1919. Trains were critically important to the Soviet method of war, being used for combat, logistics, and political agitation of the masses. Trotsky, as War Commissar, used them effectively during the Civil War and the immediately following Russo-Polish War.

an identification of the two messianisms, the messianism of
the Russian people and the messianism of the proletariat. . . .
Instead of the Third Rome in Russia, the Third International
[Comintern] was achieved, and many of the features of the
Third Rome pass over to the Third International.

Berdyaev's perception of the Soviet ethos continues to generate controversy among Western scholars, and Soviet propagandists seek to dismiss him as a renegade Marxist. The underlying
issue he expressed so cogently remains: how much of the Soviet
ethos is explicable in terms of Russian history, and how much by
the Russian intelligentsia's susceptibility to the prophetic utterances of a nineteenth century German named Karl Marx? The
evidence seems to show there is much of both.[7]

Lenin and his Bolsheviks came to power by a coup d'etat,
supported by a few ideologically inspired but still professionally
competent military units from the Latvian legions of the Imperial
Army. They were, emphatically, a minority political movement,
with only the most tenuous hold on the central levers of power.
At the time the movement came to power, it was more conspira-
torial than political; the strategic question of internal consolidation
versus external expansion was still not resolved, and the fog of
war, always dense in revolutionary times, hung thick over the
political landscape.

Lenin died in 1924, and Stalin, who succeeded him, had con-
solidated his power by the late 1920s, ostensibly resolving the
external-internal question by announcing the formula, "Socialism
in One Country." It was a useful political warfare strategy, allowing
Stalin to present the USSR to other states as a potentially responsible negotiating partner. It also allowed the party to continue
through clandestine instruments, financed and managed by both
party and state, to propagate messianic, revolutionary ideas
throughout the societies of the USSR's new diplomatic partners.
Within this dialectical framework—as a Marxist would describe
it—Soviet political warfare activity expanded rapidly behind the
facade of a nominally correct diplomatic stance.

The Soviets quickly adopted movie photography for mass agitation and used it with crude but effective manipulative intent. Both Lenin and Stalin strongly emphasized the use by Agitprop of cinematography; under Stalin the practice of photo-retouching (as illustrated in these two shots from a newsreel, showing Trotsky simply removed from the scene (bottom) after Stalin was in power) set a new standard of creative art in reshaping history for mass audiences.

Lenin had set the principles. Soviet trade opportunities, "peace before world revolution," and settlement of debts had been part of the larger diplomatic strategy floated before Western governments as early as 1919. They were offered by Lenin's Commissar for Foreign Affairs, Chicherin, at the same time that the Soviet party representatives were aggressively supporting, with funds, training, and media subsidies, the nascent communist movements of the West. The British experience when, in 1920, Soviet trade representatives Krasin and Kamenev arrived in London is justly notorious. Lenin's advice to them, by coded cable, was explicit:

> That swine Lloyd George has no scruples or shame in the way
> he deceives. Don't believe a word he says and gull him three
> times as much.[8]

The Soviets followed their instructions with gusto. Krasin assured Lloyd George in private conversations that there "were extremists on both sides" who should not be allowed to disrupt the trade talks. But at the same time, Krasin's party colleagues in the newly established Russian Trading Delegation paid out 75,000 pounds sterling to the pro-Soviet *Daily Herald* and made numerous smaller disbursements to political groups including the newly created Communist Party of Great Britain. Lloyd George, who believed the Soviet covert action was not effective and could not be stopped in any case, overrode his Cabinet's objections and continued with the trade talks.[9] Whatever the merits of the Lloyd George argument, the principle that duplicity pays seems to have been eminently clear for Lenin and Stalin.

The new Soviet political warfare style was global in scope and long term in perspective. It was also uncompromisingly self-righteous in basic outlook and remarkable for the quality of relentless political will with which Stalin and his followers imbued it. In a posture strongly reminiscent of Byzantine orthodoxy, Stalin brooked absolutely no challenge to his monopoly on truth as he defined it. Communist believers throughout the world were encouraged in their conviction, proclaimed by Marx, Engels, and Lenin, that all other systems but theirs were inherently evil and devoid of any claim to legitimacy. A pseudo-religious fervor, not reasoned judgment, became the touchstone of public opinion on foreign affairs.

Stalin's Birthday. Group portraits of the Politburo, as in this 1929 shot on the Vozhd's fiftieth birthday, became a traditional aspect of the leadership cult, harking back to Byzantine models. Proximity to the Vozhd became a vital indicator of relative status, one closely watched by rival groupings throughout the world communist movement.

The ancient wound of the West, the split between religious orthodoxy and revolt, opened anew. Since the Peace of Westphalia in 1648, most Europeans had come to accept the idea that ultimate beliefs about the universe and man's role in it were a matter between the individual and his Creator. Governments, Protestant or Catholic, from time to time had sought to use their powers to expand their confessional base, but they always had done so within a larger context of ideational pluralism, accepted pragmatically if not in principle. Such concepts and practices appeared utterly foreign to Stalin and to the mass of communist believers throughout the world at this time. During the high period of inspirational Bolshevism, marked inside the USSR by agricultural collectivization and forced-draft industrialization, this intolerant, xenophobic spirit set the standard for totalitarian practice everywhere.

During World War I, political warfare among Western countries had been stridently hostile. The "beastly Hun" theme of British and French propaganda is often cited and condemned as excessive. (As we have seen, the British in time abated this practice.) Taken in context, such extremist programming was not a root and branch condemnation of German values, but rather an assertion of some common values that the opponent violated.[10]

No such underlying assumption of commonality existed in Stalin's case, and his political warfare stance reflected this fact. His intransigence had profound implications for other nations and cultures seeking to come to terms with the international political and strategic realities posed by Soviet imperial power. A harshly Manichaean posture, it had momentous effects on relations between the Moscow regime and the subjugated nations of the empire. It also meant destruction for whole social classes and groups arbitrarily designated as "enemies of the people." Philosophical abstractions, which had been debated among intellectuals out of power, became matters of life and death when translated into flesh and blood by a totalitarian party in power.

We have a chilling example of this uncompromising—a favorite Leninist word—style in the principles Lenin drafted for admission to the Comintern, principles which were adopted without significant change: "It is the aim of the Communist International to fight by all available means, including armed struggle, for the overthrow of the international bourgeoisie and for the creation of an international Soviet republic as a transitional stage to a complete abolition of the state."[11] This inspiration was rooted in Marxism. In a letter from the 1850s, for example, Marx says, "There is only *one means* by which the murderous death agonies of the old society and the bloody birth throes of the new society can be *shortened*, simplified and concentrated—and that is by *revolutionary terror* [emphasis in original]."[12]

Bombast in this tenor was characteristic of Marx. Some later apologists have argued that he was merely guilty of loose talk; but most of his writing, including works he regarded as major contributions to philosophy and political economy, is saturated with hatred of those he regarded as the cause of all human evil, the "capitalists" and the "bourgeoisie." Lenin and other followers have taken him seriously and have put his propositions into action.

Listen, for example, to Lenin's lieutenant in Petrograd, Zinoviev, in September 1918:

> To overcome our enemies, we must have our own socialist militarism. We must carry along with us 90 million out of 100 million of Soviet Russia's population. As for the rest, we have nothing to say to them. They must be annihilated.[13]

Zinoviev's speech was not loose talk. The organizational instrument to carry out his intent was already operational, as Dzerzhinskiy, the Chief of the Cheka (now KGB), had already made quite clear:

> We [Bolsheviks] stand for organized terror, terror is an absolute necessity during times of revolution. . . . The Cheka is obliged to defend the revolution and to conquer the enemy even if its sword does by chance sometimes fall upon the heads of the innocent.[14]

The ensuing loss of life involved magnitudes previously unknown, at least to Western history before Hitler: leaving foreign wars aside, deaths through internal repressive measures conducted for ideological reasons amounted in Soviet Russia to tens of millions. By almost any estimate, the loss of life in the civil war and wars of national subjugation following the October Revolution was in the tens of millions; the later grain famine in Ukraine, imposed by Moscow in 1932-33 for reasons of Russian ethnic as well as class animosity against Ukrainian farmers, destroyed over seven million people; and the political purges and indiscriminate terror of the late 1930s probably destroyed close to twenty million.[15]

The distinction between external and internal enemies had little meaning for Bolsheviks. "Imperialists," "capitalists," and the "bourgeoisie" were all destined, in their view, for annihilation if they refused to recognize and adjust to the forces of history as Marxist ideology chose to define them. Many categories of people could not even choose survival at the price of capitulation. In most cases, class origin more than individual affirmation determined life or death.

Our purpose here is not to document the suffering of the Russian people and the subject nations, but rather to ask what significance these events had for the early Soviet style of political warfare. To that end, note that Lenin, Stalin, and their followers knew what they were doing in their conduct of mass terror, and were cognizant of the consequences. According to Stalin, as recorded later by Winston Churchill, as many as ten million peasants were "dealt with" in the collectivization campaign, and "the great bulk were very unpopular and were wiped out."[16] Party documents for the period show that other Soviet leaders, such as Kaganovich, as well as lower-level cadres also were quite knowledgeable.[17]

The outside world should have seen these events for what they were—a horrifying demographic and economic catastrophe tearing at the vitals of a great multinational empire ruled by a militant political movement with universalist messianic pretensions. But Soviet diplomacy had achieved a measure of recognition and commercial acceptance throughout the world. The Bolsheviks, observers said, for all of their inflammatory rhetoric, were being "domesticated" by the experience of rule. Many of the Western foreign offices and business communities believed further progress would advance prospects for international peace and open large new markets.

Western newspapers added to the misunderstanding. During the revolution and the civil war, they had tended to be polemically anti-Bolshevik, to the point where they seriously underestimated the broad social forces behind the revolution. Their coverage of

the military conflict was often confused and usually overly opti-
mistic on the side of the Whites. They either downplayed or un-
derreported the Reds' prospects for military victory.[18] Possibly in
overcompensation, though more likely for other reasons, many
European and American journalists tended in the next decade to
overreport the accomplishments and ignore the shortcomings of
the new Soviet regime. We will look in a moment at the consequences of such media distortion in a specific case. But let us first
approach the problem from Stalin's perspective.

Moscow needed a political warfare strategy to make further progress at the state-to-state level while continuing clandestine political
work at the ideological and social level. The task was formidable.
It required measures to divert world attention from the appalling
consequences of the ideology's application *inside* the Soviet Union
while celebrating its alleged inherent virtues among peoples and
governments *outside* the USSR. Soviet leaders and political warfare commanders in this period faced a classic case of the internal-
external tension.

Soviet success in these circumstances was remarkable. It can
be attributed to several sources. One was a sustained commitment
to propaganda and agitation as instruments of rule within the
empire and of expansion outside of it. Another was Stalin's shrewd
grasp of the Spirit of the Times. In addition, the regime received
the help of sympathetic Western leaders and media from both sides
of the political spectrum. And—above all—the Soviets had an
effective central organ for coordination and control.

The center of real power within the Soviet Union had lain
since Lenin's days in the Secretariat of the Central Committee of
the Communist Party of the Soviet Union. Two of the CPSU's
departments tended to predominate, one for organization, the other
for agitation and propaganda, or agitprop. Foreign relations were
(and are) managed by various departments insofar as they involved
elements of the Soviet state apparatus, such as the Foreign Ministry, the Cheka, the Armed Forces, and the Foreign Trade Ministry. Party relations were handled by a staff within the Secretariat,
which tended to dominate the organs of state power as well.

Atop this edifice of party power sat (and still sits) the Politburo, one of whose members held a brief for coordination of all ideological and political questions having to do with global political conflict for the movement and the national interests of the USSR. For nearly thirty years, until his death in 1982, Mikhail Andreevich Suslov held that brief. In the earlier days of Soviet power, it was held at various times by Grigori Zinoviev, Nikolai Bukharin, Andrei Zhdanov, and Stalin himself. It was probably Stalin personally who conceived much of the effective strategy for political warfare from his triumph over his rivals in 1927 until his death in 1953.

The existence, staffing, organization, and activities of this Soviet command structure for political war have never been publicly revealed. What we know of it comes mostly from careful mosaic work in a wide array of indirect documentary sources, defector reports, and third party contacts. Western research, in and out of government, has been sporadic and often self-deceptive. Western governments, lacking comparable institutions, have tended to focus their attention on those parts of the Soviet state apparatus that seemed to correspond to their own roles and missions. This combination of Soviet secrecy and Western misperception did much to strengthen Stalin's hand in his conduct of the political warfare operations of the 1920s and 1930s.[19]

Today, we have abundant evidence on the Soviet media subordinate to these party organs.[20] These media are extensive, both internally and abroad, comprising a rich array of all modern communication means. And they are highly centralized. We know they propagate the line of the party, and only that line, because Soviet party rules and the Soviet constitution require it. By comparing actual party programmatic documents and media treatment, we can tell much about the nature of the party line and about the practical correspondence between what the media receive and what they deliver. We have little direct documentary evidence of the actual policy guidance flowing from party headquarters to editors and publishers. One study, based upon interviews with emigrated Soviet journalists in the 1970s revealed that much of the day-to-day policy guidance from Agitprop officials in the Central Committee to editors in the central media is handled orally, in face-to-face meetings or by telephone.[21]

Party General Secretary Gorbachev's much-heralded policy of *glas'nost* (openness) is not intended to diminish centralized control of the media, but rather to ensure that the media—in accordance with the party's perceptions of the needs of the day—are made more diverse and lively than they have been in the past. The point is not that there is much appearing in the media under Gorbachev that was banned in the past. Rather, we need to ask, on whose initiative and for whose purposes is it appearing? Clearly, the initiative is from the Politburo. Just as clearly, the new material is in the interests of the Politburo as its members see them.

Kremlinologists in the West noted, with understandable interest, the appearance during 1987 of articles in the Soviet central press that indicated possible divergence within the leadership over how much and what kind of information to reveal about Stalin's worst excesses. The divergence, if such it was, was firmly put into context by the number two man on the Politburo, Yegor Ligachev. Asked by the editors of *Le Monde* in December 1987 about his relations with Gorbachev and why he had criticized publications that championed *glas'nost*, Ligachev replied flatly,

> There is no difference. . . . It is true that I have criticized *Ogonyok* and the *Moscow News*, but we have also criticized *Pravda, Izvestia, Sovetskaya Rossiya*, and others. We have frequent meetings with the editors of different sections of the press. We work hand-in-hand with the press. *The press is the weapon without which it would be impossible to accomplish any kind of political work* [emphasis added]. Criticism is not a lack of confidence.[22]

Ligachev's "confidence" is perfectly clear, indeed reassuring, to any editor trained in the Russian tradition of orthodoxy and party control. The party, not the editor personally, accepts ultimate responsibility for what appears in the press, however unorthodox it may seem to the uninitiated. What is new under Gorbachev is not a diminishing of party rule but a more relaxed and confident way of dealing with the inevitable cross-currents that can arise in the management of a complex, modern media empire, particularly at the time when a major new turn in the party line is being introduced.

Although the media they guided were much less extensive, these practices of centralized control were well established in

Stalin's day. Boris Bajanov served as personal secretary to Stalin and was present at many leadership sessions until he fled abroad in 1928. After his escape, he offered his British hosts in India a clear picture of Stalin's ruthless personal style, his insistence on rule by oral instructions, and his regime's strong and enduring commitment to a political warfare strategy against the British Empire, then regarded as the main enemy: Propaganda and agitation were to be the chief weapons, employed through a mix of party and state channels, overt and covert; although conventional war was inevitable, it should be delayed until Soviet military power could be enhanced, together with the industrial base on which it depended. The Politburo, Bajanov reported, was reluctantly but soberly aware of the financial, industrial, and military weakness in the Soviet position vis-a-vis the West.[23]

The Spirit of the Times had much to do with the success of Soviet political warfare in the 1930s. That spirit is well conveyed by a passage from an influential German playwright of the period, Bertolt Brecht. In *The Administrative Measure*, Brecht writes about the mass killing in the USSR resulting from the repressive measures of Stalin. He has his protagonist in the play, a party organizer sent to Germany by the Comintern to purge the German party, announce,

Terrible it is, to kill,
But not only others but ourselves we kill when it
Becomes necessary.
But we cannot, we said,
Permit ourselves not to kill. Only on our
Unbending will to change the world can we base
The Measure.[24]

Writing nearly twenty years later, a former leader of the German Communist Party offered an insight into Brecht's play and its larger significance for the spirit of the international communist movement and sympathetic European intellectuals:

In its language, in the symbols it uses, this didactic play . . .
is characteristic of the transformation of the Comintern. The
defeat [of the Chinese Communist Party by the Kuomintang]
in China and the subsequent purge are used in Germany to
indoctrinate the Party in docility to Moscow and in passivity
to the Nazis. In avant garde abstractions Brecht achieves the

transfiguration and beatification of the Stalinist Party. The audacious use of a central chorus symbolizes the intervention of the GPU [now KGB] in Party life and the voluntary acceptance of its hierarchical discipline. Stalin's reorganized Comintern is presented in the figure of the naive Communist who submits himself to final judgment by the representatives from Moscow.[25]

This totalitarian *Zeitgeist*, which led millions of Russian and European intellectuals into deeds of mass murder, was a significant part of the political warfare environment of the 1930s. Few leaders understood and used it as effectively as Stalin. Few groups suffered under it so cruelly as the old Bolsheviks, European and Russian, who had used terror themselves in coming to power and now saw it turned against them by a new generation of terrorists.[26]

This war within a war's effect on Soviet political warfare capabilities did not become fully apparent until the Great Moscow Purge Trial of 1937-38. Throughout the early 1930s, the field staffs of the Comintern, Red Army Intelligence, and the Cheka remained, on the whole, loyal and effective instruments of Stalin. So did their collaborators and dupes among Western business, media, and government circles. One of the examples of this early period may be seen in the case of the Ukrainian famine of 1932-33.

Stalin's solution to the dilemma of military and industrial backwardness lay in forced-draft industrialization. As part of this strategy, he began collectivizing the empire's still mainly private agriculture. Since the revolution of 1917, numerous small-holders, known in Bolshevik idiom as Kulaks, had held most of the Soviet Union's farms. The Ukrainian Republic, which contains the richest of the empire's grain acreage, was largely populated by such small farmers. They were—and are—a tenaciously land-proud, hardworking lot, who had done much to place the Soviet and Romanov empires among the breadbaskets of Europe. Stalin wanted them collectivized not only for ideological reasons but even more to assure complete control of their abundantly produced resource—grain—for the needs of the state. After the harvest of 1932, the

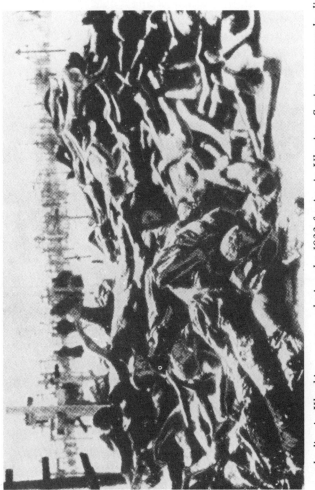

Frozen bodies in Kharkiv cemetery during the 1933 famine in Ukraine. Soviet propaganda did much to blunt international awareness of this politically motivated disaster in which over seven million people died.

Bolshevik political cadres, backed by Russian paramilitary units, simply confiscated the large stores of grain, including the reserves needed to feed the subsistence-oriented farm population through the winter.

Throughout the famine, some major Western media downplayed or simply ignored its murderous consequences. Walter Duranty of the *New York Times* and Louis Fischer of the *New Republic* seem to have actively aided the Soviets in suppressing the story, at least in the opinion of some of their Western colleagues in the Moscow foreign press corps.[27] The reasons for the journalists' actions are unclear. Probably, they had something to do with Western commercial aspirations to enter the Soviet market, some Western leaders' desire to keep Soviet Russia out of the Nazi embrace, and many intellectuals' belief that there were "no enemies on the left." A few journalists, including some of the left such as the *Manchester Guardian*'s Malcolm Muggeridge, did seek to give some sense in their reports of the scope of the disaster.[28]

General world reaction, given the lack of hard information and the contradictory reports from highly respected Western media, was one of disbelief and unconcern. The soporific effect appears to have been cumulative. Throughout the remainder of the decade, Western intellectuals who made political pilgrimages to Moscow preferred to be "understanding" about Soviet internal problems and eager to find areas where they could hail its successes.[29] As willing volunteer witnesses, less than fully approving but basically favorable, they were much more effective than the full-time overt propagandists.

The Comintern had primary responsibility for cultivating and servicing these intellectuals with media outlets, membership in organizations, and travel grants. Basic policy guidance came from the Moscow-based center, but regional authority reposed in the capable hands of the organization's West European Chief, Willi Muenzenberg. He is credited (by Western scholars, not the Soviets to whom he is still a nonperson) with having conceived and created the great network of political Front Organizations that played a major role in shaping European opinion on international issues, including the image of the USSR. Muenzenberg's Fronts, his stable of literary figures who signed petitions, protested, and wrote columns and articles for the general media as well as a string of clandestinely funded journals and newsletters, reflected the genius of a naturally gifted propagandist. Muenzenberg aptly termed his Fronts "Innocents Clubs." Following the 1939 Nazi-Soviet Pact and the turmoil of French defeat in 1940, he was murdered by Soviet agents.[30]

Soviet political warfare operations during the 1930s covered issues and targets other than those presented by Western intellectuals' reactions to the mass killings inside the Soviet Union. Operations in Asia, Western Europe, and the Americas were mounted and carried out with a variety of instruments. Black, white, and grey propaganda, assassinations and other forms of intimidation, intervention in world financial markets, including fake currency transactions—all were widely used, sometimes in combination with intelligence collection work, more often separately.[31]

The problem of separating or combining political warfare instruments, both overt and covert, with intelligence collection deserves special attention. The Soviet practice of the period is instructive. Lenin, clearly sensitive to the problems involved, sought to resolve them, at least in principle, by some measure of organizational separation. For example, his draft of the first statute of the Comintern, from 1919, contains the statement,

> Communists everywhere are obliged to create a parallel underground apparatus which should help the Party to fulfill its duty toward the Revolution.[32]

This injunction remained operative in principle, although often violated in practice, well into the Stalin era (and quite possibly later). An organization manual widely circulated in the US Communist Party during the 1930s contains a clear provision for parallel and separate party organs, one overt and the other covert. The manual does not make clear to what extent, if any, intelligence collection functions could be combined with or separated from covert propaganda and political influence work. In the Soviet operations of this period, they appear to have been combined or at least interchangeable depending upon circumstances and the ability of the people involved.[33]

Some of these Soviet campaigns of the 1930s were won, some were lost, some were allowed to fade out in confusion and uncertainty. All deserve closer analysis than they have received in the conventional diplomatic histories of the period.[34]

Amidst this welter of events, the Ukrainian famine provides a clear example of the way a totalitarian state, ruled by a messianic political movement with unlimited, millenarian pretensions, could, in the context of the times and with significant help from foreign sympathizers, markedly enhance its ability to impose its will on its opponents. Western recognition for the new Soviet state was forthcoming; awareness of the continued subversion and clandestine activity of the Comintern was obscured or diverted; advantageous commercial ties were established and expanded to the great benefit of the Soviet economy; and the overall image of the Soviet Union as a role model for the socially troubled Western societies was not tarnished by the appalling demographic crime perpetrated in one of the subject nations of the empire.

In addition to manipulating the Western democracies, Stalin in 1939 succeeded in his efforts over the decade to come to terms with his main totalitarian rival, Germany.[35] And it is to that state and its political movement, National Socialism, that we now turn for insights into yet another form of twentieth-century political warfare.

7

THE NAZIS

Leninist political warfare focused the hatred and frustration of masses of ordinary people on a "class enemy," a reification of evil collectively termed the "bourgeoisie," whose status depended not on their beliefs but on their origins. Hitler and the Nazis harbored sentiments comparable in intensity and similar in their political manifestation, but different in one point. For class hatred Hitler substituted race hatred, and he did so with success in duping the Germans to the edge of national suicide. The price in the end for the intensity of Germany's delusion was the repulsion of other nations that might—under a different strategy—have rallied to or at least supinely accepted German hegemony.[1]

Hitler's conduct of political war thus presents an example of the tension created by contrary internal and external priorities generated by a militant and aggressive power. Evidence that at one point there seems to have been over one million Soviet citizens helping the German armed forces shows the German state's potential for victory early in World War II.[2] Hitler cast aside this potential when he refused to allow a political role for the leaders of the large numbers of Ukrainian, Russian, Baltic, and Caucasian troops serving with the German armed forces. Confronted by the brutish behavior of Gestapo and SS forces, and denied any hope of a political future free of such domination, the units of former Soviet citizens still fought in the Wehrmacht's ranks, at times with surprising effectiveness.[3] Hitler wasted their larger potential as a basis for establishing viable political entities on Germany's eastern border.

Given the monumental arrogance of the Nazi leaders, it is surprising that they were as successful as they were in grasping, consolidating, and expanding their power over Germany and its neighboring nations. Their success stemmed partly from the astonishing energy and ruthlessness with which they acted, but more from hopelessness, confusion, and folly among their victims. In retrospect, Nazi political warfare style reminds us of what we may expect—in the short run—from the skillful application of duplicity and violence.[4]

In assessing Nazi strategic propaganda, we are on much firmer ground than we are in the Soviet case. The time frame is shorter —Hitler had not much over a decade in power—the policies were in most cases more straightforward, and we are able to see much of the actual documentation, notably internal policy guidance, confidential diaries, and records of meetings. What we learn from the Nazi experience is not very comforting. First, these totalitarians seem to have meant and said and did pretty much what they announced in their programmatic goals as their considered intention. The experience of rule did not "domesticate" them. When tactical political warfare objectives and Hitler's personal vision conflicted, Hitler prevailed. Second, the Nazis, and more particularly Hitler, did have a basic political warfare concept, which they persistently applied in combination with diplomacy, subversion, and economic and military power.[5]

In retrospect, the key to Hitler's policy seems to have been quite simply power—power for the movement, power for its leading cadres, and power for its *Fuehrer*. The goal was not, in essence, even nationalist as it purported to be. Hitler seems to have felt contempt for the German people, and to have felt no inhibitions in saying so, at least to his entourage.[6] This basic attitude is appallingly confirmed by Hitler's sacrifice of the German armed forces and large numbers of the civilian population in the pursuit of a war he must have known, after 1942, he could not win.

Hitler's use of strategic propaganda appears in two contexts: one offensive, from 1934 to 1942, when it was driven by aspirations for power and empire, many of which he realized; another of desperation, from 1943 to 1945, when it was a reaction to defeats whose ultimate outcome was increasingly clear. The offensive,

Adolf Hitler speaking. The Fuehrer *relied heavily on his remarkable skill in personally mobilizing mass audiences. Goebbels used public address systems, radio, and a staged setting to achieve new levels of audience exposure for a leader's image. The low camera angle in this photo accentuates the dominating image of the* Fuehrer, *something Goebbels did much to help create through recruitment of skilled photographers for his propaganda staff.*

expansionist phase was accompanied by admixtures of diplomacy, peace propaganda, and appeals to European fears of the other, Soviet form of totalitarianism. An aggressive and cynically brilliant performance, it included a coordinated use of strategic deception, practiced through combined use of propaganda, high-level diplomacy, and information filtered through intelligence channels.

Hitler's strategic objective ostensibly lay to the East: a source of raw materials, land, and slave manpower. He and his principal ideologist, Alfred Rosenberg, took every opportunity to emphasize this objective in their contacts with neighboring West European states. They argued that Germany thus served as a counterweight to the imperial ambition of Soviet Russia and the threat of class war induced through Comintern subversion. To validate this message, Hitler encouraged contacts between the growing German Air Force and Western air intelligence officers, seeking to convince the Western governments that German Air Force doctrine, training, and equipment were structured in support of a land campaign in the East and were not suitable for the long-range bombing operations that an invasion of England would require. Propaganda output, including Hitler's and Rosenberg's frequent public denunciations of Bolshevism, complemented this posture.

The English and French intelligence officers involved judged Hitler's posture to be deceptive. An inescapable corollary to Hitler's Eastern strategy, in their view, would be a prior strike at France and the Low Countries and, from the position thus gained, an invasion of or dictated peace for England. One of the officers directly concerned, who ran British air intelligence against Germany from 1933 until 1940, estimated in 1938 from personal observation of airbase and other military construction in East Prussia that the attack on Russia would be mounted in 1941, and that the essential preliminary onslaught in France thus would have to come in 1940. He reported these conclusions, without significant consequences, to the British and French governments. Winston Churchill, however, sought to use some of the information on German military preparations to stir public and Parliamentary awareness of the danger.[7]

Goebbels' role in the propaganda side of this operation seems to have been mainly to propagate the anti-Bolshevik statements of

Hitler, Rosenberg, and other top leaders to the world at large through a rapidly expanding use of radio broadcasting and print media. He does not seem to have felt much personal conviction in Rosenberg's "Nordic" and "Aryan" philosophical principles (or any other ideologies for that matter), and his strong personal rivalry with Rosenberg further diminished his Ministry's enthusiasm for the strategy of an opening to the British. In this early stage, Goebbels' oversea propaganda apparently was aimed mainly at intimidating neighboring East European nations and appealing to irredentist and chauvinist sentiments of German-speaking minorities abroad. The arrogance and exclusively German appeal of the Nazi creed was allowed to predominate, apparently making poor reading for most of Germany's neighboring nations. It did find some resonance among German-speaking communities abroad, which may explain the decision to emphasize it. The appeal seems to have been strongest in economically depressed countries like Austria and least strong in prosperous regions like Switzerland and the United States.

Nazi propaganda toward America was often self-contradictory, being split three ways during the early 1930s on both policy and organizational lines among the Foreign Ministry, the Nazi Party's Foreign Division, and the Propaganda Ministry. But the resulting failure was not complete: some credit for America's remaining at least nominally neutral until it was attacked militarily in December 1941 should go to at least one aspect of the German propaganda and covert operations campaign waged from 1937 to 1941 to bolster neutralist, anti-British sentiment in the US Congress and media.

The operations included money payments to journalists and authors, political influence operations by American fellow travelers, inducements of various kinds to members of Congress, and a covert publishing house based in New Jersey. Most of these activities were run clandestinely out of a mix of diplomatic and consular missions, trade agencies, and cultural foundations. A particularly skillful use was made of the outlet offered for unattributed, allegedly neutralist propaganda planted on sympathetic US congressmen whose statements were then published in the *Congressional Record*.[8]

This *realpolitik* strategy paralleled—but was in reality undercut by—the German Nazi Party's attempts to bolster the ideological zeal of the small, fragmented Nazi movement in North America. Most Americans—including those of German stock—were hostile or at most indifferent to the millenarian racist program of pan-German national socialism. Some might have agreed with influential anti-British journalists like H. L. Mencken, who announced that the State Department "had become an outhouse of the British Foreign Office," but being anti-British did not translate into a rejection of the cultural and historical ties binding together the English-speaking world; nor did it mean being blind to the strategic danger for America of a Nazi-dominated Europe. In time, these basic realities would have decided the German propaganda battle with Britain over North America. But time in 1939-40 was a critical strategic factor, and Germany might have done much better than it did if its political warfare commanders had grasped and acted upon these distinctions earlier in the campaign.

After 1939, circulation figures picked up markedly throughout Nazi-occupied Europe for leading German foreign-language periodicals. This rise may have resulted not only from the suppression of many competing media, notably English, but also from Goebbels' intelligent modification of the arrogant tone in some journals. His leading periodical, *Signal*, was produced fortnightly in 20 languages from 1940 to 1945. At its high point, it enjoyed a circulation in occupied Europe of three million. The core image was of Germany as a protector of European civilization against external intervention and as an economic dynamo driving a revivified European economy. German racial supremacy was softpedaled, and anti-Semitism was seldom explicit. The editors were subordinated to both Goebbels' Ministry of Propaganda and the Oberkommando der Wehrmacht.[9]

The defensive phase in Hitler's political warfare strategy took place after 1942 against a backdrop of large-scale military defeats and Axis defections, such as Italy's. Diplomatic overtures, which could have been used more effectively in both East and West to split the uneasy alliance of Western democracies and Soviet totalitarianism, were kept in clandestine and easily disavowed channels; as projected by Hitler's aides, they offered little realistic promise to East or West.[10] Political use of defected Soviet and

Joseph Goebbels at his desk during World War II, flanked by the globe and a portrait of Frederick the Great. Goebbels had a sure sense of setting, and this shot, intended for a wide European audience in his leading journal, Signal, *helped define Goebbels as a civilized European rather than a Nazi radical.*

East European forces continued to be held hostage, despite Wehr-macht objections, to Hitler's original ideological vision. Hate prop-aganda against both Eastern and Western adversaries continued strong for German domestic audiences, particularly after the aborted July 1944 attempt on Hitler's life by disaffected Wehrmacht officers. In short, Hitler's end-game propaganda was massively self-defeating. Its fitting finale was a performance of Wagner's *Twilight of the Gods* by the Berlin Philharmonic in April 1945.

It now seems clear that the main contextual element in Hitler's rise to power, given the totalitarian spirit at work inside Germany, was a failure of political will among the democratic powers. Win-ston Churchill, as early as 1935, put it plainly: "Hitler's success, and, indeed, his survival as a political force, would not have been possible but for the lethargy and folly of the French and British Governments since the war, and especially in the last three years [1932-35]."[11]

Stanley Baldwin, then Prime Minister, and the target of Churchill's remark, blamed the problem—not wholly without rea-son—on the Americans: "You will get nothing out of Washington but words: long words, but only words."[12] Baldwin was express-ing, in his usual laconic idiom, a view commonly held throughout the British establishment: that to follow America's high-sounding rhetoric against aggression would risk exposing Britain to coun-teraction by the targets of the rhetoric without any hope of Amer-ica's translating the sentiments into real support for the British.[13] One cannot help wondering what contribution Nazi propaganda might have made to German strategic aims in America if it had put more emphasis on *realpolitik* and less on racism than it did in the 1930s.

Other contextual aspects of Hitler's success in political war-fare characterized the situation in Western Europe. They included the whole problem of social disruption and political disintegration in the European state system. "The way was prepared," Hannah Arendt later observed, "by fifty years of the rise of imperialism and disintegration of the nation-state, when the mob entered the scene of European politics."[14] Arendt had witnessed, both as participant and scholar, a process in which war, inflation, and massive social upheaval shattered many of the cohesive institutions of Europe.

Together, the underlying forces, the failure of democratic leaders, and that indefinable element *Zeitgeist* set the stage. They were not, however, in themselves the actors, and to think that disembodied social and political forces were alone responsible would lead to serious miscalculation. Hitler and his chief propagandist, Goebbels, provided the political will and the insights and organizational skill needed to exploit the situation.

Hitler's vision was power, his means to achieve it clear, simple, and insane: destroy the Jews and conquer the East. Propaganda was to be a strategic weapon of first resort, which would destroy the enemy from within:

> The place of artillery preparation for frontal attack by the infantry in trench warfare will in the future be taken by revolutionary propaganda, to break down the enemy psychologically before the Armies begin to function at all. The enemy must be demoralized and ready to capitulate, driven into moral passivity, before military action can even be thought of.[15]

Many of Hitler's statements on propaganda and political warfare activities of other kinds were delivered extempore and recorded by his close associates either in memoranda at the time or in memoirs published later. The sections on propaganda in *Mein Kampf*, like the rest of the work, Hitler dictated to a close associate who joined him for the purpose in Landsberg prison in 1924. The whole work thus has an aphoristic and discursive—not to say chaotic—quality. Hitler's thought, including that on propaganda, has a clear intent, but his statements as recorded in this manner make difficult reading. The preceding quotation is probably as close as one can come to a summation.

For Hitler, the line between war and peace was no longer clearly defined as it had been in nineteenth century Europe. From 1934 to April 1940 when a general war erupted after Germany invaded France, Hitler's campaigns followed the propaganda principles worked out in his earlier struggle for power. Their application resulted in a series of striking, bloodless victories over adjacent East European states, followed by incorporation of their territory into the new German empire. By 1939 both Czechoslovakia and Austria had vanished as independent states, the Versailles Treaty limitations on German military power had been scrapped, and Germany had withdrawn from the League of Nations. Most important, Germany had struck a bargain in August 1939 with the other great totalitarian power, the Soviet Union, permitting the partition of the remainder of Eastern Europe, including Poland, and providing a strategic guarantee that allowed Hitler to turn to the West. Seldom had the Clausewitzian principle that the price of victory must be paid in blood been so strikingly confuted.[16]

Reflecting after the war on European reactions to Hitler's political warfare strategy of the 1930s, Britain's wartime Chief of Political Warfare, Bruce Lockhart, concluded that the threat of violence, though not actually applied in military conflict at that point, had much to do with Hitler's successes, as it had with those of Stalin and Mussolini:

> All over Europe, including England, there were men who had
> a sneaking regard for the super-men of violence. It was the
> respect of fear. It was like the mesmerizing fascination which
> the python exercises over the mouse-deer of the Malayan
> jungle.[17]

Throughout the 1930s, Hitler used violent threats and suasive diplomacy almost simultaneously. Examples are so numerous that one can only marvel at the tenacity of Western politicians in ignoring or explaining them away. One of the most striking cases was Hitler's speech at the Berlin *Sportspalast* on September 26, 1938, in which he denounced the Czech leader Benes in vitriolic terms, expounded on the power and purpose of the new Germany, but denied aggressive intention. He followed this propaganda thrust with a hastily arranged diplomatic summit in Munich with the British, French, and Czechs, where the Western powers in effect sold out Czechoslovakia. British Prime Minister Chamberlain, on returning to London, announced at the airport that he had achieved "peace in our time." A disgusted journalist observed that Chamberlain had demonstrated a new form of air travel: how to crawl at 250 miles per hour.[18]

Aside from their disastrous consequences at the time, the Munich agreements created legal and political complications for the future. For the first years of its wartime existence in London, the Czech government in exile, headed by Masaryk and Benes, was officially listed, for legal reasons stemming from the agreements, as "provisional," and its representatives denied official standing at the Foreign Office. The issue involved more than protocol. After the Munich summit, the Western powers needed to show in every way possible that they were firmly committed to backing the sovereignty and integrity of the Czechoslovak state. Masaryk, as "provisional" Foreign Minister, once asked his British friends whether the Czech pilots who died in the Battle of Britain should be listed as "provisionally dead." In time this situation was cleared up and the Czechs received full accreditation, along with other governments in exile. But the inherent suspicion remained and probably helped make the political elites of postwar Czechoslovakia more vulnerable than they might otherwise have been to Soviet diplomatic advances in 1945.[19]

Hitler's political warfare strategy over Czechoslovakia provides a classic case study of violence and suasion, stimulating both fear and hope. Pitched at a high key and maintained at high tempo, it used a combination of instruments, leading with propaganda and covert action, supplemented by diplomacy and backed by the threat of military force. Such a strategy is, alas, very successful against status quo, democratically based parliamentary governments. And its damage in poisoning relations within an alliance often extends beyond the immediate event.

Hitler was above all a propagandist. From his first political awakening until his *Goetterdaemmerung* in the ruins of Berlin, propaganda remained his primary instrument of political expression. His political origins, as described by a postwar biographer, make this quite clear:

> For [Hitler] power lay with the masses, and if the hold of the
> Jew-ridden Marxist parties on their allegiance was to be broken,
> a substitute had to be found. The key, Hitler became convinced,
> lay in propaganda, and the lesson Hitler had already drawn

*"Hitler the Standard-bearer," iconography in Nazi-sponsored art.
This style of painting for mass dissemination was heavily emphasized,
reestablishing—for modern times—a new totalitarian relationship for
arts and the state.*

from the Social Democrats and Lueger's Christian Socialists in Vienna was completed by his observation of the success of English propaganda during the war, by contrast with the failure of German attempts. The chapter on "War Propaganda" in *Mein Kampf* is a masterly exercise in that psychological insight which was to provide Hitler's greatest gift as a politician.[20]

For Hitler, propaganda was inseparable from the concept of power, and it combined with his conception of political opponents as embodiments of evil to make his form of politics distinctly different from that practiced in post-Renaissance Europe. For him, politics and war were inseparable, and propaganda was an instrument of war, one to be used against the enemy within as well as without the gates.

Hitler could commit propaganda blunders. A splendid example was his claim in late 1941 that victory over Russia had been achieved and that only minor military consolidation was needed. His statement was publicly made, clearly and emphatically, and disseminated in broadcast and print media throughout Europe. The British recorded it and played it back into Germany on each anniversary of its original declaration. Goebbels' standard operating procedure in such cases was *totschweigen*, that is, dead silence. It is characteristic of Goebbels that he understood the value in some cases of silence, and that he was usually capable of imposing his decision on the ideological hotheads of the Nazi regime. He offers an example of cool self control and wisdom in damage-limitation tactics that is not always followed.

One of Goebbels' most significant operational innovations was the concept of the "invisible propagandist." Goebbels and Hitler both made much in their theoretical writings of the value of strategic propaganda, and Goebbels made no attempt to conceal the existence of his Ministry of Propaganda or to downplay its importance in the structure of party and government. But in propaganda operations, he usually insisted that the propagandist must "remain invisible" in order to make people yield to propaganda "without inner resistance." In practice, this meant removing all visible traces of censorship both in German media and in the press and radio of occupied areas. Newspapers did not usually appear with those blank spaces which Europeans traditionally associated with government restrictions on freedom of the press; control over

Russian Liberation Army (ROA) commanders Igor Sakharov, Sergei Bunyachenko, and Andrei Vlasov among First Division ROA troops in February 1945. The extensive use of former Soviet citizens fighting with the Wehrmacht was kept at small-unit levels by Hitler's personal order until very late in the war, and formation of division-size units such as this, with their own insignia, came too late to have any political effect.

political content was assured instead by political selection of editors and writers, with "responsibility" for content punished by penalties or rewarded by promotion and pay.[21]

Goebbels considered writers and editors members of the elite, and expected them to use judgment and initiative in executing the confidential daily directives of the Ministry. Nazi propaganda was thus converted from a negative, reactive, and restrictive mechanism into a positive, activist political force consistently exercised in advance of events. This totalist concept of the role of propaganda in the life of the nation was a major departure from traditional European forms of authoritarianism. It remains one of the essential features of a totalitarian polity. Goebbels did not invent the practice—Lenin had initiated it in Russia before the advent of the Nazis—but he quickly grasped its importance and applied it with characteristically ruthless and relentless skill.

In tactical use of propaganda, Hitler and Goebbels emphasized simplicity and repetition above all, and insisted on a black-and-white portrayal of the world. They also sought to activate political parties favorable to Nazi ideology as instruments for mobilizing the masses. They were not much concerned with the fine points of ideology as long as the movement espousing it was contributing to the achievement of Hitler's central political vision. They did not believe truth was necessary, being contemptuous of the capacity among mass audiences for distinguishing or valuing it over emotive appeals. (Goebbels did, however, understand the utility among intellectual audiences of an image of "truth.") Hitler saw propaganda as a technical matter of persuasion, or salesmanship as he sometimes put it, in a mass market. Curiously, he seems to have perceived no incompatibility between this marketplace image and his constant fulminations against "capitalists" and "plutocracies."[22]

Like other totalitarians, the Nazis were adept at managing quick switches in propaganda lines. The main tactic in such cases was a combination of *totschweigen* on the old line and a brazen, forceful play for the new, a tactic more in line with the simplicity principle than the slow and subtle substitution of themes over time. Goebbels could be and was sometimes subtle, but it was not his preferred style. Hitler scorned subtlety. A classic example of this attitude is seen in the switch from anti-Soviet treatment common

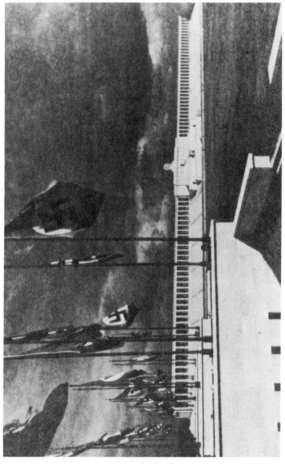

The rostrum at the Nuremberg stadium, designed by Hitler's architect, Albert Speer, for Nazi Party rallies. The use of architectural forms to symbolize imperial power was quite consciously linked to earlier Roman models. Speer's genius lay in his ability to endow the Nazi variant with an alluringly futuristic sense as well.

in Nazi political discourse throughout the 1930s to the pro-Soviet line of the August 1939 Nazi-Soviet Pact. The new line prevailed—as also in the Soviet output—until the June 1941 German invasion of Russia. In November 1940, for example, Goebbels' mass circulation *Life*-format journal, *Signal*, gave full-page photo coverage to Soviet Foreign Minister Molotov's November 12 visit to Berlin. The accompanying text read, "The historic decision of the Fuehrer and Stalin for friendship between the two great realms, which today have again become neighbors, is one of the most important factors, and one of world-wide significance, for the New Order in continental Europe."[23] When the line had changed, such statements were not explained away but simply ignored.

Goebbels differed from Hitler on a key point of character, one which—if Hitler had given it free rein—might have done much to stave off Germany's defeat. Both leaders were cynically manipulative in their use of strategic propaganda, but Hitler remained true to his ultimate political vision. Goebbels, to the contrary, was a political nihilist, lacking any moral code and utterly unconcerned with truth or principles. As Germany's situation after 1942 became increasingly desperate, he sought to persuade Hitler to turn to more effective use of satellite forces, to develop political formulas for involving the Soviet emigre military formations, and to explore avenues for a compromise peace. When it became clear that Hitler would not accept such alternatives, Goebbels pushed German propaganda operations in a more intransigent and nihilist direction, seeking mainly to keep up the fighting spirit of the German people by stimulating their fear of destruction as a nation if they surrendered. Toward the end, this posture reached the extremes of advocating the denunciation of the Geneva Convention on belligerent rights and the shooting of captured Allied airmen.

As between Hitler and Goebbels, the latter was potentially the more formidable opponent for an opposing commander; Goebbels would better stand a comparison with Napoleon and Talleyrand. Whether the world would have been a better place if Goebbels' preferred strategies had prevailed is another question.[24]

In technique and organization, Goebbels was brilliant and innovative. He immediately realized the possibilities of radio broadcasting (then still in its infancy); he explored and used effectively the new medium of cinema both at home and abroad; and he cooperated, at times abrasively, with Hitler's architect (and Goebbels' earlier protege), Albert Speer, in developing and exploiting the great potential for mass meetings and monumental settings such as the *Parteitag* events at Nuremberg. This monumental visual dimension to the Nazi mythos, harking back to Roman models, was perhaps Goebbels' most enduring contribution to the art of totalitarian propaganda. (A Slavicized version of it exists today in the symbolism surrounding the mass party gatherings in the USSR.) In the hands of Goebbels and Speer this form of symbolism not only awoke a powerful historical echo but also symbolized, with its disciplined masses of uniformed men, the incorporation of strident militarism into the totalitarian mythology. It was this doubled and redoubled symbolism of thrusting imperial will on which Hitler's Third Reich ultimately depended.[25]

Goebbels—who was trained in philosophy and law—once observed, "Jurisprudence is a science, propaganda is much more like a form of art." The statement has often been cited by students of propaganda.[26] It is worth recalling that the practice of such an art form requires materials, and that Goebbels was given scope to mobilize much of the financial, media, and cultural resources of one of the most advanced nations in Europe. The practice also required a political vision in tune with the times to animate and inform the propagandist. Hitler, for better or worse, provided such a vision. That Goebbels followed Hitler's vision to the point of personal and national self-destruction arouses a sense of wonder and revulsion. The student of political war who contemplates these events is left with an ominous conclusion: that a clever, competent, indeed gifted, statesman can be found in a highly cultivated European nation in the service of a madman.

8
BRITAIN AND AMERICA
IN WORLD WAR II

B efore leaving World War II, let us reflect for a moment on
the political warfare activities of the Allied Powers. Their
situation was confused, indeed to the point where they had dif-
ficulty formulating and pursuing any common strategy. The nature
of the problem might best be illustrated by the following passage
from a 1940 memo by the British Minister of Information:

> The policy of the British Communist Party as stated in *The
> Daily Worker* has steadily changed since the outbreak of the
> war. On September 2, 1939 *The Daily Worker* said that "the
> Communist Party would do all in its power to ensure speedy
> victory over Fascism". On October 7th, the new manifesto was
> issued reversing this policy and stating that "this is not a war
> for Democracy against Fascism; it is a fight between imperialist
> powers".[1]

The reality behind this position of the British communists,
who at that time faithfully followed Stalin's line, was quite
simple—the Soviet Union had no common interests with the democracies of the West; its position in the military conflict then
developing was purely opportunistic and would remain so. Western
governments had few illusions on this score. A Foreign Office
assessment prepared in August 1940 for Churchill noted,

> The Soviet Government have no friends in the world and no
> spiritual affinities with other governments. They merely enter
> into temporary diplomatic associations with countries for
> purely opportunistic reasons. They distrust and are distrusted
> by those with whom they associate, but take care not to let

their distrust be exploited by others (i.e., by us). Hence the anxiety they display to re-emphasize on every suitable occasion the friendly character of their relations with Germany.[2]

Subsequent events confirmed this appraisal: From 1939 to 1941 the war was a struggle by West European democracies against a de facto alliance of totalitarian powers. It changed radically in June 1941 when the German totalitarian power attacked the Russian totalitarian power. It changed again at the end of 1941 when the two strongest powers outside the Eurasian land mass entered the war: Japan in an assault on Britain and the United States in the Pacific Basin, America in support of Britain and against Japan and Germany in both the Atlantic and the Pacific regions. No war was declared between Japan and Russia until 1945.

In addition to the profound differences of values, there was thus a sizeable divergence in regional strategic orientations. Under these circumstances, the best the anti-Hitler coalition could articulate as a strategic war aim of global significance was a lowest common denominator of "unconditional surrender." The corollary to this minimal aim was a de facto limitation of political warfare to the tactical level. The idea of a common vision of the postwar world, comparable to that put forward by the Allied powers in 1918, could not be employed with any degree of credibility by the Alliance as a whole.

Allied strategy in World War II thus became a matter of applying sheer, unrelenting military power, accompanied only by tactical political warfare, to achieve the final and complete destruction in the field of all hostile military formations. The strategy was classical Clausewitz: find the opponent's *schwerpunkt*, or center of strength, smash it in battle, and be prepared to pay for the victory in blood. The strategy was totally congenial to the Soviet military leaders, whose doctrinal views, ever since Lenin, had been dominated by Clausewitz. It also corresponded to the proclivities of the American military leadership, who had traditionally subscribed to Clausewitzian perceptions of war. It did not fit the British tradition, expressed in modern times by Liddell Hart, of the indirect approach. But British influence on alliance grand strategy declined sharply after the Soviet Union and the United States entered into the conflict and was in effect subordinated to the perceptions of Britain's larger co-belligerents.[3]

Both British and Americans kept up a steady bombardment of German urban and industrial centers throughout the war. The accompanying message to the German civilian population, by airdrop leaflet and radio broadcast, was bleak. In July 1942 a British leaflet dropped over Germany, signed by Air Marshal Harris of Bomber Command, emphasized the immense productive capacity of the Anglo-American aircraft industry, the Anglo-American people's determination to end the Nazi dictator's rule of force, and the futility of German resistance. It told the German people that if they did not overthrow the Nazis and make peace they would be bombed "every night and every day, rain, blow, or snow." And they were.[4]

Given these circumstances, we cannot say that the Western powers misused *strategic* political warfare nor critique their strategic propaganda for content or style, for the simple reason that it did not exist in any meaningful way, at least after 1941. One might argue that the British had tried strategic propaganda from 1939 to 1941 and had failed. Clearly, they had expectations that a combination of maritime blockade, strategic bombing, and propaganda at various levels might help divert or diminish the German assault. Despite a nominal Franco-British predominance over Germany in numbers of tanks and planes, they knew that they lacked the military strength for a head-on confrontation.[5] An "indirect approach," as advocated by Liddell Hart, was a logical solution. It did not work in the conditions of the time.

In retrospect, the British clearly had much going against their indirect strategy: they were suffering military defeats; their leadership (before Churchill) was weak and uncertain; their domestic situation was uneasy, their global economic and military forces overextended; and the *Zeitgeist* in many ways favored the totalitarians. The organization of propaganda operations, both overt and covert, remained poor, with no order and sense of purpose being created until Brendan Brackan replaced Duff Cooper as Minister of Information in 1941.[6] An indirect strategy is not necessarily the best path to take from a position of relative weakness, but it is often adopted on grounds of expediency. Such appears to have been the case in 1939-41, and the attempt must, for whatever reasons, be accounted a failed campaign in political warfare.

In inter-Allied public diplomacy, by contrast, the British experience in 1939-41 was markedly successful. In comparison to Nazi efforts to keep America neutral, if not actively friendly to German aims, the British use of political advocacy, agents of influence, and diplomacy was handled with sensitivity and skill. The differences in style were characteristic: a typical German effort involved distribution by the German-American *Bund* of a pamphlet entitled *George Washington: An American Nazi*. The British relied heavily on personal diplomacy, beginning with the link between Churchill and Roosevelt but including numerous other levels and operations as well.

The British appraisal of American attitudes at this time was dire. Harold Nicolson, soon to be named by Churchill as Parliamentary Undersecretary at the newly formed Ministry of Information, summed up the situation in his diary entry of April 17, 1940:

> I go to the Eden Group dinner at the Carlton where they are entertaining [Minister of Information] Duff Cooper. His account of the propaganda-consciousness of the United States is terrifying. He thinks the Germans have really persuaded them that black is white. It is of course the mothers of America who dictate the tone, which is one of smug escapism.[7]

Passions in Congress ran high against British involvement in the American political and internal security arena, at times raising a question of possible impeachment of the President. The period continues to offer instructive reading in the dangers, opportunities, and high stakes involved in the conduct of public diplomacy between states sharing common values and facing a common danger but riven by uncertainty and fear.

After 1941 both the British and the Americans developed a respectable level of tactical political warfare operations. Organized in Britain under a Political Warfare Executive and in the United States under the (misnamed) Office of Strategic Services and the Office of War Information, with a military arm jointly staffed by

British and Americans as the Psychological Warfare Division of Eisenhower's headquarters, the political warfare forces offered the Anglo-American leadership an array of capabilities for operations at all levels. They were never, despite occasional high-sounding proclamations, given a sense of strategic direction and sustained high-level political will comparable to that provided by Lloyd George in 1917-18. The various operational units were numerous, often in conflict with one another, and staffed with quite differently motivated people in terms of radical-conservative preferences. The usual rivalries developed over personalities and power. Churchill took only a spasmodic interest in the mechanism. While a consummate propagandist personally, he professed little interest in organizations for propaganda's strategic application: "This is a war of deeds and not words," he would growl.[8]

In April 1939 Sir Campbell Stuart had set down three principles for British propaganda in a report to the government: It must be related to a clearly defined policy, it must be rigorously truthful, and it must never be self-contradictory.[9] Stuart's advice was never formally rejected, but he was soon returned to the retirement from which he had been summoned, and measures were adopted, more or less ad hoc in origin, that ran counter to all three principles. Strategic aims remained unclear for the reasons given above; operations that were untruthful as well as "black," both in print and over radio, were deployed for various tactical ends; and propaganda directives—at times shaped by fear of disagreement with the Soviets—tended to be self-contradictory over time. Stuart's principles presumed a strategic purpose for propaganda; without it, in an all-out military struggle propaganda was mainly useful as a tactical support element. Given that role, a quite different set of doctrinal principles applied, ones more akin to those governing military deception operations. Anglo-American propaganda and psychological operations in World War II are best judged in this light.

One might ask whether the Atlantic Charter of 1941 or later the projected United Nations did not provide a basis for strategic Allied propaganda of hope directed toward the Axis populations. Both could and arguably should have been used in programming to Germany; neither was, largely for fear of disrupting military cooperation with the USSR but also from a mistrust of any future

Bogus German police poster, produced by Ellic Howe in London and circulated throughout occupied Europe in 1944, offering a reward for apprehension of a senior SS officer (who did not exist) charged with embezzlement and desertion. Placarded by resistance forces in German-occupied cities.

German government. Bruce Lockhart's account of a talk with South African leader Jan Christiaan Smuts in 1942 is characteristic:

> Germany [Smuts said] would crack sooner or later. A hope clause was therefore necessary in our propaganda. No new Europe would be built, no permanent peace established if we merely ignored the German problem. Germany must always be an integral part of any European polity. We should not say too much at this stage. We should develop and enlarge on the Atlantic Charter. But we must get away from national concepts. Above all we should avoid saying to Germany things which played into Goebbels' hands. . . . Mr. Churchill, he said, was sound on this aspect of the problem. I [Bruce Lockhart] wondered if the South African had correctly interpreted Mr. Churchill's personal attitude toward a people who twice within twenty-five years had plunged the world into war. Doubtless at all times, and especially in war, the real inclinations of statesmen in office are restrained by considerations of public expediency. . . . That may explain why we were never allowed to enlarge in our propaganda on the Atlantic Charter, the effect of which was heavily counteracted by the policy of unconditional surrender.[10]

The Anglo-Saxon powers did not officially proclaim unconditional surrender as a war aim until the Casablanca Conference in 1943, but it was clearly in the cards earlier, and it remained in effect until the end. Harold Nicolson left the Ministry of Information in 1941, but remained active throughout the war in propaganda policy formulation both as a Member of Parliament and as a member of the BBC Board. In February 1944 he noted in his diary,

> he [Churchill, speaking in Parliament] defines what he means by unconditional surrender. The Atlantic Charter does not apply to Germany; we are not to be bound to Germany by any pact or obligation; we shall have a free hand, but that does not mean that we shall behave barbarously or against our conscience.[11]

The unconditional surrender line was reaffirmed by the British-American-Soviet meeting at Yalta in February 1945. Alliance propaganda—even at this late date—was guided accordingly, despite working-level misgivings, at least among the Americans and

British, over failure to facilitate the anti-Hitler movement at work within the German armed forces.[12]

Both British and American operators, and the agents of the exile governments in London, vigorously employed tactical political warfare during World War II. The exiles tended to focus on their homeland populations; the Anglo-Saxons programmed both to occupied areas and to enemy territory. Much of this programming is still noteworthy for examples of what can be undertaken under conditions of general war against enemy and enemy-occupied territory by an extensive alliance of (mostly) democracies.

The scope and kind of tactical operations were broad, including a full range of large-scale campaigns by Supreme Headquarters Allied Powers Europe (SHAPE). This psychological warfare, or psywar, operation of SHAPE was mainly directed toward undermining morale and sowing confusion among the enemy, mainly German, armed forces. It was staffed by uniformed personnel, operating under military discipline, with guidance determined through military chain of command. Some quite talented and committed people were involved, notably the present Chairman of the Board of CBS, William Paley, and several distinguished academics and journalists temporarily in uniform. The operation's net effect on the enemy appears, to me, to have been marginal, largely due to lack of any hope content in overall Allied strategy.[13]

The coordinating headquarters for Anglo-American political warfare operations were two organizations based in London, under British control, and two in Washington, under the Americans. The British units were the Special Operations Executive (SOE) and the Political Warfare Executive (PWE); both were initially subordinate to a newly created Ministry of Economic Warfare. The American organizations were the Office of Strategic Services (OSS) and the Office of War Information (OWI). The lines among these organizations were never clearly drawn; all, by the definition of this study, were charged with carrying out political warfare as their primary mission. All were essentially civilian organizations although some, notably SOE and OSS, were headed by general officers and included numerous uniformed personnel. All were

Safe conduct pass, developed by Psychological Warfare Division of Supreme Headquarters Allied Expeditionary Forces, based on an idea noted in Russian combat leaflets. Dropped in very large quantities, this leaflet was rated in prisoner surveys above all others for effectiveness.

linked to national policy by political figures at the sub-cabinet level, and all were to some degree loosely coordinated by inter-Allied coordinating boards or liaison officers. PWE and OWI were mainly concerned with propaganda; SOE and OSS were used for mounting direct action, that is, sabotage and paramilitary operations.[14]

Among the exile governments in wartime London the French and the Poles probably had the most extensive and effective political warfare operations underway. Both, notably the French, had running policy conflicts with their Anglo-Saxon hosts, conflicts which by *force majeure* tended to be resolved against their wills.

For Poland, the outcome of Western inability to resist Soviet pressure in 1944-45 was disastrous. In the end, the most powerful and cohesive resistance force in occupied Europe, the Polish Home Army, was crushed during the premature Warsaw Uprising of 1944. After waiting across the Vistula for the Germans to complete the job, Soviet forces occupied Poland and replaced the remnants of the nationalist-oriented Home Army with communist cadres loyal to Moscow. Facing the massive reality of Soviet military occupation, London and Washington settled for a face-saving formula that in effect sacrificed the London Poles to their communist competition from Moscow. Polish political warfare in World War II is a study in bitter glory.[15]

Although nominally independent, the political warfare operations of the other exiles were in practice incorporated, through cooptation of personnel, into the country sections of the British and American organizations. Problems of policy control, individual allegiance, and national style had to be worked out in principle between the exile governments and their official points of contact with the British and American foreign policy organs. In practice, successful resolution of issues took place at the working level, not necessarily always on the preferred Great Power lines.

The Soviets ran their own political warfare and propaganda operations in Europe during the war, rejecting or accepting only token forms of coordination with their Anglo-Saxon counterparts. As they moved west with military force, they became more active in sponsoring Marxist-Leninist or United Front types of emigre governments, which they proceeded to install in power with or without the compliance of the London-based governments. Their modus operandi of coordinated subversion by local communist parties, overt and covert propaganda, and ruthless covert action (including assassination) was strongly reminiscent of the pre-1939 Nazi style.[16] Again, the strategy was successful. The present governments of Eastern Europe, accepted as such by the democratic governments of the West whatever doubts one may have as to their legitimacy, derived from the Soviet political warfare operations of 1944-45. For the ordinary man in the belt running from the Baltic to the Black Sea, these entities are a dismal and enduring witness to the efficacy of totalitarian-style political warfare.

Political warfare and propaganda operations during World War II offer the democracies profitable study. These operations provide valuable experience in organizing manpower and matching skills found in open societies to particular tasks; balancing the conflicting demands of originality and of political control; coordinating programming with diplomacy, covert action, and military operations; practicing the special forms of intelligence collection, production, and dissemination; and coordinating emigre operations. In the history of warfare, failures (if survived) have often provided better instruction than victories, and specific examples of what has not worked can save much in lives and resources for future campaigns.

On the positive side, one of the most enduring and successful operations stemming from World War II can be heard today in the form of BBC World Service. As an example of a highly credible, world-class "white" medium using short wave as the transmission channel, it was and is outstanding. BBC's success is a sterling example of what can be accomplished, from an unfavorable position and under wartime pressures, by a combination of skill and personal commitment.

Britain started World War II far behind the Germans in concept, organization, and technology for international broadcasting. As the cartoonist Low suggested by portraying Goebbels with a microphone and Colonel Blimp with a toy balloon, Germany and Britain exemplified the two sharply contrasted styles in propaganda channels to each other and to the world. Within a few years "This is London," emerging with its Beethoven-derived "V" signature, had gained an unsurpassed reputation for accuracy, objectivity, and political relevance, appealing mostly to the upper end of the intellectual scale but also eliciting response at other levels. [17]

Today's BBC is attuned more to the needs of public diplomacy than to those of propaganda, as it was also, though to a lesser extent, in World War II. [18] As such it was (and is) subject to the criticism that it may be magnificent but it is not war. Taken in isolation, from a tactical political warfare perspective, this view may have been justified. But BBC was not operated in a vacuum. It had sister services in "grey" and "black." The combined effect was more than that of the individual parts—or it could have been, given a different grand strategy.

British and American propaganda operations at the shadier end of the spectrum were very shady indeed. They were based on the principle that the "black" operator should identify himself completely with the target, acquiring all the necessary accreditations to convince the recipients that his messages came from sources in their own homeland. These operations included radio stations allegedly run by dissident military units located in German-occupied parts of Europe, and dissemination inside Germany of a rich variety of printed materials such as faked ration cards, postal forms and stamps, military orders and announcements, and placards. One of the more innovative broadcasting techniques required use of a teamed set of powerful transmitters capable of suppressing the signal of certain German local stations and substituting a "black" signal giving false official announcements in its place. The operation was mainly tactical in effect, intended to disrupt German military operations and their rear-zone support. Some of the most successful operations included regular and scrupulously reliable reports by radio to key units, such as submarine crews, of losses in battle that had not been officially reported. The example is noteworthy of programming deceptive in origin but truthful in content, a distinction often lost from view in popular discourse on the subject.

At the outset of the war, Churchill vested broad supervisory responsibility for covert political warfare operations, including paramilitary and propaganda tasks, in a newly created Ministry of Economic Warfare, headed by Labor Party intellectual Hugh

Dalton. Speaking in retrospect, Dalton described Churchill's mandate to him as follows:

> This was to be a new instrument of war and I should be responsible for shaping it. Its purpose was to coordinate all action by way of subversion against the enemy overseas. A new organization was being created which would absorb some small elements of existing organizations but would be on a much greater scale, with wider scope and largely manned by new personnel. It would be a secret or underground organization. . . . Subversion was a complex conception. It meant the weakening by whatever "covert" means of the Enemy's will to make war and the strengthening of the will and power of his opponents including in particular guerrilla and resistance movements. . . . I accepted the Prime Minister's suggestion with great eagerness and satisfaction. "And now," he exhorted, "set Europe ablaze."[19]

Black radio operations, first under Dalton and later under the Political Warfare Executive headed by Bruce Lockhart, were run by Sefton Delmer, a journalist with extensive prewar time in Berlin. They were staffed by a mix of language-qualified Englishmen and German emigres, some of whom are known today, some not. Among them were Labor politician Richard Crossman and academic Richard Lowenthal. Broadcasting was not closely coordinated with print operations. Radio was supervised directly by Delmer; print operations were managed by a London printer and publisher named Ellic Howe, whose firm had numerous prewar connections in Germany. Most of the emigres tended to be ideological in motivation rather than mercenary, with the ideologies running from left socialist to right military-patriotic. British supervisors were often open-minded on programming techniques but insisted on close adherence to policy guidelines. Sefton Delmer, a beefy, high-living figure, with great enthusiasm and drive, was more than once accused—perhaps with cause—of acting like Henry the Eighth.[20]

American efforts in black and grey propaganda came much later into the field than the British. They were organizationally mixed with a newly created intelligence collection and paramilitary organization, OSS, on one hand, and with a primarily overt official advocacy and straight news medium, OWI, on the other hand. Yet a third element, the Psychological Warfare Division of SHAPE, when brought into existence later in the war, was the most active. Its activities, though, were predominantly in the field of military deception, tactically oriented to the short-term operational needs of the Allied invasion forces.[21]

Allied propaganda to the Axis-occupied areas of the Balkans addressed—but did not successfully resolve—the issue of radical versus conservative orientation. Churchill apparently had a radical approach in mind. Speaking to Hugh Dalton in July 1940, the Prime Minister said flatly, "All this [subversive work] must come from the Left."[22] Dalton, a Labor Party member of the coalition cabinet, presumably interpreted this injunction in the light of his own party's definition of the terms *right* and *left*. In Dalton's case, left probably meant some version of Fabian Socialism. As head of the newly created Ministry of Economic Warfare incorporating (briefly) the Special Operations Executive (SOE), with a voice— together with the Foreign Office—in setting policy for the Political Warfare Executive and for the BBC, Dalton should have been in a position to make his views prevail in operations.

In practice, the results were—and still are—less than clear. In October 1942, a policy paper signed by Lord Glenconner, the newly appointed head of SOE in Cairo, responsible for operations in the Balkans, asserted that for sociological reasons the poorer classes in any country, having less to lose and more to gain than the rich, could be expected to be more active in resistance movements; therefore, the paper concluded, "SOE finds itself for the most part drawn to collaborate with parties of the left." A marginal note on the Foreign Office copy of this document, initialed by Deputy Permanent Under Secretary Sir Orme Sargent, opined, "This is a dangerous doctrine and should be applied sparingly."[23]

The record, so far as we can judge it without access to the SOE files (closed until the year 2015), seems to be one of pragmatism involving much on-the-spot influence along personally motivated ideological grounds, complicated by an inordinate amount of bureaucratic rivalry. The Foreign Office, with its long-established personnel structure, seemed to have a strongly conservative institutional bias. The new organizations, SOE and PWE, were thrown together hastily from a mix of bankers, academics, and media and professional military men. They ranged in their ideology and attitudes from conservative merchant bankers like SOE Deputy Chief Sir Charles Hambro to convinced communist party members like James Klugman, from the Cambridge spy coterie, who served—by some accounts quite efficiently—as staff officer in SOE Cairo's regional Balkan command. Lacking access to the files, it is difficult to link names to particular issues or events. But given the loose operating style of these new organizations, we can fairly expect that communist party members, to say nothing of fellow travelers, must have had considerable room for maneuver.

The policy record is less obscure. In Yugoslavia until 1943, the British backed the Serbian ultranationalist Chetniks under Mihailovic. Having become disillusioned with Mihailovic's inaction and the mounting evidence of his collaboration with the Italian occupation forces, in 1943 the British switched their support (with Churchill's direct involvement) to the communist partisans led by Tito, a Croatian Comintern organizer. The decision was not easy. One of Churchill's private secretaries noted on January 7, 1944,

> Fitzroy Maclean, Brigadier accredited to Marshal Tito, and Randolph [Churchill] arrived. Maclean and R. are to parachute into Yugoslavia, taking with them a letter from the Prime Minister to Tito. Next to SHINGLE [Anzio] and landing craft, the Yugoslav problem, with its intricacies about abandoning Mihailovic and reconciling King Peter to Tito has been our chief interest out here.[24]

In Greece, the British backed the royalist emigres grouped around the exiled King George, who was in Cairo. As it became increasingly obvious that the King had little support and much active opposition within Greece, the British attempted to broker a coalition among the Greek resistance groups. The attempt seemed to be making some progress under the skillful guidance of Brigadier E. C. W. Myers, a British SOE officer inserted into occupied Greece, but it broke down in August 1943 at a meeting among exfiltrated Greek fighters, the British representatives in Cairo, and the royalist exile government.

The issue for most Greeks was clear and unsolvable: the King insisted that his right to return to Greece as King was not open to question; the resistance fighters—centrist as well as communist—would not have him, or at least would not accept anything short of an explicit commitment by the King (and the British) to hold a plebiscite before the King could return. Foreign Secretary Eden solidly supported the King, as did Churchill and Roosevelt. The previously promising Greek resistance fragmented, communist and royalist groups began to fight each other to the detriment of their struggle against the Germans, many of the centrists lost heart or drifted into one or the other of the extremes, and major opportunities for diverting German troops from the battle in Italy were lost. Equally tragic was the failure to use the resistance as a school for developing a vital and realistic Greek political elite in the postwar period, free of reactionary privilege and left-wing fanaticism.[25]

There is no clear explanation for Churchill's choice of a radical strategy in Yugoslavia and a reactionary (conservative is too weak a term) policy in Greece. Speculation has ranged over both strategic and personal motives, of which I find the strategic most persuasive. Greece was clearly more involved than Yugoslavia in Britain's protection of its lines of communication to Suez and beyond. Forced to choose between short-term military advantage and long-term political aims, the British opted for the military advantage in Yugoslavia, and played—however wrongheadedly—for the political prize in Greece. The Americans, who regarded the Balkans as a diversion from the main tasks in Western Europe (and the Pacific), followed the British lead, supplying some arms and aid, but always in key with British political positions.[26]

In 1945, the communists under Tito took control of Yugoslavia; in Greece, civil war erupted, requiring direct military intervention by Britain to restore the monarchy and to prevent a communist victory. The Greek problem was by no means resolved, becoming the catalyst for a major American intervention under the Truman Doctrine in 1948 (on which, more in chapter 9).

The propaganda battle of the Balkans appears no less confused and turbulent, in retrospect, than the paramilitary and political organizational conflict concerning the region. Broadcasting was the primary propaganda medium for all external actors, with the BBC, OWI, German, Italian, and Soviet-sponsored stations all on the air. In the British case, and to some extent the American as well, the content and guidance for programmers became a hotly contested public issue, with royalists, centrists, and communists using pressure in the host country press and legislature to push their contradictory claims to political legitimacy and military success against the Axis occupation forces. This intrusion of domestic politics, complicated by the existence of emotional ethnic factors in the American case, further complicated the life of London and Washington policymakers and political warfare commanders.

A dispassionate overview of the airwaves battle for the Balkans has not, to my knowledge, appeared. One conclusion, however, seems warranted: the resistance leaders in the field took foreign broadcasts very seriously, listened regularly to them, and often acted—in their own way—on the information and ideas received. A British officer with the Yugoslav partisans in 1944 reported, for example, "Listening to the BBC was regarded almost as a duty with the serious-minded partisans. It was a regular daily habit: supper, BBC, bed. Each receiving set was surrounded by a large group of eighty to a hundred."[27] I have no evidence of audience response to the Soviet-based emigre station, but as Marxist-Leninists the partisans were presumably compelled to listen to it even more than to London.[28] As recently as 1973, the Belgrade museum devoted to World War II included a symbolically arranged display juxtaposing a British Sten gun and Soviet editions of Marx and Lenin.

Mihailovic vigorously and regularly protested BBC coverage of the rival Titoists and failure to report his own exploits. He also protested, with reason, that the supply of arms and equipment dropped by SOE was nearly meaningless as a basis for serious military operations.[29] In fact, BBC in 1942 was still operating under guidance from PWE and the Foreign Office to favor the Mihailovic forces in its selection of news about Yugoslavia, and the British government had protested to the Russian government regarding reports carried over the emigre "Free Yugoslavia" station, operating from within the USSR, that accused Mihailovic (correctly, it appears in retrospect) of collaboration with the Italian occupation forces.

In fairness to all, we should also note that the British in 1940-41 were nearly destitute of military supplies, and that they had urged Balkan resistance forces to concentrate on recruitment and avoid premature engagement, which might expend their forces uselessly as well as subjecting their peoples to brutal reprisals. Neither in their paramilitary policy nor in propaganda did the Anglo-Saxon powers ever explicitly resolve the issue of suffering by civilian populations during guerrilla war. In practice, as in the case of Yugoslavia during the first years of the war, they adopted a more cautious stance than that of the Soviets, who remained harshly uncompromising.

The British shift of 1943 toward more active cooperation with Tito and a more distanced stance regarding Mihailovic, though it was not a policy announced as such to the public, was reflected in BBC news selection. Mihailovic, continuing to listen to the BBC, complained about the shift to his British liaison officers in terms of deep (and justified) suspicion. The British spokesmen became, on instructions from Cairo, increasingly explicit to Mihailovic about London's and Cairo's unwillingness to continue their support unless he cut his ties to the Italians and campaigned more actively against the Germans. Neither the policy proposals nor the propaganda treatment seem to have had any significant effect.

Throughout the war, communist-led resistance movements regarded the British posture as either duplicitous or naive. In the absence of strong inducements from the British in the form of supplies, or pressure resulting from British complaints to Moscow, these movements tended to consider their conservative counterparts as enemies and to attack them more fanatically than they did the Germans. The conservatives were equally hostile toward the communists and were often willing to cooperate—at least tacitly, sometimes explicitly—with the Germans and Italians in destroying partisan units. Neither Brigadier Myers' early attempts in Greece nor Maclean's later ties with Tito seem to have done much to resolve this dilemma.

The observer who surveys this tragedy in retrospect cannot help suspecting that the Alliance might have solved these problems in ways more beneficial to both its short-term military needs and its long-term political goals with more attention to the conservative middle, less insistence on clinging to discredited symbols of royalist privilege, less infighting among the operators, and (above all) more resources in material and means of delivery. The Balkans, however underdeveloped in comparison to Western Europe, were not devoid of a commercial middle class possessing the skills needed to ride out a foreign occupation and defend their societies from both Nazi and communist disruption.

Except in Yugoslavia, and possibly Bulgaria, it is by no means clear that the far-left forces would have prevailed without direct intervention by the Red Army. On the contrary, in countries like Romania the communists were few in number indeed, and their political constituencies were minimal. In 1944 there were less than 2,000 members of the Romanian Communist Party, most of whom were in prison or accompanying the Soviet armed forces.[30] The Soviet use of such cadres in 1944, backed by massive armed force, remains one of the more successful—although lamentable—examples of political warfare using propaganda, political organization, and subversion. The Soviet Army provided the context; it did not actually carry out the restructuring of the political, economic, and social life of each occupied country. Much of this work was completed in the Cold War, but its roots lay in World War II.

As in the Polish case, the essentially conservative Balkan governments-in-exile, which had existed in London since the outbreak of hostilities, were forced by circumstances in their homelands and the Anglo-Saxon powers' inability to change the realities of Soviet military occupation to enter into arrangements with the Moscow-backed communists. These arrangements amounted eventually, in one form or another, to political suicide. The Yalta Agreements of February 1945 provided international legitimation for these de facto settlements. Only in Greece, where the British Army intervened, were the prewar political forces able to prevail against communist-organized paramilitary operations. As in other theaters, a potential for strategic political warfare existed and the instruments to conduct it had been created and deployed; Britain and America lost a potential postwar strategic advantage through disagreement over high policy, and they cast aside an opportunity to shorten the war and save lives in the welter and confusion of working-level rivalries within the Allied—mainly British, in this case—organizations.[31]

What the Anglo-American policymakers could or should have done differently under these circumstances remains a hotly debated issue. As observers of political warfare styles and outcomes, the best we can say is that although Anglo-American strategic propaganda and subversive operations in the Balkans never reached their full potential, at least they did not disrupt the larger effort to coordinate conventional military operations with the Soviets to evict the Germans from the region.

Had Churchill's strategic preferences prevailed, giving priority to a second front in the Balkans over the 1944 landing in Normandy, a quite different political warfare strategy for the region would have been in order, and different outcomes might well have been expected.[32] To speculate on what these outcomes might have been requires assumptions removed from historical reality. The modern observer can only note that political warfare, including propaganda strategy at the theater level, must remain hostage to the central war aims of the nation or nations involved. In World War II, the Balkan theater was no exception to this rule. The case for any inherent advantage of radical or conservative strategies in political warfare operations remains unproven.

Judged by the rigorous standard of immediately perceptible results, particularly in triggering mutinies in military units, the operations against the central core of Germany must be judged failures. Hitler and the Gestapo successfully suppressed the one significant case of disaffection in the Wehrmacht, that of July 1944. And we have no very strong evidence that any of Delmer's or Howe's or SHAPE's programming stimulated this aborted mutiny. There was solid evidence at the time, in German press reaction and POW interrogation, of listening and audience awareness. In 1941 a Gestapo report put the German audience for BBC at one million listeners; by the autumn of 1944 it was estimated at between ten and fifteen million.[33] But that this exposure to allied propaganda resulted in any significant, coherent opposition to Hitler or his war aims would be difficult to prove.

Hope of German disaffection was always present among Allied forces, although it tended to fade into cynicism over time. Allied troops were aware, however, of individual moods of defeatism among German troops. Cartoonist Bill Mauldin, who probably knew front-line conditions throughout the American part of the war as well as anyone, recorded his views in 1945:

> We were all bursting with enthusiasm about the attempted [July 1944] assassination of Hitler. We felt that this was a sure indication that Germany was cracking, and we would be home by Christmas. I should have remembered we felt the same enthusiasm at Salerno when we first set foot on continental Europe and began pushing inland. The Germans were disorganized after the push started, and they all told us they surrendered because they knew it would be over by Christmas and they didn't want to get killed in the last days of the war.[34]

American propaganda analysts were also aware of a large German audience. Two of these analysts noted, in a research report completed in New York in 1944, "Black listening must have increased, because both Fritsche and Goebbels referred to it as though it was a widespread practice in Germany. Fritsche [Goebbels' Deputy for News] went so far as openly to denounce Radio Moscow and obliquely to denounce 'Gustav Sigrified Eins,' a clandestine anti-Nazi station."[35]

The German military opposition to Hitler, regardless of how it arose, was a political fact of major importance in 1944. Nearly all of the Wehrmacht high command in the West was either directly committed to it or at least aware of it and unwilling to betray it to Hitler and the Nazi Party. The scope of the conspiracy, the determination of several of the activists, and the stature of some of its leaders suggest that the plot would have succeeded if not for simple bad luck on one critical point—Hitler's physically surviving the July 20, 1944, assassination attempt by von Stauffenberg. Anglo-American propaganda may or may not have

Two cartoons drawn by Bill Mauldin for Stars and Stripes. The cartoon on the left, dated August 30, 1944, was captioned, "Maybe the sun's comin' up, Joe"; the one on the right, no date, was captioned, "Sure they's a revolution in Germany. Git down so they won't hit ya wit' a wild shot."

contributed to this event and the political background to it; the critical issue for the British and American political warfare commands was how to play it once it had occurred.

Propaganda, for the German conspirators, was a weapon with several uses. Three of the senior conspirators—Rommel, Stulpnagel, and von Rundstedt—had agreed on a plan for armistice negotiations with Eisenhower and Montgomery, with a provision for Allied radio stations to explain to the German people the military and political situation and the crimes of their leaders.[36] The overall proposition as contemplated by the German generals was not likely to be acceptable to Roosevelt and Churchill (if they ever saw it as a real proposal). The important point, though, was that a powerful group, willing and able to act to change the nature of the war, existed within Germany. And that group sought to work with Anglo-American propaganda media, in cooperation with their own use of military force, as part of the operation. The political weapon clearly had a potential in the eyes of the senior German military command; that fact in itself gave it a significance that should be taken into account in assessing its role and mission in the Allied conduct of the war.

Beyond the military level, Germany's political leaders were also aware in 1943 and 1944 of the potential of enemy—or at least British—propaganda. Goebbels, who was not aware of the July 20, 1944, conspiracy among the military leadership, presumably would have denounced it if he had had the opportunity; but he was privately on record as early as 1943 regarding the dangers. On November 28, 1943, he noted in his diary, "Soldatensender Calais, which evidently originates in England and uses the same wavelength as Radio Deutschland—when the latter is out during their air raids—gave us something to worry about. The station does a very clever job of propaganda."[37] It seems fair to ask how many of the political leaders of Nazi Germany would have stuck by Hitler if they had been faced with a successful military coup coupled with an assertive Allied propaganda barrage, through both white and black media, including hope as well as intimidation themes.

It is unclear in retrospect, as it was during the war, where Allied propaganda might have led given the right conditions. At the time,

British officials differed in their opinions. Ivone Kirkpatrick, head of the Political Section of the German Control Commission and formerly Foreign Office liaison to the BBC, "gave a damning account of the inefficacy of both SOE and PWE, both of which have been loud in self-advertisement during the war." He was speaking informally to one of Churchill's private secretaries, Sir John Colville, who noted the comment in his diary entry of April 3, 1945. Colville added, subsequently, as an explanatory note, "Political Warfare Executive, responsible for anti-Nazi propaganda. Richard Crossman was one of its leading lights, thereby avoiding active service. It was not considered a very effective organization."[38] Both the original entry and Colville's subsequent gloss reveal—whatever the merits of the case—some of the personal and political tensions present within the British government over the utility of PWE.

It could be argued (in my view, with reason) that the failure was not in the weapon nor in how it was wielded, but rather in the unwillingness—justified or not in terms of high policy—to program to Germans at any level above that of bleak despair, and in Goebbels' ability to make use of this failure through intensive fear-based counterpropaganda. Together, these two elements reinforced a pervasive mood throughout the German population, aware in varying degrees of the horrors perpetrated in concentration camps and occupied areas by the Gestapo and SS, that defeat was likely to bring unbearable retribution for the entire nation.

For Italy, Allied policy remained officially committed to unconditional surrender, but in practice Italian audiences were given much more hope content than were the Germans. Under BBC guidelines, for example, the Italian public was never given the impression that its guilt was inseparable from that of its leaders, particularly Mussolini; there was to be "no preaching," and listeners were to be given "a sense of hopefulness."[39] As always, causality is impossible to demonstrate. But Italy collapsed before Germany, surrendering in 1944. The removal of Italian armed forces from a combat role in 1944 significantly increased the pressures on German forces and lightened the tasks of Allied forces. If, as seems likely, this shift resulted from the Allied propaganda posture, we should credit the role of propaganda as a force multiplier at the theater level.

Winston Churchill on a British Ministry of Information placard in World War II. British and American leader images tended to be naturalistic, in contrast to the iconographic totalitarian imagery. The backdrop of armed force sets off Churchill's stolidly civilian dress to make a political point.

Firm policy control over Allied programming to Germany,[40] though it may have prolonged the war, provides a useful example, together with Goebbels' counterstrategy, of outcomes to be expected in such a context. For the channels had been created and the audiences were on the line and listening; a potential thus was present, had the Anglo-Saxon leaders chosen to use it, for strategic political warfare. Propaganda, more so than other weapons, depends upon having the necessary forces deployed in an effective posture for engagement or maneuver. World War II British and American operations offer an interesting study of such forces in being but never committed—with the possible exception of in Italy—to action in the manner that would have made them strategically effective.

No account of political warfare waged by the English-speaking peoples would be complete without noting the personal style of Winston Churchill. Dubious on policy grounds of organized political warfare (or perhaps merely aware of its limitations at the time), he was still, himself, a superb rhetorician. Seldom have words been so soundly marshaled for the uses of war. The style is unmistakable; deployed in the service of unconditional surrender, it may have prolonged the struggle and helped to devalue the coming peace. But for his own peoples, and for the broader democratic alliance of which they were the center, his speeches minimized the pessimism that came with military reverses; they kept alive the spark of hope in ultimate victory; and they swelled the tide of triumph in the hard times at the end.

The best organized, most technologically advanced, and lavishly funded propaganda can remain dead without an animating spark. Churchill provided it when he rallied a world rotted with appeasement, capitulation, and fear by speaking in 1940, to Parliament and the world, for "Victory at all costs, in spite of all terror; victory however long and hard the road may be."[41] Churchill had no reluctance to speak of *victory* and of *defeat* for it was clear, given the enemy, what they meant. And free men responded, not from class hatred or ethnic animosity, but from some deeper ethos in their history.

9

THE COLD WAR

N ow 'e's gone too bloody far," rumbled Britain's Foreign
Secretary, Ernie Bevin, after the London Foreign Ministers'
Conference at the end of 1947.[1] The object of Bevin's displeasure
was Vyacheslav Molotov, Politburo member and Foreign Minister
of the USSR, who had delivered another self-righteous, vitriolic
attack on the Western powers' efforts to resolve the problems of
postwar Europe. Bevin's remark symbolizes as well as anything
the turning point in British and American attitudes toward Soviet
political warfare campaigns of the 1940s.

Bevin, a self-educated labor organizer who had done much
to make Allied victory over Germany possible by organizing Britain's labor force, had few personal illusions about the Soviets:
"Molotov," he once observed, "was like a communist in a local
Labor Party. If you treated him badly, he made the most of the
grievance and, if you treated him well, he only put his price up
and abused you next day."[2] Bevin's chief, Prime Minister Clement
Attlee, also had misgivings, at least in private, about Stalin: "Re-
minded me of the Renaissance despots—no principles, any methods, but no flowery language—always Yes or No, although you
could only count on him if it was No."[3]

In postwar Europe few Western leaders wanted to confront
the Soviets. Troubled by major internal problems resulting from
the war, hoping for cooperation from the Soviets in rebuilding
Europe, and uncertain as to American policy, they sought to turn
aside or ignore the mounting signs of Soviet aggression in Eastern
Europe and the Middle East. The internal problem was possibly
the most compelling. As Bevin's biographer put it,

Even those in the West, who suspected that Stalin was neither a revolutionary idealist nor a doctrinaire Marxist but a hardened and cynical politician, could not afford to ignore the advantages which he derived from Russia's revolutionary image: a "Russian" party in every country—in France and Italy a mass party attracting millions of votes—providing a receptive audience for Soviet propaganda and a potential fifth column weakening and confusing resistance to Soviet pressure.[4]

A growing number of observers, both European and American, saw evidence of the danger. In July 1947, two French statesmen, Herve Alphand and Couve de Murville, told the American Ambassador that the Soviets were counting on a profound depression to put an end to American aid and to European reconstruction. The European economies would disintegrate, and economic and social chaos would follow. Given these circumstances, the Soviets expected to expand their control through the well-organized communist parties.[5]

In a talk with Bevin, French President Vincent Auriol emphasized the extent to which French opinion was dominated by the fear of war, including civil war that could annihilate the elite of the nation. The Western powers, Auriol said, were too weak to run risks and must not give the Soviet Union any excuse for precipitate action.[6]

Bevin had his own problems, as revealed in an observation he had made, at the January 1946 UN General Assembly meeting in London, on Soviet intervention in British politics:

Indeed, I know when I displease the Soviet Government because all the shop stewards who are Communists send me resolutions in the exact same language . . . one of those strange coincidences that occur.[7]

Soviet emphasis on political war as an instrument for achieving their aims in Europe, particularly in Germany, should have been long understood by knowledgeable observers. Contacts between Soviet and Western occupation commanders had presented some quite specific indicators. "He who controls the press and radio is the master of Berlin," announced Marshal Zhukhov to Field Marshal Montgomery in 1945.[8] The communists quickly and fully deployed throughout Europe the organizational weapon to make such control possible. It included the full array of "nonpolitical" Fronts, organized from above and below, "spontaneous" mass appeals and resolutions, subsidized media, and manipulated politicians serving hidden agendas.

Moscow set the policy line for this apparatus and promulgated it through a multilateral organization of European communist parties having a central bureau sited first in Belgrade and later in Bucharest. The principle of "democratic centralism" applied, and the line of command ran from the Secretariat of the Communist Party of the Soviet Union (or CPSU) in Moscow, backed by the clandestine operations of the KGB and—for Eastern Europe—the occupation forces of the Soviet military. In theory, the organization, named the Communist Information Bureau, or Cominform, set policy through negotiated agreement of the permanent representatives from member parties. The organization maintained a Secretariat and operated a monthly journal entitled *For a Lasting Peace, For a Peoples' Democracy*.[9] The policy line was then promulgated further throughout Europe by the official media, educational, and cultural establishments in Eastern Europe and by a growing network of Front Organizations in Western Europe.[10]

The "two camps" thesis of a world divided along classic Manichaean lines, into an evil capitalist half and a virtuous socialist (that is, Soviet) half, formed the basic policy content for the Soviet campaign. As stated in the September 23, 1947, Declaration from its first formal meeting, the Cominform saw a world consisting of

> The imperialist and anti-democratic camp having as its basic aim the establishment of the world domination of American imperialism and the smashing of democracy, and the anti-imperialist and democratic camp having as its basic aim the undermining of imperialism, the consolidation of democracy, and the eradication of the remnants of fascism. . . . A special place in the imperialist arsenal of tactical weapons is occupied by the utilization of the treacherous policy of the right-wing socialists.[11]

Whatever reality the Cominform may have had as a genuine multilateral organization was soon destroyed by its obvious subservience to the Soviet party and intelligence officials who ran it and by the noisome defection of its Yugoslav member from the Soviet orbit. Relocated to Bucharest, it lingered on as a part of

"Proletarians of all Countries, Unite!" A universalist slogan dating from the Communist Manifesto *of 1848, conveying the ethos of the Soviet ideocratic party-state. The slogan is printed on the state seal shown on most Soviet currency, official documents, and party media such as* Pravda. *The version shown is on a Soviet gold coin, the* Chervonetz, *minted in 1976 in the Russian Republic of the USSR. Soviet gold, long mined by forced labor, is an important source of hard currency for political warfare operations.*

the flimsy facade behind which the CPSU Secretariat ran its campaign to consolidate communist rule in Eastern Europe and to disrupt the American-financed reconstruction of the West. It was this American presence which now produced a full-scale political conflict.

America's entry as a committed, fully cognizant actor in the political battle for Europe required the scrapping, in fact if not in form, of several myths derived from the global humanist vision of a peaceful world in which major disputes would be regulated by negotiation rather than war. In one of these myths, the Soviet Union and the United States were converging societies that, given time and patience, would eventually evolve into compatible if not identical post-capitalist and post-communist industrial societies. In the West, characteristically, no ideological authority ever thrashed out this issue; various scholars and visionary politicians continued to hold such a view in one form or another. But in terms of practical international (and domestic US) politics, President Harry Truman's March 1947 address advocating US aid to Greece and Turkey buried the myth. Its key passages, later known as the Truman Doctrine, stated,

> At the present moment in world history nearly every nation must choose between alternative ways of life. The choice is too often not a free one. One way of life is based upon the will of the majority. . . . The second . . . is based upon the will of a minority forcibly imposed upon the majority. It relies upon terror and oppression, a controlled press and radio, fixed elections and the suppression of personal freedom.
>
> I believe that it must be the policy of the United States to support free peoples who are resisting attempted subjection by armed minorities or by outside pressure. I believe that we must assist free peoples to work out their own destinies in their own way.[12]

British and American policymakers were at odds on a number of major issues in 1947, much more seriously so than it appeared to many Americans at the time. Issues of colonial policy, free trade, currency convertibility, the Middle East, and nuclear weapons all offered varying degrees of divergence. But on European reconstruction and security their interests converged. So did their emerging perceptions of the threat posed to their interests, however divergent, by Soviet political warfare elsewhere, particularly in the Mediterranean region. Winston Churchill had stated the seriousness of the challenge in his Fulton, Missouri, speech of February 1946, warning of Soviet actions to impose an Iron Curtain over Europe.

Attlee's Labor government, vulnerable in 1946 to the strongly pro-Soviet element still in its ranks, could take no action on this warning from a Conservative politician who had recently suffered a resounding defeat at the polls. Nor had the government abandoned hope of working out an arrangement with Stalin. By late 1947, after experiencing Soviet aggression in Turkey and Persia and feeling the threat of Soviet-inspired subversion in Greek and Italian political life, Attlee and Bevin saw things differently. Moreover, they believed their constituencies at home and their allies abroad would share these perceptions if given the facts.

The way now open for a strategic political warfare campaign in Europe, Bevin acted to create the mechanism that could wage it on Britain's behalf and to cooperate with the United States in its operation. Following a Cabinet meeting in February 1948, he handed a long list of questions to his principal private secretary, (later Sir) Frank Roberts. Among the issues addressed were the feasibility and costs of recreating the World War II Political Warfare Executive; of mobilizing the support of major religious groups, beginning with the Christian churches but including Buddhists and Muslims; of forging instruments to combat communism within the United Kingdom; and of devising new constitutional formulas for independence within the Commonwealth that could enable Britain to keep India, Pakistan, and Ceylon as members now that they had become independent.[13]

As part of this British initiative, a covert information operation, the Information Research Department (IRD), was created in late 1947. Under the directorship of Christopher Mayhew, a Foreign Office official, IRD was charged with providing, confidentially and without attribution, background information on the Soviet Union and related communist affairs for use by selected foreign contacts, including journalists. Official confirmation of IRD's activities remains closely held: it would appear to have operated in both European and what are now known as Third World areas until renamed and drastically reduced in scope in 1977. Research reports produced by IRD, such as the series on Communist Fronts, were consistently accurate and reliable. IRD also sponsored and subsidized a series of books on communist affairs.[14] But despite the sustained high quality of its products, IRD lacked the financial resources to mount a full-scale challenge to Soviet political warfare, at least as American policymakers saw it.

The American body politic also contained an element of pro-Soviet or simply pacifist opinion that could be expected to resist any commitment of resources to political warfare directed against the USSR. This constituency, ranging from CPUSA members through no-enemies-on-the-left liberals to global humanists, had no broad support in American politics, as the failed 1948 presidential campaign of Henry Wallace demonstrated. But it retained a strong negative—or blocking—potential, having a significant presence in key sectors of society, notably in the media and cultural world and among some influential figures in the Executive Branch.[15]

It did not include Harry Truman, who instinctively distrusted communism as an ideology and the Soviet Union as its embodiment in the international arena. His instincts, moreover, had been strongly reinforced by his belief that Franklin Roosevelt, his predecessor, had concluded just before his death that America would have to adopt a stiffer posture toward the USSR.[16] Truman, in the view of some of his advisers, overstated his case, leading to a public posture, as revealed in the Truman Doctrine, that was more universalist, even Manichaean, than many of them thought wise or necessary.

The Truman Doctrine provided the ostensible basis for American political warfare operations of the Cold War period. Because its wording was open to a universalist interpretation, much of the related writing that transmitted and amplified the Doctrine for domestic and foreign audiences has been judged in retrospect to have a universalist aim as its core vision. There is some justice in this view. American perceptions of the US role in the world have from time to time included such sentiments, and Harry Truman, like Woodrow Wilson, was clearly a leader who came from that school. This universalist school was not, however, the most dominant element in America's world view, and it did not in this instance prevail in practice.[17]

What emerged, behind the scenes, was an operational strategy for political warfare much in the tradition of Elizabethan limited aims and pragmatic methods. Most of the American policymakers involved did not regard this tension between an outer posture of universalist appeal and an inner operational core of pragmatism as necessary or desirable for America's long-term policy interests. In practice, the uneasy combination of the two strains of policy offered advantages as well as posing dangers. In any event, the combination was fortuitous rather than intentional, growing out of an interplay of political and bureaucratic forces at work within the American polity, not linked in a larger sense to any overriding ideology or strategic plan. This course of development, too, was rooted in Anglo-Saxon historical patterns of political war.

American strategy for political war in the 1940s period of the Cold War had two main aims: to restore Western Europe through military, economic, and political support, and to weaken the Soviet hold on Eastern Europe through propaganda. The two aspects were mutually reinforcing, and the result was expected to be a "containment" rather than destruction or total transformation of Soviet power. George Kennan, who drafted many of the seminal policy documents, liked to speak of an "imperial analogue," portraying international communism as similar to classical imperialism of the Roman period. Drawing on the words of Edward Gibbon's *Decline and Fall of the Roman Empire*, he argued, "there is nothing more contrary to nature than the attempt to hold in obedience distant provinces."[18] The approach, in short, was a rejection of the Clausewitzian concentration on the enemy's strongest point, and a reversion to the classic "indirect strategy," as British military analyst Basil Liddell Hart later termed it. This approach amounted to significantly less than the universalist pretensions read into the

Truman Doctrine. It was also more effective and clearly more feasible.

The American strategy was inherently defensive, but it was applied as a form of active defense. The most forward aspect of it was its appeal to the nationalism still strong throughout the now-subject nations of Eastern Europe.[19] Such a strategy had much in its favor, for nationalism had always been strong among the quite diverse nations of the region—strong enough never to be successfully contained or suppressed by either German or Russian domination. Which was most hated usually depended on which was in occupation, and after World War II that meant the Soviets.

Concerning nationalism *within* the Soviet empire, American policy remained ambivalent—and ineffective. Articulated later as "non-predetermination," the approach had little prospect of reducing the Soviet empire to its constituent national republics, as British political warfare had done in World War I against the Hapsburgs. For various reasons, Americans and Europeans were reluctant to play the nationalities card for all it was worth. Among the warring Soviet emigre communities, the problem proved intractable: Russians insisted on the integrity of any post-Soviet empire, non-Russians insisted on either full autonomy or complete secession.

The outcome, as incorporated in the principles of a "Working Alliance" between representatives of the American Committee for Liberation (AmComLib) and the emigre groups, included "a succinct expression of 'non-predetermination,' which had always been the policy of the American Committee and which it was felt any emigre group must accept in order to work with the Committee."[20] By trying too much to keep all options open, the American formula procured the hostility and suspicion it sought to diminish. There was never an effective, much less unified, democratic political opposition to Soviet power among the Soviet emigres as there was among many of the East Europeans.

For the 1940s, the Soviet issue as such remained secondary. The first priority was economic and social reconstruction in Western Europe; second was loosening the hold of local communist regimes in Eastern Europe. Any effort—which Kennan and others thought unlikely to have any early effect—designed to liberalize the Soviet regime came behind these higher priorities. Such were

*Head of Stalin, image on a 100-crown silver coin minted probably in
1953 in Prague. Portrayal of a foreign political leader on a country's
coinage can be an effective device for inculcating a sense of
subordination among the population and establishing visible and
enduring evidence of diminished sovereignty. This is an interesting
example of a political warfare method in modern times that dates in
origin to Hellenistic Greek practices under Alexander of Macedon.*

the broad outlines of "containment" within which America
launched political warfare operations in Europe in the late 1940s.[21]

American instruments for directing a political warfare campaign
were rudimentary at best. The United States lacked adequate command structure at the top, experienced staffs, and forces in being
to carry out the strategy when articulated. Writing in retrospect,
an American war planner, General A. C. Wedemeyer, described
the situation with candor:

> In the American system, the military departments handled
> strategy, the State Department foreign policy. No one, with
> the exception of a single grossly overextended human individ-
> ual, the President, was charged with the most difficult task of
> all—the intelligent relating of military power to political pur-
> pose. Some of the implications of this absurd state of affairs
> were brought to my attention during my three years as a stra-
> tegic planner in the Plans Division of the War Department
> General Staff.[22]

At the next level down, the staffs and operating units which
had existed briefly from 1942 to 1945 were gone in the hasty
demobilization after victory. No infrastructure had endured for
political warfare staffs, as for the uniformed military, to sustain
the capability. Robert Sherwood, the wartime head of OWI's Over-
seas Service, has left a memoir of the situation American force
planners had faced in 1941 when engaged in planning talks with
the British:

> Although, in the plan known as A. B. C.-1, "Subversive Ac-
> tivities and Propaganda" were listed as item number three in
> the primary measures to be taken against Germany, the United
> States Government had no plans for any propaganda organi-
> zation or, indeed, any idea where such an organization would
> be put in the Administration. In July, 1941, Roosevelt author-
> ized Colonel William J. Donovan to organize the Office of
> Coordinator of Information but the word "Information" applied
> to intelligence rather than propaganda.[23]

The situation Sherwood described was doubtless what most
Americans would think of as "normal" for their country, and by

1947 the nation's affairs in this regard were clearly "normal." With conceptual planning, as practiced by George Kennan and others, done in an organizational vacuum, the first steps to move the nation and its allies into a more effective posture suffered accordingly. The launching of the Marshall Plan, America's central initiative in the entire campaign, is revealing. Bevin's biographer described how the Foreign Secretary learned of the plan:

> Nothing was done to draw attention to Marshall's [June 5, 1947] speech in advance. The American news agencies dismissed it with a few lines and it was not broadcast by the American networks. . . . The British Embassy in Washington did not think it worth the cable charges to send an advance copy of the speech to London and, in face of the lack of interest shown by the American press, only three British correspondents thought it worth paying serious attention to it . . . it was on a small wireless set by his bedside that Bevin first heard of Marshall's speech in the BBC's American commentary.[24]

With characteristic enthusiasm—and haste—America built a political warfare capacity. In 1947 a National Security Act was passed creating, among other things, a National Security Council that would, if wisely administered, solve the problem described by General Wedemeyer. Henceforth, one might expect, the instruments of policy—military, propaganda, public diplomacy, economic, covert action, and diplomatic—could be used in their most effective combinations. Henceforth, grand strategy could be broken down into regional and functional operating plans and activities by the agencies of the Executive Branch. Henceforth, policy control and verification could be practiced by the Commander in Chief through a staff both knowledgeable and competent to interpret his vision of the world and of America's role in it. And henceforth—although this was not specifically spelled out in the Act—the Legislative Branch would have a single authoritative point of reference to which it could relate and refer in deciding whether laws and appropriated funds were or were not being wisely and lawfully administered.

Both Truman and Eisenhower used the NSC apparatus in this sense, and both, by and large, used it successfully to fight the Cold War. The various subcommittees and boards that they developed and used for this purpose changed in name and specific duties over the years. They cannot be reported here in detail.[25] At the outset, in addition to Kennan's studies, inputs came from a Washington lawyer, Lawrence Houston, who had been counsel to the old OSS, from Allen Dulles and John Warner, both formerly with OSS, and somewhat later from Dulles' former Deputy in OSS, Frank Wisner. Wisner was given charge of a new operational unit misleadingly entitled the Office of Policy Coordination (its media operations were soon dubbed "Wisner's Wurlitzer"), which became the covert action arm of the newly created Central Intelligence Agency. Many of the senior figures had known each other from university days at Princeton; Wisner was a lawyer trained at the University of Virginia. High-level policy backing within the administration came mainly from Secretary of State George Marshall and Secretary of Defense James Forrestal.

A reinvigorated Voice of America (VOA), as an official US government broadcast medium, held primary responsibility for overt political advocacy, disseminating public diplomacy to allies and neutrals and some forms of propaganda to adversaries. In 1953 VOA was subordinated to a newly established US Information Agency (USIA), which extended public diplomacy operations into print and other media. The Department of Defense, with growing responsibility for bases and military units abroad, developed and deployed an extensive network of oversea English-language radio stations, stations which not only broadcast to American forces but also enjoyed a large local eavesdropping audience.

Among these activities, the grey and black propaganda operations subordinate to the CIA were most intensively deployed and probably most influential in achieving America's specific political warfare goals. The whole campaign was broadly based, diversified, and better coordinated than might be expected from its hasty origins. Above all, it was a campaign in which the effect of the whole was greater than the sum of its parts. Considering its essentially limited objectives, as noted above, it was successful in its central purpose.

No one has yet written a full, objective account of American political warfare operations for the Cold War, and though much of the evidence is now in the public record, or available on request, it has not been subjected to dispassionate scholarly analysis. Until it is, any comparative appraisal, in historical perspective, must remain tentative. That being understood, I would argue that modern commanders can profitably note several aspects of the campaign. Among them are the research, broadcasting, and print media operations conducted from Western Europe, against Eastern European targets, under control of the New York-based Free Europe Committee and the similarly based American Committee for Liberation or AmComLib.

Both Free Europe and AmComLib were hybrid organizations: partly government, beholden to the CIA and through it to the new National Security Council, partly supported by a private corporation drawing funds from business and individual donations. Free Europe was launched in 1949 and aimed at Eastern Europe; AmComLib was incorporated in 1951 and targeted on the USSR. (Both have undergone changes of title and mission since their early days; they are currently combined as Radio Free Europe/Radio Liberty, subordinated to a Board for International Broadcasting funded by direct, fully overt Congressional appropriation.) In their prime, both were very much within the Anglo-Saxon tradition, dating from Elizabethan days, of mixed government and private support. In modern form they involved participation by a spectrum of government officials and private talent, and represented a joint endeavor by Americans and Europeans.[26]

The spirit, organization, staffing, and operation of Radio Free Europe (or RFE) and Radio Liberty (RL) in their most effective period, the 1950s and 1960s, offer useful instruction in retrospect for students of political war. They were, from top to bottom, infused with a spirit appropriate to their task. As cooperative endeavors, mixing East Europeans and Americans, they were motivated by a sense of purpose that necessarily involved sensitivity and compromise to achieve a common aim. Such compromises required some accord on principles and constant adaptation to changing events. Central policy units within each radio provided this evolving sense of purpose, enhancing its effect where there was unity, and diminishing or defusing problems of divergent interest or perception. The record of these units was sometimes mixed, but over time one of them, RFE, did the job. RL, I would argue, was less successful, mainly for the conceptual reasons associated with non-predetermination strategy.

The two radios were for good reasons kept organizationally separate. They were aimed at quite different cultures and had essentially different roles. Internally, they were quite different. RFE was a network of separate broadcast divisions, each with its own director, research unit, and programming staff made up mostly of emigres. RL was operated as a single station, functioning with Russian as its main language service, with adjunct minority-language desks. (This structure confirmed the suspicion among non-Russians that US policy in practice favored Russian imperialism.) RFE was larger in staff and facilities; it also had a highly professional central news service with more bureaus at key points throughout Western Europe. Both radios maintained strong radio monitoring units. Editorial offices were in Munich, with transmitters in Germany, Spain, and Portugal.

Staffing depended upon the central managements. All personnel were employed by the parent New York corporations and recruited on the basis of skills and commitment to the common goals. Some American personnel, but by no means all, were recruited, secretly, from US government agencies, mostly from the CIA. Europeans were often recruited on recommendation by East European governments-in-exile or emigre groups, but were also recruited at large from ethnic communities throughout the world. The Europeans thus represented two broad categories: *emigres*, who felt a primary allegiance to their native countries and had often quite strong views regarding the systems of governance they hoped to see replace communist rule in Eastern Europe; and *emigrants*, who retained the language skills and culture of their places of origin but had formally transferred their allegiance to new homelands in the West. All concerned needed to keep these distinctions in mind, particularly in crises. The successful, albeit often tentative and mutually unsatisfactory, resolution of these tensions was probably management's most important task.

Officially, the US government denied any responsibility for the radios and took care to conceal the channels of funding, personnel recruitment, and policy influence. Obviously, the major support was American, but it was plausibly not official American, and it could be excluded from diplomatic intercourse and international legal complications. Key members of Congress were knowledgeable about the radios, and important sectors and individuals in American private media were heavily involved. But the amenities of formal international life were preserved, thus facilitating a switch to state diplomatic channels of communication if the Soviets chose to respond seriously to Western feelers for a political settlement of the Cold War and to dismantle their own political warfare capability.

The radios and their associated operations thus were—in the American government's view—"grey" operations; they remained such until their cover was destroyed and their existence publicly attacked by "New Left" activists in America during the late 1960s. How and why these revelations and attacks occurred goes beyond the bounds of this study. But it is worth noting that these actions destroyed or radically revised much of the *raison d'etre* and sense of purpose in the radios.

During Radio Free Europe's strongest period, the Polish emigres saw themselves as emigres, not as emigrants; to these Poles, the Polish Service of RFE was emphatically not a grey operation. They enjoyed a great deal of autonomy, were quite explicit on the air as to who they were and what they stood for, and did not consider the concealed US government subsidies to in any way impair their intellectual integrity or national allegiance. They could (and did) assert their autonomy when they believed their US colleagues acted without due regard for the interests of Poland as seen by Poles. In essence, these same attitudes prevailed throughout all of the national staffs of the radios.

Operating the radios presented challenges that grew in scope and significance as the radios became more effective in shaping roles as surrogate voices for their subjugated countrymen. And very effective voices they were. After initial startup problems, they eventually achieved an audience and influence exceeding that of many official stations operating under communist rule.[27]

With influence came responsibility. Even the most aggressive anti-communist, European or American, was keenly aware that incitement to revolt, however justified by repression, was self-defeating when it exposed unarmed civilians to brutal reprisal from Soviet military units and Soviet-backed internal security forces. Less clear and more difficult to resolve were questions of relative advantage: how much, for example, should the professional elites of Eastern Europe do or not do to enhance the efforts—however inept—of local communist regimes to rebuild and expand their countries' economic and social bases? For the peoples of Eastern Europe, the communist approach to modernization represented complex challenges.

RFE broadcasters, American and European alike, soon realized that a responsible and finely tuned approach was necessary, one based on careful interaction reflecting mutual awareness of what was and was not feasible and desirable *from the point of view of those actually living in the country*. For unlike USIA media, like the Voice of America, which reported and commented on events from the American viewpoint, the Munich radios were based on a premise of reflecting the interests of the nations they addressed. In a long view, such interests were seen by the American sponsors as compatible with the basic aspirations of the East European peoples. In the short term, conflicts could appear, or be made to appear (as was often the case), in regime counterpropaganda. Given the suddenness with which events moved in Eastern Europe and the rapidity with which broadcast media must respond, the policy officers and broadcast directors on the spot often had to resolve such conflicts.

Attention to these distinctions and concern for the well-being of peoples living under a communist tyranny did not have to mean complicity in abuse of police power, violation of national traditions, destruction of religious faith and institutions, or submission to violations of national sovereignty. It did not mean ignoring the economic distress caused by Stalinist exploitation disguised as rapid industrialization. Nor did it mean lack of awareness of the corruption and ineptitude rife among the newly installed communist elites of Eastern Europe. Personal corruption and individual abuses of power were fair game for RFE and RL in their most effective years, subject of course to the requirements of good journalistic standards.

Compared to 1960s standards of "investigative" journalism in the West, RFE programming guidelines were—despite occasional lapses—remarkably responsible. To have acted otherwise would have been self-defeating. In overall style, RFE reflected a mix of responsible Central European and American broadcast journalism, with program level tending toward the upper end of the scale. Radio Liberty also aimed upscale, but faced more difficulties in establishing its radio personality, if only because large numbers of its listeners, after a half-century of Soviet rule, were less clearly part of modern Europe.

CIA staffs in Western Europe undertook a parallel "grey" propaganda operation, not against West Europeans but in cooperation with them. This cooperative effort worked against Soviet propaganda operations and local communist groups loyal to Stalin rather than to their own governments. It differed from the effort in Eastern Europe in scope, style, and media used. Because it was carried out on the territory and inside the societies of allied nations, it had to be conducted with the compliance, formal or tacit, of the host governments and in consonance with their traditions and culture.

Print media were the main instrument, in subsidized journals like the London-based *Encounter*, for English-speaking readers, and *Der Monat*, published in Bonn for German speakers. The massively organized local communist Fronts put great pressure on intellectuals in postwar Europe, particularly on the anti-Stalinist left, and financial support was thin or nonexistent in their still war-damaged societies. Help, in various forms, could make a difference, enabling many of them to survive and pursue interests that were essentially individual and not necessarily "left" as defined by local communists in educational and media establishments.

The basic American intent was not to produce—as the Soviet opposition did—a chorus of sycophantic apologists. Rather, the United States hoped to aid in rebuilding a lively and diversified intellectual life in Europe, which could, for its own reasons, in its own idiom, and on its own terms, defeat Soviet—including local communist—incursions on their freedom. Many intellectuals simply needed a forum for discourse and a place for publication free of obvious and explicit ideological demands. Given such opportunities, European intellectuals could and did do the rest for themselves, free of any sense of patronizing foreign pressure. A grey operation, subtly managed, could best meet this need; it was particularly effective when intelligently coordinated with USIA and VOA programming for public diplomacy purposes.

In the 1950s, the Voice of America and its sister print media operated by the US Information Agency developed a world-class, round-the-clock, credible voice for communication to and between audiences all over the globe. The guiding principles worked out in these years, as formally sanctioned in 1960 under Director George V. Allen, were clear and forthright:

1. Our news will be accurate and comprehensive—meaning we must report the bad with the good.

2. We must be the Voice of America, not merely the Voice of the Administration. We must provide a balanced reflection of all significant and responsible segments of American society— even when they disagree with an administration policy.

3. As the official radio, we must clearly state U.S. policy and argue for it as persuasively as possible.[28]

Maintaining such principles against all pressures, foreign and domestic, was no easy task, but it was an essential one. Without such control, the more sharply targeted political warfare campaign in Europe would have been out of balance, lacking the context of overall American credibility and integrity necessary for responsible world influence. VOA broadcasting, and USIA's International Press Service wireless files and world-circulation magazines, provided a good media mix, rounded out by a growing program of educational and cultural exchange.

The Western defense of Europe thus took many forms. The Marshall Plan and organization of NATO provided economic and military aspects. The West also used public diplomacy in relation to allied populations, propaganda through internal defense measures in Western Europe and external assertion by radio to Eastern Europe, and diplomacy through the bilateral and multilateral contacts needed to achieve the understanding—and cooperation where mutually desired—for such actions and policies. The campaign was successful, and what had been feared by European and American statesmen in 1946 no longer presented a serious threat in

1956. Europe had recovered, at least in the West, to a position of economic vitality, cultural self-esteem, and political stability favorably comparable to regional conditions anywhere else on the globe, and clearly superior to those in the still-communist-dominated East. Therein lay a new challenge.

American Cold War perspectives, as noted earlier, included an inherent tension between an ostensibly universalist vision and a limited operational strategy. It was a tension never explicitly addressed and never finally resolved. In the event, American policy contained some element of both at all times; in any specific case, no one (including the Americans involved) seemed able to say which would prevail. For differing reasons, some Americans, many Europeans, and most Soviets found this disturbing. Marxist-Leninists regarded it as duplicitous and denounced it as a form of capitalist cunning. Most politically informed people in the West saw it as inherently Anglo-Saxon at best and ineptly American at worst. All regarded it, in varying degrees, as dangerous. And they were right, at least in the sense that all warfare, not least political, is dangerous and not to be undertaken lightly. Nor was it.

The Hungarian Revolution of 1956, and other less violent upheavals in Soviet-dominated Eastern Europe, resulted from many things; American political warfare operations were clearly, in my view, among them. How and why this was so, and with what results, deserves close attention by students of political war.

In the early 1950s American policy had shifted toward a more universalist posture. Soviet military force, either directly threatened as in the Berlin blockade of 1948-49 or indirectly applied as in the North Korean attack of 1950, convinced most Americans that ruling communist parties were not to be relied upon. To rest hopes of a secure peace on agreements negotiated with them through diplomatic channels was evidently dangerous. In 1952 the Eisenhower administration came into office on a proclaimed policy of "rolling back" communist power, a formula widely interpreted as a strong affirmation of the universalist strain in America's outlook.

But the commitment was not total. Following Stalin's death in 1953, when signs appeared in Moscow of a desire to ease tensions and to explore (and exploit) some of the possibilities always present for improved relations, the Americans and their European allies responded. Various steps that followed included state visits by the new Soviet leaders and a summit meeting in Geneva. The Cold War appeared to be moderating.

The propaganda battle in Europe, East and West, continued, but in a different context than that of the 1940s. What had been a Western active defense of Western Europe now subtly shifted, in response to the new context, into something resembling an offense. The more assertive official posture of President Eisenhower and his aides, the restored confidence and economic well-being of Western Europe, and the infighting among Stalin's successors added to the mounting sense of malaise and suppressed national resentment throughout Eastern Europe. The correlation of forces had shifted from East to West. Because the forces set in motion by the American political warfare planners were mainly economic and attitudinal, thus endowed with a momentum and dynamism of their own, they would probably continue to shift with glacial impetus until some event or events ripped open the surface of the international political landscape.

The Soviet leadership triggered the avalanche. At a Party Congress in February 1956, party leader Nikita Khrushchev denounced Stalin in an extended but secret speech. Khrushchev described the public acts and private character of the former *Vozhd* in graphic and selective terms that, in effect, placed all of the shortcomings of Soviet life on Stalin's head. By implication, Khrushchev also absolved the new leadership from responsibility for the present consequences of those shortcomings. A gambler's move, it reflected deep insecurity and uncertainty about the stability of the Soviet system. As such, it was intended as a propaganda statement, in the technical sense of ideas for a few elites only. Agitational exploitation would result from it, but the speech as Khrushchev gave it to the Congress and the foreign communist leaders present was strictly secret. Had there been no Western propaganda exploitation, it would presumably have remained so.

Within weeks, though, word of the attack surfaced in Western media. In June the US government released a text as "recently

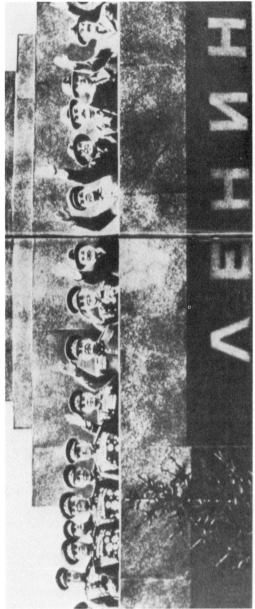

Lenin's Tomb, May Day Parade, 1947. Appearance of the Vozhd, or Leader, with **Politburo members and marshals** for the annual mass parade provides visual evidence of the combined ideological and imperialist claims of the Soviet leadership. Stalin, portrayed here in marshal's uniform, was buried in the tomb in 1953 and his name added under Lenin's. Removed to a resting place in the wall behind the tomb after being denounced by Khrushchev in 1956, Stalin remains a troublesome symbol for Soviet foreign propaganda operations. During the Cold War consolidation of Soviet client states in Eastern Europe, replicas of this Muscovite ritual in Eastern European capital cities provided a main symbol of legitimacy for local party leaders.

obtained from a confidential source." What Khrushchev had intended as a relatively candid, if self-serving, propaganda guidance
for party elites thus became a revealing indictment not only of the
Soviet leadership but also of its replicas in occupied Eastern Europe. A wide range of Western media now revealed and explored
the realities behind the speech, including many events known in
the West but still suppressed in the speech as well as in the official
communist legend. Radio Free Europe and Radio Liberty, which
reported the debate extensively together with other Western broadcasters, used the occasion to review for their audiences the Stalinist
origins and deeds of their local communist rulers. Few of those
rulers were able to respond with any credibility.

The "Secret Speech" engagement was important as a propaganda battle not only for its effect on perceptions at the time,
but even more for the credibility it gave to long-standing Western
accounts of Soviet history—accounts the Soviet media had vocif-
erously denied for years. Seldom has the principle been so strikingly proven, that a political scandal concealed is infinitely worse
over time than one revealed at once. Khrushchev, showing some
appreciation of this truth, sought to defuse the danger. But what
he did by saying too little, too late, and in the wrong way made
matters worse. And the Western political warfare commanders
made the most of the event—not stridently, but coolly, consistently,
and steadily—using scholarly research to back up journalism,
providing texts and commentary disseminated through a range of
both broadcast and infiltrated print media. Because much of the
exploitation was through "grey" media, it did not interrupt ongoing
diplomatic contacts or create obstacles to further Soviet movement
in the direction of detente.

These events affected Eastern Europe more than Washington or
Moscow anticipated, possibly because both underrated or mis-
understood the underlying forces for change. Whatever the assessments—and what they were is still unclear—events moved
quickly. In October 1956 two of the client governments of Eastern
Europe were in disarray. In Poland, change came mainly within
the ruling party elite and, following quick personal intervention

by Khrushchev and other Politburo members, produced a new modus vivendi. The new arrangement maintained communist rule and Warsaw Pact membership, but provided for less rigid Soviet control and promised a better life for the common man and his family.

Radio Free Europe's Polish Broadcast Division, under the cool and capable leadership of experienced Polish emigre Jan Nowak, did much to bring about these changes. Its programming kept the Polish population informed and encouraged, without inciting the outbreak of suicidal bravery some Poles occasionally demonstrated. The result for the people of Poland was not freedom; but it was an improvement over what they had suffered under before, and it was much better than the death and destruction they would have faced if provoked into triggering full-scale repression by units of the Red Army.

For students of political warfare, the operations of RFE's Polish Service are instructive: the chief was an experienced, technically proficient political journalist with the stature required for credibility among his staff and their audience; the staff represented a respectable level of ability, both functional and cultural; and the relations between the American policy officers and the emigre programmers were essentially sound, based on a sense of mutual— if wary—respect. Such capabilities are not the result of only one personality, nor are they thrown together in a crisis. They result, as they did in this case, from the careful and conscientious professionalism of several echelons of management and the personal commitment of many individuals. These capabilities are critically important to the conduct of political war.

Hungary was different. Unlike Poland, the explosion in Hungary was not contained within the ranks of the party apparatus. It started among non-party intellectuals and quickly spread to a wide spectrum of society, including most but not all of the industrial labor force and the military. The local leadership was weak, uncertain, and even less loved than that in Warsaw. And the Soviets, despite the cleverness of their man on the spot, Yuri Andropov, were apparently less certain as to what was happening and how to respond.

A new party leader, Imre Nagy, emerged and, facing widespread revolt, announced Hungary's withdrawal from the Warsaw

Pact and his intention to hold free elections. Some days later, the Soviet occupation forces were supplemented by an invading tank army and the revolt was crushed. Over 100,000 insurgents fled across the border to Austria and Yugoslavia; many others, including Nagy and the commander of the revolted army, were imprisoned, with some later killed by Soviet order. Another Moscow-loyal local communist was installed, and Hungary was brought to order, Soviet style. Over time, Moscow gradually introduced measures of economic liberalization and tolerated some modest increases in civil rights, changes which most observers believe would never have taken place without the pressures from below that erupted so violently in October 1956.

Radio Free Europe responded differently to Hungarian events than it did to those in Poland, and did so for understandable reasons. Hungary, to begin, had long been more tightly sealed, and there were fewer sources of news on the spot. The degree of popular involvement in the revolt was much greater, matters quickly became more violent than in Poland, and there were fewer signs as to how the local communist rulers or the Soviets would react. The Polish crisis soon resolved itself into a case of pressures for liberalization *within* the party apparatus. In Hungary, the pressures came from *outside* the party, amounting to demands from broad sectors of society for liberation from party rule.

The Hungarian Service of RFE was smaller in staff and neither as experienced nor as politically astute as the larger Polish Division. And it faced a major dilemma. Lacking the Poles' rich array of local sources and unable to expand its own, the Hungarian Service either had to operate in the dark or had to rely mainly on rebroadcasting accounts from the many small "Freedom Fighter" stations that came on the air during the fighting, which took an understandably combative line. It is surprising that the RFE broadcasts (subjected after the fact to exhaustive critique) were not more inflammatory. Nowhere in the tapes reviewed by post-facto investigative commissions did any explicit incitement to revolt occur. Neither was there any explicit promise of Western intervention; but the implication was, in some cases, clearly there, and desperate men would, understandably, have chosen to interpret things as they wished and hoped.

In the context of a larger ambivalence in America's strategic posture, propaganda operations did much to precipitate and sustain a Hungarian nationalist uprising against a despised foreign occupation—and they did so in consonance with Hungarian hope of massive help from abroad. Whether events going as far as they did was in either Hungarian or American interests is debatable. Lives were lost, as they may be in war; but not all of those fighting died, and a new balance was struck that many today in both countries can think of with gratitude.

From the European viewpoint, the outcome of the 1956 events was not total tragedy. Much was achieved in setting limits on how Muscovite imperialism, on the march since 1945 (and earlier), would be able to define victory and defeat. The imposition of its peculiar, ideocratic despotism on ever-growing numbers of previously independent nations had been a feature of Russian imperialism since the inception of the medieval Muscovite state.[29] In 1945, under a new and vigorous ideology, the state had launched another major expansion, subjugating and incorporating new territories and peoples. Many scholars have argued that it did so from an endless quest for security, stemming from an innate conviction that only by domination could it prevent encroachment in return. But the consequences for those subjugated were nonetheless dismal.

The political warfare in Eastern Europe that culminated in the events of 1956 showed Moscow that there were limits to its imperial domination. It may also have showed a generation of Soviet elites, on reflection, that failure to achieve total domination need not endanger their own legitimate security interests. If the rulers of Muscovy could have grasped this point, both halves of the classical ecumene might have reached a brief point of equilibrium in their eternal conflict.

As this book's epigraph indicates, war is a state of mind. Whether a state of war exists among political entities depends upon their several states of mind. For a period of twenty years, more or less, two modern states with their respective allies and clients both regarded themselves, although in varying degrees, as being at war, in fact if not under international law. During this period of conflict, each side developed and wielded the weapons they thought best for their purposes, in some cases taking the initiative, in others responding to the moves of the opponent.

The operations of both sides covered the globe but were most visible and focused in Western Europe and Northeast Asia. Surveyed in retrospect, the Western powers seemed to have been stronger in capabilities but weaker in intent; the Eastern powers seem to have been clearer in their intent, but weaker in capability. The struggle's immediate outcome was inconclusive, and the longer-range consequences remain unclear. For the observer of political warfare, the interest in the period lies in the basic fact that both, rather than one of the parties, saw themselves as engaged in this particular form of warfare.

10
TODAY AND THE FUTURE

War is not a reasonable activity. Its origins lie deep in the human psyche, and its conduct is dictated by aspects of the human condition that depend upon custom, tradition, and instinct more than upon conscious planning. Scholars in various periods of history have suggested keys to an understanding of the individual and social forces behind conflict. Their views have seldom stood the test of reality. There is little reason to believe that their theories are an adequate guide to policy.

We have therefore turned to history, and looked at what others thought and did in response to conditions comparable to our own. Our purpose is not to construct a truth machine but to see where it is possible to link cause with effect in a particular context, and to ask what worked and what did not, given the intent of the actors in the drama. Some analysts will, no doubt, reject this approach, judged by some modern schools of strategic thought to be hopelessly outmoded, more in keeping with the thought of the nineteenth century than that of today.

The greatest threat to peace in this century, though, comes from a political and military establishment, located in Moscow, that is firmly rooted in the concepts of nineteenth century thinkers like Clausewitz and Marx, as well as in the political culture of an earlier age. Moreover, much of Clausewitz remains in the war college curricula of their Western opponents,[1] and the political propositions of Marx and Lenin still have a profound (if pernicious) influence throughout many intellectual communities in the West.[2] One does not have to accept the validity of these influences in order to recognize that any description of political conflict embracing both East and West must take them into account. And for that purpose a historical perspective clearly has much to recommend it.

For Americans, a historical perspective to statecraft has respectable antecedents. Addressing the Constitutional Convention of 1789, John Dickerson of Delaware advised, "Experience must be our only guide. Reason may mislead us."[3] The conduct of political warfare against Marxist-Leninists requires a clear understanding of history because much of their ideology and propaganda depend upon exaggerated claims to historical legitimacy. There is absolutely no reason why commanders and statesmen working within the civic cultures of the West should abandon this ground to the ideologues of the East.[4]

Certainly, general theories of history, especially positions on the problem of causality, vary. Those who, like Stalin, are committed to the view that history "never does anything of moment without some particular necessity" stand at one end of a spectrum.[5] At the other end are those who would agree with the view that history is "just one damn thing after another." This study is based on a middle position that argues for and from the existence of some form of causality, however complex, and however imperfectly we may perceive it. Perceiving the causal links in history is part of being aware of experience as a guide to action. We can benefit from such insights, recognizing that each historical event is unique, without attempting—as Marxists do— to establish inexorable laws of historical development. One does not have to accept "historical inevitability" in order to learn from experience.

War is possibly the most enduring aspect of human culture. Modern fears of a nuclear apocalypse may have helped change some aspects of war, but they have not eliminated it and may have enhanced it in some forms. Political war is one of those forms. Anticipating unacceptable consequences from general war, men and societies have sought to pursue their aims through less materially destructive forms of conflict, among them political war. As in earlier periods, they have often practiced war while professing peace, an approach well suited to political warfare.

Some modern writers have stressed the inhibiting fear of biological extinction thought to be inherent in general nuclear war, arguing that this dilemma makes man's previous experience of war irrelevant. A corollary to the argument holds that man must change his nature or cease to exist, a line of argument often associated with advocacy of radical forms of social engineering such as Marxism-Leninism. Others argue from a basis of revealed religious truth promising salvation, if not strategic security, through moral regeneration.

No one can prove that the continued survival of the human race in the nuclear age has resulted from application of such theories. Nor has war ceased to be a continuing form of human activity. The reality seems to be that man continues to practice war at times and in ways which offer him its benefits without exacting unacceptable penalties, and that the fear of nuclear Armageddon has not prevented him from using considerable ingenuity in practicing numerous forms of non-nuclear combat. Earlier patterns of conflict thus retain their meaning for the present.

Scenarios offered for the outcome of political war today include convergence of the superpower participants, up to and including the transformation of one or both of them. Put another way, the expansionist power might come to redefine its concept of national security, either explicitly or in practice, to the point where the superpower relationship was symmetric, resulting from the existence of two status quo powers. Many smaller powers have long feared such superpower collusion, perhaps more than they feared the consequences of conflict, though few have been prepared to say as much in public. If the historical examples of this study are relevant to present conditions—and I would say they are—there is little reason to fear such an outcome. Much more likely is an extended struggle with increases and decreases in intensity and wide swings in the fortunes of the respective sides.

In such an extended-struggle scenario, all elements of national purpose will continue to be deployed: economic inducements and pressure; subversion and paramilitary operations of varying shades and tints; diplomacy, both bilateral and multilateral, ranging up and down the scale from traditional foreign office contacts through special envoys and summits. Crisis centers, hot lines, and other innovative devices will be used, abused, and discarded. Propaganda will continue as a primary weapon, always reflecting the differences between the two social systems and historical traditions in which it originates. Coordination will be tight and closely linked to orthodoxy on one side, loosely structured and strongly influenced by trends in individual conscience on the other. Political warfare, in short, will be the primary form of interaction between the superpowers, and its outcome and side effects will shape the environment in which other powers must struggle to survive.

Such a scenario may be likely, but it is by no means certain. Two great uncertainties, always attendant on politics and war, must be contemplated. And it is a curiosity of the present times that the two superpowers both deny their existence as uncertainties: the Soviets because they insist on the basis of revealed truth that victory is certain; the West, apparently, because it chooses to regard the concepts of both victory and defeat as irrelevant. Neither position seems to hold up in historical perspective. Victory and defeat must be contemplated as real possibilities, either for oneself or for the conditions existing in the territory of one's defeated opponent. Seen in this light, the relationship of the superpowers is markedly asymmetrical.[6]

Soviet concepts of political victory are clear, and the Soviets' practice in applying their concepts to concrete situations, as in Eastern Europe and Southern Asia, is well documented. Whether they would seek to transform the society, economy, and political life of Chicago as they did that of Warsaw should not be open to doubt. They would. Their doctrinal writings clearly provide for such an event, and their present political warfare capability is designed, given an appropriate increment of scale and the assistance of local collaborators and opportunists, to make the attempt possible. The "world socialist system," to be attained through the "world revolutionary process," is globally open-ended. There is no reason to believe that its future scope, as intended by the International Department of the CPSU, excludes Chicago or any other part of the non-communist world.[7] On the contrary, the "coming triumph of socialism on a world scale" is a principle long and firmly embedded in the ideology and practice of the CPSU.

All of which is not to say that the present Soviet Politburo, with its troubles, contemplates such a victory over the West as a direct and current object of policy. As of the late 1980s the Soviets give indications of being on the tactical defensive. But those who would argue that the Politburo has dropped *victory* from its list of long-range priorities, or that they no longer define *victory* in Marxist-Leninist terms, or that they no longer believe in the ideology, should contemplate the lesson of Hitler. They should also pay less attention to spokesmen like Georgiy Arbatov, and take the trouble to read carefully the introductory chapters to the Party Program of the CPSU, which roundly announces, "The International Communist Movement is the vanguard of the workers movement and all forces of the world revolutionary process."[8]

Victory, as noted earlier, is not a term in the official Western lexicon. Nor is *defeat*. Given the diverse nature of the Western world and the rotation of governments through the electoral process, with concomitant shifts in policy perceptions, one looks in vain for any definitive statement of global or even regional war aims.[9] The North Atlantic Treaty, signed in 1949 and still in effect, offers one of the few enduring expressions of common Western political will. The core of the Treaty is a commitment to maintain "individual and collective capacity to resist armed attack," a commitment limited to events in the Treaty area. In short, the political vision of the nations of the West was conceived after World War II in regionally limited, status quo terms, and it has consistently remained so for nearly forty years.

At the national level, an observer looks in vain for any signs of an official American program that would justify a government in Washington attempting to reorganize the politics and society of Minsk. Nor is there much evidence of any presidential intent over the years to advise a post-communist Soviet leader on the preferred system of political economy in the territory of the present Soviet empire.

In the 1950s, when Washington came as close as it ever will to articulating a vision of post-communist Russia, it coined the term *non-predetermination*. One cannot help wondering how many dispossessed Ukrainian farmers or underpaid Russian workers in labor camps would be willing to fight and die for non-predetermination. The term was little more than bureaucratic fudge, cooked up in planning staffs as an exercise in lowest-common-denominator politics. Its one virtue (and it is not one to be scorned) lay in its essential honesty. If that was all that was possible in the American, and Alliance, domestic political context, it was best to say so, lest people under communist rule be misled into expecting more external support than was possible.

One thus confronts a dilemma facing all status quo powers, namely, how to conduct political warfare in the absence of a stirring vision of the future to match the millenarian claims of the opponent, or even any specific and enduring idea of who or what the opponent might be.[10]

Of several solutions, the most obvious is to distinguish between defensive and offensive strategies and to concentrate on defense. The strategy has much to recommend it, if consistently pursued. Defense (as Clausewitz and others have noted) is often an inherently stronger posture than offense. But it should be a posture of active defense, and it requires at least a clear idea of the enemy. Too often the concept of defense has been insensibly translated, as we have seen, into appeasement in one form or another.

Complacency, derived from reliance on some presumably impregnable main weapons system or defensive line, is a fatal trap. If democracies have an inherent strategic weakness, it is a proclivity toward such complacency. Strategic defense in political war, although in theory the democracies' strongest and most appropriate posture, becomes in practice a less than satisfactory solution. Elizabeth I's strategy against Spain is probably the best historical example of successful use of an active and indirect strategic defense.

Anglo-Saxon rulers have from time to time tried offensive political warfare strategies, but with mixed success. Lloyd George (possibly because he was a Welshman) used the offensive briefly and with spectacular success as part of a larger end-game strategy. He and Wilson failed in their attempts to follow through into a consolidation of the victory.

Other than in wartime, American and British efforts to assert the international validity of Gladstonian or Wilsonian liberal idealism have seldom enjoyed sustained domestic support. Despite occasional rhetorical flourishes, the English-speaking peoples probably are unwilling to sacrifice blood or treasure in large amounts to impose this vision on the world at large. Business communities tend to react like a distinguished American banker, who observed *a propos* the USSR, "Who knows which system is best; all we care is, do they pay their bills?" The man in the street may regard liberal values as desirable for all, but given a choice he will usually choose to spend his tax dollars or pounds at home.

Another solution might be called the Franklin Option, after Benjamin Franklin's observation, regarding the government of George III, "a great empire, like a great cake, is most easily diminished at the edges."[11] In the idiom of modern policymaking, this idea might be translated into a strategy of unremitting pressure at regional and local levels based upon alliances with local movements sharing common concerns, keeping open the option of a later attack on the strategic center—a conceptual approach more akin to the thought of Liddell Hart than to that of Clausewitz. American policy during the 1950s tended in this direction, and the whole history of East-West conflict in the Third World might be interpreted in this light, with the initiative usually on the Soviet side, as in Korea, Vietnam, and Afghanistan. The problem for the West has not been so much finding pressure points but linking those found to some central strategic aim.

To some degree, all of the above strategies have at one time or another informed American policy. But seldom has any policy line survived the ebb and flow of domestic political life. What one administration asserted in an attempt to give form and focus to America's presence in the world, the succeeding administration would promptly reject or ignore. And adding to this alternation over time was the continuing struggle between the legislature and the executive over control of policy. Such circumstances are not conducive to the conduct of political war, which not only requires continuity of basic policy but also depends on advance planning to create and deploy equipment and manpower. Taking into consideration the problems of foreign basing, appropriations, construction, manning, and training, ten-year lead times for operational modern mass communication facilities for oversea use are by no means excessive.

Perhaps the best solution to these problems lies in creating the political warfare instrument on long-term premises, while retaining flexibility on when and how to use it. Policy content can be adjusted to changing circumstances and needs, so long as the basic capability remains in working order. Such an approach appears to underlie the sustained commitment since the 1940s to American military power.

No such commitment has existed for political warfare capability, where there has been a history of organizations created, used for a time, and then destroyed in fact if not in form. Psychological operations capabilities created in World War II were never used for more than tactical purposes. Others were created in the late 1940s, made operational in the 1950s, and disrupted in the 1960s; by the late 1970s they were in serious disarray. By the early 1980s US Army Psyop existed mostly in skeletal form. Radio Liberty, Radio Free Europe, and related research capabilities, such as the Munich-based Institute for the Study of the USSR, existed, but in much different form; their sense of purpose and status had lost much of its original impetus. CIA support of operations around the world had been drastically reduced or abandoned.[12]

America fared better in maintaining its public diplomacy capabilities. The Voice of America and most related USIA and State Department programming in other media remained as instruments of long-term cultural exchange and general service news programming. USIA's oversea presence, the US Information Service (USIS), under close State Department control, was often primarily concerned with the useful but limited task of providing public relations services for diplomatic missions. The 1980s brought a major expansion of VOA facilities, and the beginning of satellite TV programming known as "Worldnet." The National Endowment for Democracy, funded by the Congress, with bipartisan backing, was established in the late 1970s to give support at modest levels to democratic political and social activities in selected foreign countries; it offers a restrained potential for a systematic effort to propagate the principles of democracy abroad in cooperation with several similar organizations maintained for similar purposes by other Western democracies. Many believed these activities still lacked sufficient sense of strategic purpose, but they clearly gave America a more effective voice at the country level. America by the beginning of the 1980s had begun to update and expand its public diplomacy capability; it had only remnants of a political warfare force.

America had also shifted part of its attention from Europe to Asia. The ambivalence was inherent in America's geography, and the alternation East or West was part of American history. The nature of the Asian involvement from the late 1960s to mid-1970s was unusually controversial, and for various reasons of an internal nature it was unusually self-destructive.

American posture during the Vietnam War showed little or no sense of strategic purpose. Nor was there any internal consensus on which to base the national purpose. Political warfare forces were shaped and deployed, but they were mainly regional in scope and tactical in nature. North Vietnam's efforts, by contrast, were strategically oriented, well supported (usually) by their larger communist allies, and effectively targeted on US domestic, politically partisan weaknesses. Seldom has a small power succeeded so spectacularly in exploiting the internal divisions of a major opponent through classic political warfare operations. When the Vietnam War ended in 1975, America's primary focus reverted to the Atlantic, and some measure of domestic harmony was restored.

By the beginning of the 1980s, it was not clear what the American body politic had concluded about the utility of political warfare, or indeed whether it was even aware of it as such. The term itself was only applied to the history of World War II "black" operations. The present-day practice of psychological operations had strictly tactical meaning, and then only in conventional military usage. *Propaganda* remained in the popular lexicon, but almost exclusively as a term of partisan abuse. Suggestions that it had more meaningful historical referents than those associated with Hitler and Goebbels met, at best, with incomprehension.

The partisan nature of foreign policy discourse continued to cloud the issue. Those inclined toward a global-humanist perception of the world asserted, despite the historical record, that propaganda was unworthy and un-American. Power realists sometimes advocated propaganda, usually on the grounds that "the Soviets practice it." Often, what they seemed to have in mind were forms of mass counterpropaganda for American domestic audiences. Such efforts seldom elicited any solid congressional support, and

often generated sharp controversy. America—but not the world—
had returned to normal.

By the late 1980s, significant change had begun in the Eastern
half of the East-West world that is the focus of this study. Economic, social, and political reforms associated with the Soviet
leader, Mikhail Gorbachev, were announced and to a limited extent
implemented by attempts at structural change. The essence of the
reforms was a qualified renunciation of many of the most repressive
features of Stalinism, notably arbitrary police rule, atrophied political institutions, and a stagnant, overcentralized command economy. In external relations the Soviets declared their intent to engage
the West in detente, to liberalize controls over Eastern Europe,
and, selectively, to cut back on the number and kind of their
commitments in less-developed countries—most notable being the
withdrawal of conventional military formations from Afghanistan.

The Gorbachev reforms were summed up, characteristically,
in slogans: "Reconstruction" for the economy, "Openness" for the
society, and "New Thinking" for the intellectual and (partly) political life of the empire. The Soviet Union announced an attempt
to relaunch detente under the traditional Marxist- Leninist slogan,
"peaceful coexistence"; the West did not welcome the term, its
leaders recalling the deceptive use to which Brezhnev had put it
in the 1970s. On substance, however, the West demonstrated a
strong interest in meaningful reduction of tension, particularly
military tension.

Gorbachev's political vision, if carried forward successfully
by his followers, would amount to a renewal and reinvigoration
of imperial Russian rule comparable to and possibly exceeding in
scope the New Economic Program of Lenin in the 1920s. It would
also produce a different basis for Eastern posture toward the West.
The resulting posture would presumably—taking the East's declarations at face value—be designed to reduce tensions and increase the levels of mutually beneficial East-West interaction.
Whether Gorbachev would prevail in full, or even in part, in

pushing through this broad and fundamental program of change remained for many observers an open question.

The West needs to ask what significance these changes in Soviet domestic and foreign policies might actually have for the political warfare posture of the CPSU's International Department and for the paramilitary capabilities and intentions of the Soviet state. Would the CPSU, for example, reduce, redirect, or eliminate the support it had traditionally provided, in one form or another, for what it currently calls the "World Revolutionary Process"? As of this writing, the emphasis of such Soviet support has changed and some of the instruments have been moderately reduced in scope; but the basic capability, as defined by support for organizational weapons like ruling and non-ruling communist parties, deployment of propaganda weapons like the array of Front Organizations, and the supply of weapons for armed insurrections, remains very much in place.

The basic doctrinal commitments to world revolution, to the "leading and guiding role" of communist parties in all dimensions of international life, and to the maintenance of massive military power to support such a world view persist. The capabilities and intentions of the Soviet leadership to carry on global political warfare *may* be affected by Gorbachev's reforms *if* he survives and *if* he is able to put his program into effect for any extended period. These three levels of uncertainty remain very serious problems for the West.

The Gorbachev program might well change the posture of the Soviet party and state—but whether it would be able to change the underlying political and cultural patterns that have traditionally stimulated an assertive Soviet role in the world is less clear, indeed much less clear. The nineteenth century saw the emergence of a German empire, rooted in militarism and aggressive forms of territorial expansion, that withstood several monumental defeats before it was decisively crushed, with the social order on which it rested being reconstituted along peaceable, democratic lines in the aftermath of World War II. The changes that finally came in Germany were not the result of conventional military power alone; they required massive external intervention in the political, economic, and social structures of German society. There is no reason to expect any such level of external intervention by the West in Soviet life, with or without military conflict.

Present Western programs of public diplomacy and minimal propaganda fall far short of what is required to produce fundamental change. Barring major intervention, will the elites of the modern Soviet Union succeed, on their own, in carrying out changes in their historically determined ways of life? For the West to answer such a question would be an act of hubris; to ignore it, an act of folly.

Political war remains a fact of international life. Among the three great categories of war—nuclear, conventional, and political—only political war lies outside the realm of East-West negotiation. And yet of all types, it is the one most closely linked to the political visions at the root of conflict. Men are not hostile, it is often noted, because they are armed; they are armed because they are engaged in hostility. What use is it for the opponents in the present drama to pursue nuclear and conventional disarmament while they ignore the continued presence and deployment of political warfare capabilities? And what are the prospects for meaningful reduction in overall tension when the most threatening form of hostility remains undisclosed, unrestrained, and unacknowledged by those who practice it most aggressively?

The apocalyptic horrors of nuclear holocaust continue to attract the attention of foreign and defense analysts and to mesmerize the population at large, at least in Western cultures. Shifting the emphasis in conflict from nuclear to conventional levels is occasionally suggested as a means of assuring biological if not national survival. Armored vehicles, it is argued, have less potential for getting out of control than nuclear weapons. The argument has a neat and plausible consistency. It is usually unappealing to those who must contemplate facing the consequences for themselves and their countries of large-scale armored warfare. Disarmament analysts presume both forms of war—nuclear and conventional—to be more destructive of life and property than political war. The presumption is profoundly mistaken.

Political war has resulted in massive loss of life during the twentieth century—certainly more than has resulted from nuclear war, perhaps more than from conventional war as well. The Nazis' near-genocide of six million European Jews in World War II was a political, not military act. It was committed against a defenseless people for purely ideological motives, by paramilitary units, without the intervention of the German Army. Stalin's destruction of four to six million Ukrainian farmers in the 1932-33 collectivization campaign was imposed by paramilitary formations under the control of party activists pursuing ideological aims; the Red Army was seldom involved. The destruction of several million Cambodian citizens by the Khmer Rouge in the late 1970s was carried out for essentially ideological reasons, again under the control and at the initiative of a fanatically motivated Marxist-Leninist-Maoist political movement. It was not an act of conventional war between disciplined military formations of hostile states, nor was it strictly speaking a civil war. The butcher's bill in Afghanistan remains to be calculated. It will not be small.

Political war usually has as its object the destruction of a social order, and the elimination or forcible reorientation of large classes of people. Even in its most restrained forms, as practiced by states acting under the restrictions of rules of just and limited war, it presumes loss of life. Carried out by millenarian movements from motives of race or class hatred, it almost inevitably requires physical elimination of whole categories of human beings, in all age groups and of both sexes. Political war is one of the most destructive and bitter forms of combat, and it remains one of the least successfully regulated. It is a lethal weapon.

In the decades to come, Western statesmen may or may not engage in political war. Those who do so may act from offensive or defensive motives. Whatever their choice, the West's use of political warfare weapons will be purely external. Any massive internal use of propaganda by a Western nation would require an abandonment of the nation's values and a change in its nature comparable to that which occurred in Rome under the Caesars. The prospect is not inconceivable; it is certainly not desirable, nor does it at present seem plausible.

Eastern statesmen, Marxist or otherwise, may after long commitment to an offensive political warfare strategy adopt a posture of strategic defense, or even—conceivably—mothball the weapon for a decade or more. It is difficult to see who among the present Soviet rulers might succeed in scrapping the machinery of propaganda and agitation aimed at controlling the empire's mounting internal tensions. Soviet power was conceived in terms of propaganda as a primary weapon against *both* internal and external disruption. Moscow cannot abandon the instruments of internal propaganda without destroying the empire those instruments bind together or profoundly changing its nature. The proud traditions of Imperial Russia, as well as those of Lenin, make any such prospect highly implausible.

Both West and East may strive to ignore or to deny the existence of political war in their mutual discourse. But if there is to be any genuine hope for reduced tension through the remainder of the century, political warfare, at least in its external form, must become part of the agenda.

NOTES

1 THE NATURE OF POLITICAL WAR

1. There is a precedent for this sense of the term in American practice, euphemisms and neologisms of the past several decades notwithstanding. One of the basic documents creating the US Office of Strategic Services (OSS), issued by the Joint Chiefs of Staff in October 1943, authorized the new agency to maintain liaison with Allied intelligence services, to get information from and give support to underground groups, to conduct propaganda, and to accumulate and analyze economic, political, and military information that would be used to prepare studies on how "*to enforce our will upon the enemy by means other than military action.*" As cited in William Casey, *The Secret War Against Hitler*, Washington DC, Regnery Gateway, 1988, pp. 11-12.

2. Philip Selznik, *The Organizational Weapon: A Study of Bolshevik Strategy and Tactics*, New York NY, Arno Press, 1979, (Rand, 1952), p. 2.

3. See John S. Pustay, *Counterinsurgency Warfare*, New York NY, Free Press, 1965.

4. A recent study by a former staff member of the US Congress notes, "The history of covert action might be loosely grouped into three categories: Propaganda . . . paramilitary operations . . . political action . . . [and] in total numbers, propaganda probably has represented about half of all covert actions in the postwar period, political (and related economic action) a third, and paramilitary operations the remainder, though the last have been the most expensive and often the most controversial." Gregory F. Treverton, *Covert Action: The Limits of Intervention in the Postwar World*, New York NY, Basic Books, 1987, p. 13. The author is speaking of the United States; I know of no comparable estimate for the USSR, but I would not be surprised to discover that the proportional weight of propaganda has been higher in the Soviet case.

5. I have accepted the definition, and accompanying discussion, of Brian Vickers, *In Defence of Rhetoric*, Oxford, Clarendon Press, 1988, p. 1.

6. For an extended discussion, ibid., pp. 83-213.

7. There is no generally accepted definition. For examples see the appropriate entries in major encyclopedias of the world. Soviet usage has distinctive features, as I explain later. For general background, see Harold Lasswell, Ralph Casey,

and Bruce Lannes Smith, eds., *Propaganda and Promotional Activities: An Annotated Bibliography*, Chicago and London, University of Chicago Press, 1969. The term, despite partisan attempts to endow it with pejorative and tendentious connotations, remains in use for serious discourse and official documents, both in the United States and abroad. See, for example, the usage in documentation presented in William M. Leary, ed., *The Central Intelligence Agency: History and Documents*, Montgomery AL, University of Alabama Press, 1984, including the study drafted in 1974 by a staff member of the Church Committee of the US Congress.

8. For US and NATO military usage, see US Department of Defense, Joint Chiefs of Staff Publication 1, *Dictionary of Military and Associated Terms*, Washington DC, USGPO, 1 June 1979. Also, US Department of the Army, *The Art and Science of Psychological Operations: Case Studies of Military Application*, 2 vols., Washington DC, USGPO, 1976.

9. A National Security Council Directive of January 14, 1983 (NSDD77) defines the term as "Those actions of the US Government designed to generate support for our national security objectives." (As cited by Hans N. Tuch in Richard Staar, ed., *Public Diplomacy: USA versus USSR*, Stanford CA, Hoover Institution Press, 1988, p. 52.) See also Gifford Malone, *Organizing the Nation's Public Diplomacy*, Lanham MD, University Press of America, 1988, and Hans N. Tuch, "Public Diplomacy: What It Is and How It Works," in *Murrow Reports: Occasional Papers of the Edward R. Murrow Center of Public Diplomacy*, Tufts University, Medford MA, Fall 1985. In accordance with the NSC practice, these authors use a somewhat broader definition than that stated here. Both distinguish between *public affairs*, which encompasses domestic advocacy, and *public diplomacy*, which should apply only to communication directed abroad.

10. As cited in J. H. Plumb, *England in the Eighteenth Century*, London, Penguin, 1950, p. 21. '

11. From "Windsor Forest" (1704-13). As John Bailey notes in his Introduction to the *Poems of Alexander Pope* (London, Thomas Nelson and Sons, undated), p. viii, "For a century after the Restoration there was in this country such an intimate relation between governing classes and the men of letters as has seldom existed anywhere."

12. William V. O'Brien, *The Conduct of a Just and Limited War*, New York NY, Praeger, 1983, p. 16.

13. Ibid., p. 38.

14. Zbigniew Brzezinski, in Foreword to M. A. Albright, *Poland: The Role of the Press in Political Change*, Center for Strategic and International Studies Paper 102, Georgetown University, Washington DC, 1983.

15. *Bol'shaya Sovetskaya Entsiklopediya* (Great Soviet Encyclopedia), Moscow, BSE Publishing House, third edition, vol. 5, pp. 832-33. As translated into English in the American edition, vol. 5, New York NY, 1979, pp. 646-49. The article is by M. I. Galkin and P. I. Trofimenko.

16. V. I. Lenin, "The Proletarian Revolution and the Renegade Kautsky;" (1917), *Collected Works*, translated by George Hanna, London, Lawrence and Wishart, 1963.

NOTES

17. V. I. Lenin, *Selected Works*, edited by J. Fineberg, New York NY, 1935-1939, vol. 10, p. 91.

18. V. I. Lenin, *Collected Works*, translated by Julius Katzev, April/December 1920, London, Lawrence and Wishart, 1966, vol. 31.

19. V. I. Lenin, *Sochineniye* (Collected Works), Third edition, Leningrad, Partizdat, 1935, vol. 25, p. 36.

20. For English-language translations, see *Current Digest of the Soviet Press* (Columbus OH). An appropriate selection can be found in Albert Weeks and William Bodie, eds., *War and Peace: Soviet Russia Speaks*, New York NY/Washington DC, National Strategy Information Center, 1983.

21. For a discussion by an East European intellectual, see the Introduction by Czeslaw Milosz to Abram Tertz [Andrei Sinyavskiy], *On Socialist Realism*, New York NY, Vintage/Random House, 1960, p. 138.

22. R. H. Bruce Lockhart, *Comes the Reckoning*, London, Putnam, 1947, p. 265.

23. See Gladys D. Ganley and Oswald H. Ganley, *Global Political Fallout: The First Decade of the VCR 1976-1985*, Cambridge MA, Harvard University Center for Information Policy Research, 1987. The authors believe, "this new medium will have an important, perhaps critical, global political impact of wide range and scope."

24. US Central Intelligence Agency Study, "Soviet Covert Action and Propaganda." Presented to the Oversight Subcommittee, Permanent Select Committee on Intelligence, House of Representatives, 6 February 1980, by the Deputy Director for Operations, Central Intelligence Agency. Appendix I to Hearings before the Subcommittee on Oversight . . . Ninety-sixth Congress, Second Session, February 6, 19, 1980, Washington DC, USGPO, 1980, p. 60.

25. In command economies, introduction of new mass communications technology is (usually) strictly controlled; in free-market economies it often has a momentum of its own, as in the case of satellite disk reception. See "A Look at Satellite TV," *Consumer Reports* (Mt. Vernon NY), vol. 51, no. 9, September 1986, p. 617. The asymmetry is noteworthy.

26. Bernard Law Montgomery, *Memoirs*, London and Cleveland OH, 1958, p. 82.

27. *Victory* and *defeat* are not terms in the official US military lexicon. Neither term appears in the *Dictionary of Military and Associated Terms*, JCS Pub. 1.

2   ANTIQUITY

1. Michael Walzer, *Exodus and Revolution*, New York NY, Basic Books, 1984, p. 81.

2. See, for example, Barbara Tuchman, *Bible and Sword: England and Palestine from the Bronze Age to Balfour*, New York NY, Funk & Wagnalls, 1956, ch. 5, "The Bible in English."

3. Karl Marx, *Class Struggles in France*, in *Selected Works*, Moscow, 1951, vol. 1, p. 193, as cited in Walzer, *Exodus and Revolution*, p. 54. Rigorously construed, Marx's teaching rejects the idealist concept of a telos, or ultimate end; yet his concept of historical materialism amounts to much the same thing.

4. The term is used here in its widest sense as a form of syncretistic theosophy diffused throughout the Levantine world rather than the specific cults which went by the name. See Henry Chadwick, *The Early Church*, Harmondsworth/Baltimore, Penguin, 1967, pp. 33-41.

5. Ibid., p. 169.

6. Walzer, *Exodus and Revolution*, p. 102.

7. Joseph Goldberg, *Understanding of Politics in Ancient Israel*, Thesis, Seattle WA, University of Washington, pp. 259, 281, passim.

8. *Oxford Companion to Classical Literature*, Oxford/New York NY, Oxford University Press, 1984, p. 302.

9. Summaries of these concepts may be found under entries for Aristotle, Lucan, Rhetoric, Oratory, and others, in the *Oxford Companion to Classical Literature*. For an extended discussion, see Vickers, *In Defence of Rhetoric*.

10. The episode is a famous one, recounted in most texts on classical Greece. For a summary, see *Oxford Companion to Classical Literature*, p. 141.

11. A discussion of this and other examples of coinage as propaganda can be found in Richard G. Doty, *Money of the World*, New York NY, Grosset and Dunlap, 1978; on the Alexander coinage, see p. 34. Whether the head shown is actually Alexander or an idealized Hercules is disputed, but the effect was the same.

12. *Oxford Companion to Classical Literature*, p. 141.

13. Tacitus, *The Annals of Imperial Rome*, translation by Michael Grant, Harmondsworth/Baltimore, Penguin, 1956. On Roman style in dealing with neighboring peoples, see the example of Tiberius' use of diplomacy, deception, and force against the Parthians (pp. 210-14).

14. The case for continuity has been put concisely by Arnold Toynbee, in *Civilization on Trial*, New York NY, Oxford University Press, 1948, ch. 9, "Russia's Byzantine Heritage." Toynbee's judgment has been the topic of much debate by later scholars, some of whom have offered useful qualification but few of whom have (in my view) refuted his basic thesis. See also Nicholas Berdyaev, *The Russian Idea* (1947), Boston MA, Beacon Press, 1962, and Nicholas Berdyaev, *The Origin of Russian Communism* (1937), Ann Arbor MI, University of Michigan Press, 1966. A different view of Byzantium and its heritage, influenced by the *Annales* school of structural analysis, will be found in Alexander Kazhdan and Giles Constable, *People and Power in Byzantium*, Washington DC, Dumbarton Oaks Center for Byzantine Studies, Harvard University, 1982.

15. See Michael Grant, *The Roman Emperors: A Biographical Guide to the Rulers of Imperial Rome 31 BC-476 AD*, New York NY, Scribner's, 1985, pp. 227-33. On Constantine's military policy, see Edward N. Luttwak, *The Grand Strategy of the Roman Empire: From the First Century AD to the Third*, Baltimore MD/London, Johns Hopkins University Press, 1976. On the political and religious relationships, see Chadwick, *The Early Church*, pp. 125- 29. For

the cultural background of early imperial Rome, see Michael Grant, *The World of Rome*, New York NY, World, 1960, part 4, "Literature and the Arts."

16. See B. H. Liddell Hart, *Strategy*, second revised edition, New York NY, Praeger/Signet Reprint, 1974, ch. 4, "Byzantine Wars—Belisarius and Narses," pp. 39-54.

3   THE REFORMATION

1. As cited in Herbert Richmond, *Statesmen and Seapower*, Oxford University Press, 1946. For a discussion of the context, see Michael Howard, "The British Way in Warfare: A Reappraisal," in *The Causes of Wars and Other Essays*, Cambridge MA, Harvard University Press, 1984, p. 181.

2. Thomas Heywood, *An Apology for Actors*, London, 1612, as cited in A. L. Rowse, *William Shakespeare: A Biography*, New York NY, Harper and Row, 1963, p. 411. See also Roy Strong, *Splendor at Court: Renaissance Spectacle and the Theater of Power*, Boston MA, Houghton Mifflin, 1973.

3. Paul Johnson, *Elizabeth I*, New York NY, Holt Rinehart & Winston, 1974, p. 234.

4. G. B. Harrison, *Introducing Shakespeare*, New York, NY, Penguin, 1947, p. 16.

5. Rowse, *William Shakespeare*, p. 359.

6. Harrison, *Introducing Shakespeare*, p. 52.

7. Shakespeare was a master of classical rhetoric, using a rich variety of techniques extending far beyond those noted here. An instructive listing of rhetorical figures and tropes, all illustrated from Shakespeare's works, can be found in Vickers, *In Defence of Rhetoric*, pp. 491-98.

8. Critics have long been impressed by Shakespeare's skill in characterization. Samuel Johnson, for example, observed in his *Preface to Shakespeare* (1765), "In the writings of other poets a character is too often an individual; in those of Shakespeare it is commonly a species." D. Nichol Smith, ed., *Shakespeare Criticism: A Selection*, Oxford University Press, 1946, p. 80.

9. C. W. Hodges, *The Globe Restored*, p. 15, as cited in Rowse, *William Shakespeare*, p. 291.

10. For detailed sources, see Alfred Harbage, *Shakespeare's Audience*, New York NY, Columbia University Press, 1941 (1958), pp. 86-87.

11. See the Introduction by A. L. Rowse to Emilia [Bassano] Lanier, *The Poems of Shakespeare's Dark Lady: Salve Deus Rex Judaeorum*, New York NY, Charles N. Potter, 1979.

12. Rowse, *William Shakespeare*, p. 291.

13. For background to the political and military events of this period, see Geoffrey Parker, *Europe in Crisis 1598-1648*, Ithaca NY, Cornell University Press, 1979, pp. 131-44. The diplomatic history is described in Conyers Read, *Mr. Secretary Walsingham, and The Policy of Queen Elizabeth*, 3 vols., Oxford,

Clarendon Press, 1925, and ibid., *Lord Burghley and Queen Eilzabeth*, London, Jonathan Cape, 1960.

14. For background on the Elizabethan age, see S. T. Bindoff, *Tudor England*, Harmondsworth/Baltimore, Penguin, 1950, and A. L. Rowse, *The Expansion of Elizabethan England*, London/New York NY, Macmillan, 1965. For the Jacobean context, see C. V. Wedgewood, *The Thirty Years War* (1938), New York NY, Anchor Books, 1956, and Sir George Clark, *The Seventeenth Century*, Second Edition, Oxford University Press, 1947/1969.

15. Sir John Harington (1561-1612), as cited in Rowse, *William Shakespeare*, pp. 129-30. For a more skeptical view of Elizabeth's political style than that taken by Harington (and his biographer, Rowse), see Charles Wilson, *Queen Elizabeth and the Revolt of the Netherlands*, Berkeley CA, University of California Press, 1970, p. 6, passim.

16. G. M. Thompson, *Sir Francis Drake*, London, Futura, 1976, offers a compelling account of the role of Walsingham's intelligence organization and the struggle between him and Burghley over policy toward Spain and the effect upon it of Drake's operations in the Americas.

17. Marjorie Cox, "The Background to English Literature: 1603-1660," in Boris Ford, *The Pelican Guide to English Literature, vol. 3, From Donne to Marvell*, Harmondsworth/Baltimore, Penguin, 1979, pp. 27-28.

18. As excerpted in M. H. Abrams, et. al., eds., *The Norton Anthology of English Literature*, fourth ed., vol. 1, New York NY, Norton, 1979, p. 1034.

19. As cited in H. G. Koenigsberger, "Philip II," in *Encyclopedia Britannica* (1968), vol. 17, p. 841.

20. As cited in Sir Charles Petrie, *Philip II of Spain*, London, Eyre & Spottiswoode, 1964, p. 184. Petrie's view of Philip is basically sympathetic. For a more hostile version, see the account written by William the Silent, who led the Dutch revolt against Philip (and was assassinated by Philip's agents in 1584): *The Apologia of 1580 of William of Orange*, in John C. Rule and John J. TePaske, *The Character of Philip II: The Problem of Moral Judgments in History*, Boston MA, D. C. Heath and Co., 1963, pp. 8-10.

21. A vivid, authentic, albeit partisan account by a participant in the English Jesuit operation can be found in *The Hunted Priest: Autobiography of John Gerrard*, translated by Philip Caraman, SJ, introduction by Graham Greene, London, Fontana, 1959. For a scholarly appraisal of the operation and its political context, see the biography of Father Robert Parsons, SJ, by A. L. Rowse, *Eminent Elizabethans*, Athens GA, University of Georgia Press, 1983, pp. 41-74.

22. T. S. Healy, SJ, *John Donne: Ignatius His Conclave*, London/New York, Oxford University Press, 1969, p. 131.

23. John Donne, *Pseudo-Martyr. Wherein out of certaine Propositions and Gradations, This Conclusion is evicted. That those which are of the Romane Religion in this Kingdom, may and ought to take the Oath of Allegeance*, London, 1610.

24. Paul Johnson, *Elizabeth I*, New York NY, Holt Rinehart & Winston, 1974, pp. 277, 470, citing *CSP Domestic*, vol. 232, no. 12, and Conyers Read, *Mr Secretary Walsingham*, III.

25. A. L. Rowse, *Christopher Marlowe; His Life and Work*, New York NY, Harper and Row, 1964.

26. Edward Lucie-Smith, ed., *Penguin Book of Elizabethan Verse*, London/Baltimore, Penguin, 1965, pp. 272-74, has samples of his poetry.

27. "When the [Elizabethan] bishops made a survey of religious loyalties in 1564, they discovered that, of 850 JPs [Justices of the Peace] surveyed, only about half supported the regime in religion; 264 were set down as neutral, and 157 as definitely hostile." Mary Bateson, ed., "A Collection of Original Letters from the Bishops to the Privy Council," *Camden Miscellany* 9 (London, 1895), as cited in Paul Johnson, *Elizabeth I*, London/New York, Holt Rinehart & Winston, 1974, p. 152. See also Petrie, *Philip II of Spain*, p. 72, who notes, "the greater part of the [English] nation was probably still Catholic."

28. A letter from Philip II to his Council of September 26, 1593, commands them to "wholly rid themselves, in all affairs, of passion and affection and of private interest or aims, looking only to the service of God and the good of my affairs and of those of these realms and the others beyond, which are all one." See text in L. Cabrera de Cordoba, *Felipe II, Rey de Espana*, vol. IV, pp. 67-68, as cited in Petrie, *Philip II of Spain*, p. 309.

29. John Buchan, *Cromwell*, London, Sphere Books, 1970, p. 37.

30. Isaac Walton, *The Life and Death of Dr. John Donne*, London, 1640, reprint of the 1675 edition in the World's Classics Series, Oxford University Press, 1962, pp. 44-45.

31. Healy, *John Donne: Ignatius His Conclave*, p. xxvi.

32. Ibid., pp. xi-xvii.

33. Donne's essays, sermons, and political satires offer a rich conspectus of rhetorical techniques in the English idiom. For samples, see John Donne, *Selected Prose: Chosen by Evelyn Simpson, Edited by Helen Gardner and Timothy Healy*, London, Oxford University Press, 1967. For a biography, see John Carey, *John Donne: Life, Mind and Art*, London/New York, Oxford University Press, 1981.

34. See Petrie, *Philip II of Spain*, pp. 280-81.

35. Rowse, *Expansion of Elizabethan England*, p. 311.

36. Petrie, (*Philip II of Spain*, p. 188) notes, "it will be a mistake to conclude that [Philip's] proceeding, or even the Inquisition itself, was unpopular with Spaniards. On the contrary, Philip seems in this, as in most other things, to have been a perfect embodiment of the feeling of his country at the time."

37. Rowse, *Expansion of Elizabethan England*, p. 332.

38. Ibid., p. 243. See also Rowse, *Christopher Marlowe*, p. 86.

39. A. O. Meyer, *England and the Catholic Church Under Elizabeth*, translation by J. R. McKee, London, 1916, pp. 269-71, 489-91, as cited in Johnson, *Elizabeth I*, pp. 241, 468. The Meyer book carries the imprimatur of the Catholic authorities.

40. Rowse, *Expansion of Elizabethan England*, p. 364.

41. For a sympathetic account, in a larger context, see Petrie, *Philip II of Spain*.

42. Milton's propaganda role has been documented in most standard biographies. On Thurloe, see Buchan, *Cromwell*, p. 457.

43. John Milton, *Areopagitica* (1644), in K. M. Burton, ed., *Prose Writings by John Milton*, London/New York, Everyman, 1958, p. 180.

44. On the growth of a popular press and its use for propaganda, see Maurice Ashley, *England in the Seventeenth Century*, Harmondsworth/Baltimore, Penguin, 1952; also, J. M. Clyde, "Parliament and the Press," *Transactions of the Bibliographical Society*, March and June 1933, and Clyde, "Struggle for the Freedom of the Press," 1934, as cited in Buchan, *Cromwell*, p. 264. For more recent scholarship on the period and the press, see J. P. Kenyon, *Stuart England*, Harmondsworth/Baltimore, Penguin, 1978, p. 349.

45. Maurice Ashley, *The English Civil War*, London, Thames and Hudson, 1974, p. 124.

46. Buchan, *Cromwell*, p. 493.

47. Ibid., p. 466.

48. Ibid., p. 330. On extremists in the New Model Army, see G. E. Aylmer, ed., *The Levellers in the English Revolution*, Ithaca NY, Cornell University Press, 1975. The idiom of political radicalism in the context of military discipline is instructive, as were Cromwell's methods for dealing with it.

49. Buchan, *Cromwell*, p. 347.

4   THE NAPOLEONIC ERA

1. Carl von Clausewitz, *On War* (1832), Paret and Howard translation, Princeton NJ, Princeton University Press, 1975, book 1, ch. 1, p. 87.

2. Ibid., book 6, p. 370.

3. Edmund Burke, *Letter on a Regicide Peace* (1796-97).

4. Burke wrote extensively on the French Revolution and its philosophic origins. For a selection, see Edmund Burke, *Selected Writings and Speeches*, edited by Peter J. Stanlis, Chicago IL, Regnery Gateway, 1963.

5. G. Vellay, ed., *Discourses et Rapports de Robespierre*, Paris, 1908, p. 332.

6. As cited in J. H. Plumb, *England in the Eighteenth Century*, London, Penguin, 1950, p. 210.

7. Gustave Le Bon, *The Crowd: A Study of the Popular Mind*, (1895), translation and introduction by R. K. Merton, New York NY, Viking Press, 1960, p. 19.

8. As cited in David Thomson, *England in the Nineteenth Century*, London, Penguin, 1950, p. 226.

9. Ibid., p. 555.

10. Le Bon, *The Crowd*, p. 31.

11. Ibid., p. 6.

12. See James H. Billington, *Fire in the Minds of Men: Origins of Revolutionary Faith*, New York NY, Basic Books, 1980, ch. 11, "The Magic Medium: Journalism," pp. 306-23.

5   WORLD WAR I

1. Paul von Hindenburg, *Out of My Life*, London, Carrell & Co., 1920.

2. As cited in a newspaper interview granted to the *Berlin Morgenpost*, August 25, 1918.

3. Erich Ludendorff, *My War Memoirs 1914-1918*, London, 1919. For an assessment of these German opinions by one of the British propaganda leaders, see Sir Campbell Stuart, *Secrets of Crewe House: The Story of a Famous Campaign*, 2d ed., London, Hodder and Stoughton, 1920, pp. 93, 120, 128.

4. Michael Howard, "Strategy and Policy in Contemporary Warfare," in Michael Howard, ed., *Studies in War and Peace*, New York NY, Viking Press, 1971, p. 191.

5. CMND 9161, 1918, as cited in Cate Haste, *Keep the Home Fires Burning*, London, Allen Lane, 1977, p. 21.

6. Stuart, *Secrets of Crewe House*, pp. 207-08.

7. Ibid., p. 2.

8. Heinrich Kessmeier, *Der Feldzug mit der Anderen Waffe*, Hamburg, Falken Verlag, 1940.

9. David Lloyd George, *War Memoirs*, vol. 2, London, Odhams Press Limited, 1942 (1936), pp. 1873-74.

10. Ibid.

11. See Christopher Andrew, *Her Majesty's Secret Service: The Making of the British Intelligence Community*, New York NY, Viking, 1986, chapter 7.

12. Ibid., p. 288.

13. See A. J. P. Taylor, *Beaverbrook*, New York NY, Simon and Schuster, 1972, pp. 144-48, for a summation of Beaverbrook's role, the relations among the three arms, and some information on the Ministry of Information's staffing and operations. The citation here is on p. 148.

14. For figures on these and other operations, and a dispassionate appraisal of the impact, see George G. Bruntz, *Allied Propaganda and the Collapse of the German Empire in 1918*, Hoover War Library Publications No. 13, Stanford CA, Stanford University Press/London, Oxford University Press, 1938, reprint by Arno Press, New York NY, 1972.

15. Wickham Steed presented the basic policy proposal to Northcliffe in mid-February 1918. See text in W. Steed, *My War Memoirs*, London, 1919, vol. 2, pp. 187-88. On the debate that followed with the Foreign Office, see Z. A. B. Zeman, *Breakup of the Hapsburg Empire 1914-1918*, London, Oxford University Press, 1961/New York NY, Octagon Books, 1977, pp. 186-89.

16. Leo Valiani, *The End of Austria-Hungary*, New York NY, Knopf, 1973, pp. 235-36.

17. Ibid., p. 237.

18. Arthur J. May, *The Passing of the Hapsburg Monarchy 1914-1918*, Philadephia PA, University of Pennsylvania Press, 1968, vol. 2, p. 720.

19. Ibid., p. 597.

20. Leo Valiani, *The End of Austria-Hungary*, pp. 238-40.

21. The term *organizational weapon* has a specific meaning in political warfare. For an analysis of the basic concept see Philip Selznik, *The Organizational Weapon: A Study of Bolshevik Strategy and Tactics*, New York NY, Arno Press, 1979 (Free Press, 1960; Rand, 1952), pp. 2-3. In sum, it means "organizations and organizational practices . . . used [as weapons] by a power-seeking elite in a manner unrestrained by the constitutional order of the arena within which the contest takes place. . . . In this usage 'weapon' is not meant to denote *any* political tool, but one torn from its normal context and unacceptable to the community as a legitimate mode of action." Allied use of Austro-Hungarian emigre groups in 1918 clearly falls within this definition, even though the term was not yet current.

22. For a discussion of the political context for Allied operations, particularly the Italo-Yugoslav situation, see May, *Passing of the Hapsburg Monarchy*, vol. 2, pp. 595-611, 820-21.

23. J. A. Spender, *Fifty Years of Europe*, p. 389, as cited in Thomson, *England in the Nineteenth Century*, p. 211.

24. On England, see Thomson, *England in the Nineteenth Century*, p. 176; on Austria-Hungary, see Zeman, *The Breakup of the Hapsburg Empire*, ch. 1, "Before the War." See also, John Williams, *The Other Battleground: The Home Fronts: Britain, France and Germany 1914-1918*, Chicago IL, Regnery, 1972.

25. A. J. P. Taylor, *The Hapsburg Monarchy: 1809-1918*, Harmondsworth, Penguin, 1964, p. 264.

26. As cited in S. T. H. Wilton, "World War I," *Encyclopedia Britannica* (1968), vol. 23, p. 714.

6   MARXISM-LENINISM

1. For a philosopher's view, see Hannah Arendt, *The Origins of Totalitarianism*, new edition with added prefaces, New York NY, Harcourt Brace Jovanovich, 1973. For a journalist's perspective on the Italian and German variants and their influence on various European countries, see Elizabeth Wiskemann, *Fascism in Italy: Its Development and Influence*, second edition, London/New York, Macmillan/St Martin's Press, 1970.

2. Introduction by A. J. P. Taylor to Karl Marx and Friedrich Engels, *The Communist Manifesto* (1848), Harmondsworth/Baltimore, Penguin, 1967, p. 27.

3. V. I. Lenin, Speech to the 8th Soviet Congress, December 22, 1920, *Selected Works*, vol. 8, pp. 257-65, as cited in Nathan Leites, *A Study of Bolshevism*, Glencoe IL, Free Press, 1953, p. 374.

4. RSFSR Criminal Code of May 1922, as cited in Y. Felshtinsky, "The Legal Foundations of the Immigration and Emigration Policy of the USSR 1917-1927," *Soviet Studies* (Glasgow), July 1982.

5. As interviewed in *The Proletarian Revolution* (Moscow), no. 10, October 1922, p. 99, as cited in Adam Ulam, *Expansion and Coexistence: Soviet Foreign Policy 1917-1973*, second edition, New York NY, Praeger, 1974, p. 54.

6. For an introduction to the voluminous scholarship on the early history of the Comintern, see Ulam, *Expansion and Coexistence*, pp. 111-25. The organization as such no longer exists, and the ninety or more parties that grew out of it are known today in Moscow as the "world revolutionary process." For an account of its history and of the Soviet party organ responsible for relations with it today, see Robert W. Kitrinos, "International Department of the CPSU," *Problems of Communism* (Washington DC), September-October 1984, pp. 47-75.

7. Berdyaev wrote perceptively on a wide range of philosophical issues. Those interested in this aspect of his work may wish to look at his *The Origin of Russian Communism*, translated by R. M. French, Ann Arbor MI, University of Michigan Press, 1960. For a different view, see John Dunlop, *The Faces of Contemporary Russian Nationalism*, Princeton NJ, Princeton University Press, 1983, pp. 284, passim.

8. Signal intercept, as decrypted by Britain's GC & CS, cited in Andrew, *Her Majesty's Secret Service*, p. 262.

9. Ibid., pp. 267-68.

10. The distinction is an important one for political warfare analysis. For a discussion of it in another context, see Ernst Kris and Hans Speier, *German Radio Propaganda: Report on Home Broadcasts During the War*, London, Oxford University Press, 1944, pp. 213-32.

11. V. I. Lenin, "The Terms of Admission into the Communist International," in *Collected Works*, vol. 31, Moscow, Foreign Languages Publishing House, 1960, p. 208; and "Statutes of the Communist International Adopted at the Second Comintern Congress," in Jane Degras, *The Communist International: 1919-1943, Documents*, vol. 1, Oxford University Press, 1956, p. 163.

12. Karl Marx, "Victory of the Counterrevolution in Vienna," *Neue Rheinische Zeitung*, no. 136, November 7, 1848, as reprinted in Karl Marx and Friedrich Engels, *Collected Works*, vol. 7, 1848, New York NY, International Publishers, 1977, p. 506.

13. Grigori Zinoviev, Speech, reported in *Severnaia Kommuna* (Petrograd), no. 109, September 19, 1918, p. 2, as cited in G. Leggett, *The Cheka: Lenin's Political Police*, London/New York, Oxford University Press, 1981, p. 114.

14. Felix Dzerzhinskiy, Press Interview, June 1917, as cited in Ronald Hingley, *The Russian Secret Police; Muscovite, Imperial Russian, and Soviet Political Security Operations 1565-1970*, London, Hutchinson, 1970, p. 122.

15. Ukrainian losses have been the subject of recent investigation in the light of general concern over genocidal acts. See James E. Mace, "Famine and Nationalism in Soviet Ukraine," *Problems of Communism* (Washington DC), May-June 1984, pp. 37-50; for other periods see S. Maksudov, "Losses Suffered

by the Population of the USSR in 1918-1958," *Cahiers du Monde Russe et Sovietique* (Paris), no. 3, 1977. For a definitive overview in English, see Murray Feshbach, *The Soviet Union: Population Trends and Dilemmas*, Washington DC, Population Reference Bureau Inc., vol. 37, no. 3, August 1982, pp. 6-7.

16. Winston Churchill, *The Hinge of Fate*, Boston MA, Houghton Mifflin, 1950, p. 498. The statement was made to Churchill during his visit to Moscow in 1944.

17. Leonard Schapiro, *The Communist Party of the Soviet Union*, London, Eyre and Spottiswoode, 1960, p. 386; and Lev Kopelev, *The Education of a True Believer*, New York NY, Harper and Row, 1980, pp. 224-86.

18. See, for example, Phillip Knightley, *The First Casualty: From the Crimea to Vietnam: The War Correspondent as Hero, Propagandist, and Myth Maker*, New York NY, Harcourt Brace Jovanovich, 1975, ch. 7, "The Remedy for Bolshevism is Bullets 1917-1919," pp. 137-70.

19. For an introduction to scholarship on the central organs of the CPSU, see Leonard Schapiro, *The Communist Party of the Soviet Union*, pp. 447ff; for an extended description of Moscow's central organs for the conduct of political war today, see Richard H. Shultz and Roy Godson, *Dezinformatsia: Active Measures in Soviet Strategy*, Washington DC, Pergamon-Brassey's, 1984.

20. For a summary of basic historical statistics on the growth of Soviet communications media, see Ellen Mickiewicz, *Handbook of Soviet Social Science Data*, New York NY, Free Press, 1973, pp. 177-94.

21. Ljlita Dzirkals, Thane Gustafson, and A. Ross Johnson, *The Media and Intra-Elite Communication in the USSR*, Santa Monica CA, Rand Corporation, 1983. See also Leonid Vladimirov, "Problems of the Soviet Journalist," *Conflict Studies* (London), no. 56, April, 1975, pp. 3-10.

22. *The Washington Post* (Washington DC), August 21, 1988.

23. For a summary of Bajanov's interrogation by British officers in India, see Gordon Brook-Shepherd, *The Storm Petrels: The Flight of the First Soviet Defectors*, New York/London, Harcourt Brace Jovanovich, 1977, pp. 36-39.

24. Bertolt Brecht, *Die Massnahme: Kritische Ausgabe mit Einer Spielanleitung von Reiner Steinweg* (The Admininstrative Measure: Critical Edition with an Introduction to the Play by Reiner Steinweg), Frankfurt am Main, Suhrkampf Verlag, 1972 (from the 1930 edition text).

25. Ruth Fischer, *Stalin and German Communism: A Study in the Origins of the Party State*, Cambridge MA, Harvard University Press, 1948, p. 624.

26. For a classic portrayal, in English, see Arthur Koestler, *Darkness at Noon* (1941), New York/London, Bantam Books, 1975. The characters in the work are fictitious, but "the historical circumstances which determined their actions are real. . . . Several of them were personally known to the author," according to Koestler's foreword. For corroborative memorial accounts, see, among others, Elizabeth Poretsky, *Our Own People: A Memoir of Ignace Reiss and His Friends*, London, Oxford University Press, 1969; and, Walter G. Krivitsky, *In Stalin's Secret Service: An Expose of Russia's Secret Policies by the Former Chief of the Soviet Intelligence in Western Europe*, New York NY, Harper, 1939.

27. Mace, "Famine and Nationalism in Soviet Ukraine," p. 38.

28. Malcolm Muggeridge, *Winter in Moscow*, Boston MA, Little Brown, 1934, pp. 39-57, 150, et passim; Muggeridge, *Chronicles of Wasted Time*, vol. 1, *The Green Stick*, New York NY, William Morrow, 1973, pp. 205-76.

29. Paul Hollander, *Political Pilgrims: Travels of Western Intellectuals to the Soviet Union, China, and Cuba 1928-78*, London/New York, Oxford University Press, 1981.

30. An intimate but partisan account of Willi Muenzenberg's life has been published by his widow. See Babette Gross, *Willi Muenzenberg: Eine politische Biographie, mit einem Vorwaert von Arthur Koestler*, Stuttgart, Deutsche Verlags-Anstalt, 1967.

31. For an authentic personal account, see Krivitsky, *In Stalin's Secret Service*. For additional evidence, both primary and secondary, see Witold S. Sworakowski, *The Communist International and Its Front Organizations: A Research Guide and Checklist of Holdings in American and European Libraries*, Stanford CA, Hoover Institution, 1965; and Branko Lazitch in collaboration with Milorad M. Drachkovitch, *Biographical Dictionary of the Comintern*, Stanford CA, Hoover Institution, 1973.

32. Cited in David Dallin, *Soviet Espionage*, New Haven CT, Yale University Press, 1955, p. 16.

33. J. Peters, *The Communist Party: A Manual on Organization*, New York NY, Workers' Library Publishers, no date. A description of this publication, now a bibliographic rarity, will be found in Alan Weinstein, *Perjury*, New York NY, Vintage Press, 1979, p. 61. The description in Weinstein's book of the handling of Whittaker Chambers by Comintern and Soviet intelligence operators gives some indication of the problem of coordination, a problem that contributed to the defection of Chambers and others from the apparatus.

34. Solidly researched studies of the diplomatic history exist, but even the best offer sparse coverage of the political warfare dimension. One of the best is Ulam, *Expansion and Coexistence*; its index contains no entry for *propaganda*.

35. Both Fischer (*Stalin and German Communism*) and Krivitsky (*In Stalin's Secret Service*) offer eyewitness evidence of Stalin's moves toward an early accommodation with the Nazis, in the German case at the expense of those German Communist Party leaders who resisted his policies. See also Raymond James Sontag and James Stuart Beddie, eds., *Nazi-Soviet Relations 1939-1941: Documents From the Archives of the German Foreign Office*, Washington DC, US Department of State, 1948, for a documented account of the outcome.

7   THE NAZIS

1. For an analysis of these similarities and differences, see Arendt, *The Origins of Totalitarianism*.

2. Alex Alexiev, *Soviet Nationalities in German Wartime Strategy, 1941-1945*, Santa Monica CA, Rand Corporation, August 1982, p. 3.

3. For an authentic account of these forces by a German Army interpreter who worked with them, see Sven Steenberg, *Vlasov*, New York NY, Alfred A. Knopf, 1970.

4. For further analysis of some of the points in this chapter, see Michael Mihalka, *German Strategic Deception in the 1930s*, Santa Monica CA, Rand Corporation, Note N-1557-NA, July 1980. For the larger strategic background, see B. H. Liddell Hart, *Strategy*, second revised edition, London, Faber and Faber, 1967, New York NY, Praeger, 1974, particularly part 3, "Strategy of the Second World War."

5. For further exploration of the relationship between German wartime strategy and the regime's propaganda themes, see one of the seminal works in the field by Alexander L. George, *Propaganda Analysis: A Study of Inferences Made from Nazi Propaganda in World War II*, Evanston IL, Row, Peterson and Co., 1959, particularly pp. 16, 24. See also Kris and Speier, *German Radio Propaganda.*

6. This paradox has been noted by various observers, perhaps most trenchantly by Eberhard Jaeckel, *Hitler in History*, Hanover VT, University of Brandeis Press, 1984, p. 89.

7. The British side of the affair has been described in a memoir by one of the participants, Group Captain F. W. Winterbotham, in *The Nazi Connection*, New York/London, Harper and Row, 1978. His appreciation, in 1938, of the Nazi timetable is given on pp. 170-78.

8. A full description, based on research in both German and American archives, can be found in Klaus Kipphan, *Deutsche Propaganda in den Vereinigten Staaten 1933-1941* (German Propaganda in the United States 1933-1941), Heidelberg, Carl Winter Universitaets Verlag, 1971.

9. For a reprint, with commentary by an American historian, of selected issues of the English-language edition, see S. L. Mayer, ed., *Signal: Hitler's Wartime Picture Magazine*, Englewood Cliffs NJ, Prentice-Hall, 1976.

10. For an account of one of the channels to the United States, see Alan Dulles, *The Secret Surrender*, New York NY, Harper and Row, 1966. A separate channel to the British—which may or may not have been known to Hitler—was conducted by Abwehr Chief Canaris personally. Activated just prior to the June 1944 Normandy landing, it led nowhere. Canaris commented, on receiving a reply from his London contact, *"Finis Germaniae."* See Anthony Cave Brown, *C: The Secret Life of Sir Stewart Graham Menzies, Spymaster to Winston Churchill*, New York NY, Macmillan, 1987, pp. 583-92.

11. Winston S. Churchill, *Great Contemporaries* (1937), London, Fontana Books, 1959, p. 213.

12. As cited in D. Cameron Watt, *Succeeding John Bull: America in Britain's Place 1900-1975*, Cambridge/New York NY, Cambridge University Press, 1984, p. 63.

13. Ibid.

14. Arendt, *The Origins of Totalitarianism*, p. 351.

15. As cited in Hermann Rauschning, *Voice of Destruction*, New York NY, G. P. Putnam, 1940.

16. For background on the political and strategic significance of these events, see Liddell Hart, *Strategy*. Another useful summation is that by a senior historian in the Office of Military History of the US Army, Maurice Matloff, published in "Strategy," *Encyclopedia Britannica* (1968), vol. 21, p. 295.

17. R. H. Bruce Lockhart, *Comes the Reckoning*, London, Putnam, 1947, p. 23.

18. Ibid., p. 13.

19. For an authoritative account of these relationships in wartime London, see ibid.

20. Alan Bullock, *Hitler: A Study in Tyranny*, revised edition, New York NY, Bantam, 1961, p. 32.

21. Kris and Speier, *German Radio Propaganda*, p. 24.

22. For an extended analysis see Z. A. B. Zeman, *Nazi Propaganda*, London/New York NY, Oxford University Press, 1964.

23. Mayer, *Signal: Hitler's Wartime Picture Magazine*.

24. For a concise summary of Goebbels' strategic views in comparison to Hitler's, see Wilfred Knapp, "Goebbels," *Encyclopedia Britannica* (1968), vol. 10, p. 521. Goebbels' own perceptions, relatively uninhibited, can be found in the volumes of his personal office diary recovered after 1945. See Louis Lochner, ed., *The Goebbels Diaries*, New York NY, Doubleday, 1948; Fred Taylor, ed., *The Goebbels Diaries 1939-1941*, New York NY, Putnam, 1982; Hugh Trevor-Roper, ed., *Final Entries 1945: The Diaries of Joseph Goebbels*, New York NY, Putnam, 1978.

25. The importance of visual and architectural means in totalitarian propaganda is often underrated in the English-speaking world. For a sensitive and thoughtful account, in retrospect, of what it meant in Nazi Germany, see Albert Speer, *Inside the Third Reich*, translated by Richard and Clara Winston, New York NY, Macmillan, 1970. The photos following p. 166, including models for the Nuremberg stadium, are noteworthy.

26. See M. Balfour, *Propaganda in War 1939-1945*, London, Routledge Kegan Paul, 1979, p. 14.

8   BRITAIN AND AMERICA IN WORLD WAR II

1. Sir John Reith in a memo of April 1940, as cited in Ian McLaine, *Ministry of Morale*, London, George Allen Unwin, 1979, p. 56.

2. As cited by Sir John Colville in *The Fringes of Power: 10 Downing Street Diaries 1939-1955*, New York NY, Norton, 1985, p. 212 (entry for August 8, 1940).

3. See Clausewitz, *On War*, and Liddell Hart, *Strategy*.

4. Bruce Lockhart, *Comes the Reckoning*, p. 158.

5. The confusion and uncertainty over such net assessment problems in the British political leadership is described, in Winston Churchill's *The Gathering Storm*, Boston MA, Houghton Mifflin, 1948; see also, F. W. Winterbotham, *The*

Nazi Connection, for a personal memoir by one of the Air Staff intelligence officers responsible for making the assessment.

6. See Andrew Boyle's biography of Brendan Bracken, entitled *Poor Dear Brendan*, London, Hutchinson, 1974, p. 267.

7. Harold Nicolson, *Diaries and Letters 1939-1945*, New York NY, Fontana, 1970, p. 68.

8. Bruce Lockhart, *Comes the Reckoning*, p. 68; also pp. 126-27, 170-71, 180-81.

9. Charles Cruickshanks, *The Fourth Arm: Psychological Warfare 1938-1945*, London, Oxford University Press, 1981, p. 44.

10. Bruce Lockhart, *Comes the Reckoning*, p. 202.

11. Nicolson, *Diaries and Letters 1939-1945*, p. 354. See also Bruce Lockhart, *Comes the Reckoning*, p. 330.

12. Ibid., p. 338.

13. Daniel Lerner, *Psychological Warfare Against Nazi Germany: The Sykewar Campaign, D-Day to VE-Day*, Cambridge MA, MIT Press, 1949/1971.

14. The bibliography on these organizations is copious but fragmentary. Among the original sources, several stand out: on PWE, Bruce Lockhart, *Comes the Reckoning*; on SOE, M. R. D. Foot, *Resistance*, London, Grenada, 1978; and on OSS, Corey Ford, *Donovan of OSS*, Boston MA, Little Brown, 1971. On OWI, Alan M. Winkler, *The Politics of Propaganda: The Office of War Information 1942-1945*, New Haven/London, Yale University Press, 1978, is carefully researched, although not written by a participant. For a recent reprise, from the perspective of a senior American intelligence official, who had served on the OSS staff in London, see Casey, *The Secret War Against Hitler*.

15. The political framework to these events can be found in any of the standard histories of the period and in the voluminous literature on the Yalta accord. For a remarkably insightful eyewitness account by a Polish Home Army officer active in both London and Warsaw, including the 1944 uprising, see Jan Nowak, *Courier From Warsaw*, Detroit MI, Wayne State University Press, 1982. See also Josef Garlinski, *Poland, SOE and the Allies*, London, Allen Unwin, 1969.

16. For an overview account, see Ulam, *Expansion and Coexistence*, ch. 8. For an eyewitness account of the process in, for example, the Soviet-occupied parts of Germany, see Wolfgang Leonhard, *Child of the Revolution*, London, Collins, 1957.

17. The definitive work is Asa Briggs, *The History of Broadcasting in the United Kingdom*, 3 vols., vol. 3, *The War of Words*, London/New York, Oxford University Press, 1970.

18. For an inside view, admittedly sympathetic but not uncritical, see Gerrard Mansell, *Let Truth Be Told: 50 Years of BBC External Broadcasting*, London, Weidenfeld and Nicolson, 1982.

19. Hugh Dalton, *Memoirs*, 3 vols., vol. 2, *The Fateful Years*, London, 1957, p. 366.

20. On broadcasting, see Sefton Delmer, *Black Boomerang*, New York NY, Viking, 1962; on print media, see Ellic Howe, *The Black Game*, London, Michael Joseph, 1982.

21. Lerner, *Psychological Warfare Against Nazi Germany*. Coordination between psywar operations and the officially designated unit for deception operations was not well developed. See J. C. Masterman, *The Double Cross System*, New Haven CT, Yale University Press, 1972, New York NY, Avon Books, 1972, pp. 51-52.

22. B. Pimlott, ed., *The Second World War Diary of Hugh Dalton*, p. 60, as cited in Anthony Glees, *The Secrets of the Service*, London, Jonathan Cape, 1988, pp. 81, 406.

23. J. G. Beevor, *SOE: Recollections and Reflections 1940- 1945*, London, Bodley Head, 1981, pp. 96-97.

24. Colville, *The Fringes of Power*, pp. 463-64.

25. For an exploration of the fragmented documentation in the public domain, plus commentary by a number of the participants, see Phyllis Auty and Richard Clogg, eds., *British Policy Towards Wartime Resistance in Yugoslavia and Greece*, New York NY, Harper & Row, 1975. The Afterword by G. H. N. Seton-Watson ventures a convincing but still tentative summing up.

26. See Walter R. Roberts, *Tito, Mihailovic and the Allies 1941-1945*, New Brunswick NJ, Rutgers University Press, 1973.

27. Mansell, *Let Truth Be Told*, p. 172.

28. I would be grateful for suggested sources of evidence on wartime attention in the Balkans to German, and Italian, occupation propaganda. The little I have seen is too inconclusive to justify mention here.

29. S. W. Bailey, "British Policy Towards General Draza Mihailovic," in Auty and Clogg, eds., *British Policy Towards Wartime Resistance in Yugoslavia and Greece*, pp. 69, 75.

30. See, for example, Robert Lee Wolff, *The Balkans in Our Time*, Cambridge MA, Harvard University Press, 1956, pp. 449-74.

31. For a candid account by a participant, see "Statement by Brigadier Sir Fitzroy Maclean," in Auty and Clogg, eds., *British Policy Towards Wartime Resistance in Yugoslavia and Greece*, pp. 221-28.

32. Whether Churchill did or did not officially press for a Balkan priority in World War II is much disputed. Several writers believe he did, several others say not. See for example, F. W. D. Deakin, "The Myth of an Allied Landing in the Balkans during the Second World War (with particular reference to Yugoslavia)," in Auty and Clogg, eds., *British Policy Toward Wartime Resistance in Yugoslavia and Greece*, pp. 93-116. Much seems to depend upon a distinction between Churchill's *preferences* and his actual *policies* as shaped in the light of American opposition (and Soviet unresponsiveness) in 1944. Whatever the case, from the standpoint of the potential offered for Allied political warfare operations, the consequences were the same. The resources needed were simply not available.

33. Balfour, *Propaganda in War 1939-1945*, p. 96.

34. Bill Mauldin, *Up Front*, New York NY, Henry Holt and Co., 1945, p. 30.

35. Kris and Speier, *German Radio Propaganda*, p. 211.
36. Casey, *The Secret War Against Hitler*, p. 116.
37. Lochner, ed., *The Goebbels Diaries 1942-1943*, 1948, p. 535.
38. Colville, *The Fringes of Power*, pp. 581-82.
39. Mansell, *Let Truth Be Told*, pp. 174-76.
40. For evidence on how often, at what levels, and on what terms the "hope clause" issue was debated see Lockhart, *Comes the Reckoning*, pp. 158, 289, 330, 372-73. The "Supplementary Essay" by Richard Crossman in Lerner, *Psychological Warfare Against Nazi Germany*, is illuminating on this topic.
41. Hansard, May 10, 1940.

9   THE COLD WAR

1. David Thomson, *England in the Twentieth Century*, Harmondsworth/ Baltimore, Penguin, 1968, p. 237.
2. To Hugh Dalton on September 9, 1946, as cited in Alan Bullock, *Ernest Bevin: Foreign Secretary*, London/New York, Norton, 1983, p. 311.
3. Ibid., p. 25.
4. Ibid., p. 8.
5. Ambassador Jefferson Caffery to Secretary of State Marshall, July 3, 1947, in *Foreign Relations of the US*, 1947 (3), pp. 308-09, as cited in Bullock, *Ernest Bevin*, p. 423.
6. Bullock, *Ernest Bevin*, p. 540.
7. Ibid., p. 220.
8. Lockhart, *Comes the Reckoning*, p. 365.
9. For an eyewitness account of Stalin's role in the formation of the Cominform, see Milovan Djilas, *Conversations with Stalin*, New York NY, Harcourt, Brace & World, 1962, pp. 127-29; 132.
10. See Clive Rose, *Campaigns Against Western Defence: NATO's Adversaries and Critics*, London, Macmillan/Royal United Services Institute, 1985. Part 2, "Adversaries: International Front Organizations and Soviet Peace Campaigns," offers concise, well-documented historical perspective on the prewar and Cold War origins of the present Soviet use of these instruments. For a listing of the Fronts in the 1980s, see *Soviet International Fronts*, US Department of State Publication 9360, Washington DC, August 1983.
11. Royal Institute of International Affairs, *Documents on International Affairs: 1947-1948*, edited by Margaret Carlyle, London, 1952. pp. 122-46.
12. Address to Congress, March 12, 1947, *Congressional Record*, Washington DC, USGPO.
13. Bullock, *Ernest Bevin*, p. 527.
14. For information on (later Sir) Christopher Mayhew and a brief summary of the major operations, see Lyn Smith, "Covert British Propaganda: The Information Research Department: 1947-77," *Millenium: Journal of International Studies* (UK), vol. 9, no. 1, 1980, pp. 67-83. The judgment on quality of the

products is my own, based on occasional access to some of them over several decades.

15. For a sensitive memoir by a participant, see William Barrett, *The Truants: Adventures Among the Intellectuals*, New York NY, Anchor Press/ Doubleday, 1982. On communist influence in the American foreign affairs community, see Alan Weinstein, *Perjury: The Hiss-Chambers Case*, New York NY, Vintage/Random House, 1978, 1979. For an account by the head of the Federal Bureau of Investigation unit responsible for counterespionage, see Robert J. Lamphere and Tom Schachtman, *The FBI-KGB War: A Special Agent's Story*, New York NY, Random House, 1986.

16. John Lewis Gaddis, *Strategies of Containment: A Critical Appraisal of Postwar American National Security Policy*, New York NY/Oxford, Oxford University Press, 1982, p. 15.

17. For an exploration of the philosophical origins of the American world outlook, including its streak of messianism, in comparison to communist perspectives, see Reinhold Niebuhr, *The Irony of American History*, New York NY, Charles Scribners's Sons, 1952.

18. Gaddis, *Strategies of Containment*, p. 47.

19. Ibid., p. 48.

20. *Negotiations For an Effective Partnership: A Study of the Negotiations between the American Committee for Liberation from Bolshevism and Leaders of the Emigration from the USSR to Create a Central Emigre Organization for Anti-Bolshevik Activity*, June 30, 1956, p. 171, American Committee for Liberation document, unpublished. (On AmComLib's status and funding, see below.)

21. The classic statement of "containment" appeared, in public, as an article, by George Kennan, writing as X, "The Sources of Soviet Conduct," *Foreign Affairs* (New York NY), vol. 25, no. 4, July 1947, pp. 566-82.

22. General A. C. Wedemeyer, US Army (ret.), in a letter to the editors of *Commentary* (New York NY), January 1986, pp. 8-9.

23. Robert E. Sherwood, *Roosevelt and Hopkins: An Intimate History*, New York NY, Grosset & Dunlap, 1948, 1950, p. 951n.

24. Bullock, *Ernest Bevin*, p. 404.

25. For a description, from the perspective of a former Deputy Director of the CIA, see Ray S. Cline, *Secrets, Spies, and Scholars: Blueprint of the Essential CIA*, Washington DC, Acropolis Books, 1976, pp. 97-104. For documents, see William M. Leary, ed., *The Central Intelligence Agency: History and Documents*, Montgomery AL, University of Alabama Press, 1984.

26. Two memoirs offer both general background and a participant account of Radio Free Europe and Radio Liberty: Cord Meyer, *Facing Reality: From World Federalism to the CIA*, New York NY, Harper & Row, 1980, and Sig Mickelson, *America's Other Voice: The Story of Radio Free Europe and Radio Liberty*, New York NY, Praeger, 1983. Both books, I suspect, tend to overstate the role at the outset of US Government agencies, and to understate that of RFE's parent organization, the privately incorporated Committee for Free Europe. The political influence at the Eisenhower White House of several of the committee's

board members, notably C. D. Jackson and Lucius Clay, was formidable, and few US government officials were willing or able to challenge them, even if they had wanted to.

27. Most international broadcasters, including Radio Free Europe, carry out audience research and occasionally circulate reports based upon it. Interested scholars can usually obtain access to the reports upon application to the respective parent organizations.

28. John W. Henderson, *The United States Information Agency*, New York NY/London, Praeger, 1969, p. 164.

29. Historians may differ as to *why* Russia is and long has been expansionist; looking at a map, it is difficult to dispute the simple fact that Russia *is* expansionist. For a discussion by a pair of modern strategic analysts, see Rebecca V. Strode and Colin S. Gray, "The Imperial Dimension of Soviet Military Power," *Problems of Communism* (Washington DC) vol. 30, no. 6 (November-December 1981), pp. 1-15. For an appraisal by an earlier observer, accredited to the Imperial Russian Court in 1588, see Giles Fletcher, *Of the Rus Commonwealth* (London, 1591), facsimile edition, Cambridge MA, Harvard University Press, 1961.

10   TODAY AND THE FUTURE

1. See the Introductory Essays by Michael Howard and Bernard Brodie to Carl von Clausewitz, *On War*, edited and translated by Howard and Paret. For Clausewitz' views on the uses of history, see book 2, ch. 5, p. 156.

2. For a fresh appraisal of something which may seem self-evident, see Paul Johnson, *Modern Times: The World from the Twenties to the Eighties*, New York NY/London, Harper and Row, 1983.

3. For a reminder of the relevance of Dickerson's observation to modern times, by an American constitutional scholar, see Walter Berns, "In Times of Crisis How Much Power Does the President Have?" *The Washington Times*, June 3, 1987.

4. For an exploration of this subject from a non-Marxist philosophical position, see Patrick Gardiner, *The Nature of Historical Explanation*, London/ New York NY, Oxford University Press, 1980 (1952).

5. *Pravda*, June 20, 1950, as cited in Leites, *A Study of Bolshevism*, p. 67.

6. See Richard Pipes, *US-Soviet Relations in the Era of Detente*, Boulder CO, Westview, 1981, ch. 6 "Why the Soviet Union Thinks It Could Fight and Win a Nuclear War," as amplified by the same author's "Team B: The Reality Behind the Myth," *Commentary* (New York NY), October 1986, pp. 25-40. Vadim Zagladin, Deputy Chief of the International Department of the CPSU, in a Moscow press conference on June 25, 1988, offered a recent confirmation of the continued Soviet adherence to a concept of victory when he announced, "While we rejected nuclear war and struggled to prevent it, we nevertheless based

our policy on the possibility of winning one." (As reported by Michael Parks in the *Los Angeles Times*, June 26, 1988.)

7. For an authoritative statement, used as a text in the system of party higher education, see V. V. Zagladin, *Mezhdunarodnoye Kommunisticheskoye Dvizhe- niye: Ocherk Strategii i Taktiki*, (The International Communist Movement: Sketch of Strategy and Tactics), 2 vols., second edition, revised and supplemented, Moscow, Politizdat, 1972.

8. An English-language translation of the current program, adopted at the 27th Party Congress in March 1986, appears in the US Foreign Broadcast In- formation Service *Daily Report*, FBIS-SOV-86-046, Monday, 10 March 1986, vol. 3, no. 046, supplement 051. The citation appears on p. 06.

9. The *Dictionary of Military and Associated Terms* has no entries for *victory* or *defeat*. Since the dictionary is agreed usage for NATO forces, unless otherwise noted, the omission is presumably common policy.

10. The *Dictionary of Military Terms* does use the term enemy, if only adjectivally, as in enemy capabilities. There is no entry for *enemy* as a noun.

11. Benjamin Franklin, "Rules by Which a Great Empire May be Reduced to a Small One," *Gentleman's Magazine* (London), September 1773, vol. 43, p. 441.

12. A senior NSC staffer in the first Reagan administration has observed, "I can recall no instance during the two years that I served on the National Security Council when this matter [propaganda] came up for serious discussion." Richard Pipes, "Dealing With the Russians," in Arnold Horelick, ed., *US-Soviet Relations: The Next Phase*, Ithaca NY/London, Cornell University Press, (Rand/ UCLA Center for the Study of Soviet International Behavior), 1986, p. 283.

SELECTED BIBLIOGRAPHY

Alexiev, Alex. *Soviet Nationalities in German Wartime Strategy, 1941-1945*. Santa Monica CA, Rand Corporation, August 1982. An instructive account of one of the outstanding examples in modern history of political blindness and confusion in the management of emigre relations during military hostilities. Also useful for its reminder of the magnitude and diversity of defection from the Soviet cause.

Andrew, Christopher. *Her Majesty's Secret Service: The Making of the British Intelligence Community*. New York NY, Viking, 1986. A very thorough, carefully documented, well-balanced book, mainly concerned with intelligence collection and analysis, but useful to students of political warfare for coverage of foreign propaganda and disinformation operations against Britain, and of Britain's erratic efforts to assess and counter them.

Arendt, Hannah. *The Origins of Totalitarianism*, second edition, with added prefaces. New York NY, Harcourt Brace Jovanovich, 1971. First published in 1951 by a German refugee scholar who saw, in retrospect, an essential congruence between the Nazi and communist variants of totalitarianism. Despite numerous efforts to explain the phenomenon away, it is still with us, though in further modified forms. Arendt's book remains one of the best efforts to describe it in intellectually rigorous terms.

Auty, Phyllis, and Clogg, Richard, eds. *British Policy Toward Wartime Resistance in Yugoslavia and Greece*. New York NY, Harper & Row, 1975. A revealing, sometimes partisan, still incomplete, but very useful recounting by a group of surviving participants of the British political warfare campaign of World War II in the Balkans. Much of the discussion turns on the issue of radical versus conservative approaches. The Afterword, "Thirty Years After," by G. H. N. Seton-Watson, is helpful although necessarily tentative as a summing up, given the continued embargo on SOE files.

Balfour, Michael. *Propaganda in War 1939-1945: Organisations, Policies, and Publics, in Britain and Germany*. London, Routledge

Kegan Paul, 1979. A carefully researched, generously documented account of German and Anglo-American propaganda organizations and operations. The author is an English academic who served in the Political Warfare Executive and as Deputy Chief of Intelligence, SHAEF Psychological Warfare Division.

Barrett, William. *The Truants: Adventures Among the Intellectuals*. New York NY, Anchor Press/Doubleday, 1982. An introspective account, by a former editor of *Partisan Review*, of the intellectual odyssey of an influential sector of the American literary elite, as they shifted under the effect of Stalin's abuses from various forms of pro-Soviet feeling to become what was known as the anti-Stalinist Left. Useful to students of political warfare for the insights into the circulation of attitudes and ideas within a Western intellectual elite and the key role played by a few small-circulation "little" magazines.

Berdyaev, Nicholas. *The Origins of Russian Communism*. Ann Arbor MI, University of Michigan Press, 1966. First published (in Russian, 1937) by a Russian-emigre press in Paris. A cogent description of the twin roots—Byzantine and Marxist—of the modern Soviet world outlook. The author was a leading Russian academic, well versed in Marxist dialectics as well as classical Russian philosophy. Recommended for anyone interested in tracing the philosophical origins of modern Soviet agitation and propaganda.

Bittman, Ladislav. *The KGB and Soviet Disinformation: An Insider's View*. McLean VA, Pergamon-Brassy's, 1985. A scholarly account, based upon personal experience in the Czech intelligence service, supplemented by subsequent research in the West. Particularly valuable for its account of the principles and practices of KGB coordination and control in Eastern Europe. The author is a Charles University-educated lawyer who left Czechoslovakia after the 1968 Soviet invasion.

Briggs, Asa. *The History of Broadcasting in the United Kingdom*, 3 vols. London/New York/Toronto, Oxford University Press, 1970. The definitive work, offering a mine of detailed information for the researcher as well as perceptive insights. Volume 3, *The War of Words*, covers World War II. Students lacking time for the full treatment in these volumes may wish to refer instead to the Mansell book cited below.

Bruce Lockhart, R. H. *Comes the Reckoning*. London, Putnam, 1947. A vivid, forthright, and occasionally disillusioned account of British and American political warfare operations during World War II by a journalist who headed Britain's Political Warfare Executive. The author was a friend and associate of Lord Beaverbrook, who often lent him political support.

Bruntz, George G. *Allied Propaganda and the Collapse of the German Empire in 1918*. Hoover War Library Publications No. 13, Stanford University Press/Oxford University Press, 1938. A scholarly attempt, in retrospect, to assess the effects created by military and civilian operators through various media, particularly balloon drops.

Buchan, John. *Cromwell*. London, Sphere Books, 1970. A perceptive and scholarly biography of an English leader with an instinctive feel for the uses, and limits, of radical politics in war. The author was a statesman, and writer, who served as public relations adviser to Lloyd George during World War I.

Casey, William. *The Secret War Against Hitler*. Washington DC, Regnery Gateway, 1988. A well-informed participant's description of and commentary on Anglo-American political warfare and special operations in Europe during World War II. Particularly valuable for its coverage of issues like unconditional surrender as applied to propaganda policy at both tactical and strategic levels. Also unusual for its sensitivity to the problems of linking propaganda, special operations, and conventional force to the use of strategic bombardment. The author was a staff aide to OSS Chief David Bruce in wartime London, and served as Director of the CIA in the Reagan administration.

Cave Brown, Anthony. *C: The Secret Life of Sir Stewart Graham Menzies, Spymaster to Winston Churchill*. New York NY, Macmillan, 1987. Major biography of a leading and hitherto shadowy figure in World War II. Sheds new and stronger light on the problems inherent in coordinating political warfare and intelligence collection in wartime, managing agents of influence in allied countries, and developing channels to opposition figures in enemy leadership circles. The author is a journalist specializing in coverage of intelligence and deception operations.

Clausewitz, Carl von. *On War*, Paret and Howard translation. Princeton NJ, Princeton University Press, 1975. This elegant edition of a classic first published in 1832 corrects errors and omissions in earlier translations and offers several insightful commentaries. Clausewitz was sensitive to the role of politics, but his essential strategic concept accorded a key role to overwhelming armed force aimed at the critical point (*schwerpunkt*) in the enemy defense. Students of political warfare may want to compare such concepts to the "indirect" strategy advocated by Liddell Hart.

Cline, Ray S. *Secrets, Spies, and Scholars: Blueprint of the Essential CIA.* Washington DC, Acropolis Books, 1976. Offers a description, from the perspective of a senior US intelligence manager, of the inception and evolution of American strategic intelligence, including the National Security Council's various subcommittees developed under the Truman and Eisenhower administrations to fight the Cold War.

Cruickshanks, Charles. *The Fourth Arm: Psychological Warfare 1939-1945.* London, Oxford University Press, 1981. An academic study, summarizing much of what is known from memoirs and the official records released to date on Allied psychological operations in support of military campaigns. The author concludes that radio broadcasting, particularly BBC, was probably the most effective medium.

Delmer, Sefton. *Black Boomerang.* New York NY, Viking, 1962. One of the few relatively forthright accounts by an expert of a major black broadcasting operation conducted during and in support of large-scale military operations. Instructive for its description of the problems inherent in working with a mix of personnel who may be animated by quite different motives. Although aware of the limitations, Delmer still believed in retrospect that black operations contributed much to the disorientation of German morale.

Donne, John. *Selected Prose: Chosen by Evelyn Simpson, Edited by Helen Gardner and Timothy Healy.* London, Oxford University Press, 1967. Essays, sermons, and political satires by a Jacobean clergyman, diplomatic agent, and polemicist. Donne is best known today for his privately circulated and posthumously published poetry. Both poetry and prose offer rich examples of the rhetorical techniques Donne introduced to the English literary idiom as a propagandist for James I. See also the introductory essay in T. S. Healy, SJ, ed., *John Donne: Ignatius His Conclave*, Oxford University Press, 1969.

Doty, Richard G. *Money of the World.* New York NY, Grosset and Dunlap, 1978. A solidly researched study, by a curator of the Smithsonian Institution's coin collection. The numerous illustrations include useful examples of coinage and paper used for propaganda purposes.

Drachkovitch, Milorad M. *Biographical Dictionary of the Comintern.* Stanford CA, Hoover Institution, 1973. A carefully researched Who's Who of Marxist-Leninist political warfare operators and their collaborators between the two World Wars.

Dzirkals, Lilita; Gustafson, Thane; and Johnson, A. Ross. *The Media and Intra-Elite Communication in the USSR.* Santa Monica CA,

Rand Corporation, 1983. Offers a rare and convincing look at the links between CPSU policymakers and the chief editors of Soviet media. Based upon a series of interviews with emigre Soviet journalists. The main emphasis is on Soviet domestic media.

Fernandez-Armesto, Felipe. *The Spanish Armada: The Experience of War in 1588.* London, Oxford University Press, 1988. New documentary evidence, particularly from Spanish archives, covering morale and motivation as well as strategy, naval tactics, and weapons. Chapter 2, "The Image of the Enemy," concludes that the war, which had not started as a war of religion, soon became one, and "in Spain, the notion that Englishmen were irremediably tainted with heresy was strengthened by the foregone conclusions of the Inquisition. In England, Foxe's efforts to inspire horror of the Inquisition as an internal 'engine of tyrrany' were confirmed." It was, as well, the images of the rival monarchs, Philip and Elizabeth, that fixed the hostile perceptions on religious lines.

Fletcher, Giles. *Of the Rus Commonwealth* (London, 1591), facsimile edition. Cambridge MA, Harvard University Press, 1961. A systematic account of Russian politics, society, economy, and international conduct in the sixteenth century. Remarkable for the similarities it offers to modern Soviet conditions, of which the accounts of Russian imperial dominance, mistrust, religious orthodoxy, and repression in occupied areas are most striking. Fletcher wrote the account for his government (which hoped for commercial advantage and possible strategic assistance from Russia against Spain) while serving as Ambassador to Moscow in 1588. Suppressed by Burghley (who feared damage to his trade initiative), it later surfaced and served as a basis for a history of Muscovy written by Milton. A useful reminder for modern students of the enduring nature of national styles in political war.

Foot, M. R. D. *Resistance.* London, Grenada, 1978. The standard (albeit incomplete) source, by an officer in Britain's World War II Special Operations Executive, on British efforts to disrupt the German occupation of Europe through support of emigre governments and underground resistance. Instructive on the problems of tactical coordination in large-scale political warfare, particularly when read in conjunction with the accounts, by Bruce Lockhart and Sefton Delmer, of covert propaganda operations.

Ford, Corey. *Donovan of OSS.* Boston, Little Brown, 1971. There are more recent and more detailed accounts of the formation and World War II activities of the US covert action capability, but for students with limited time this is still probably the best introduction. See also the book by Donald F. Troy cited below.

Gaddis, John Lewis. *Strategies of Containment: A Critical Appraisal of Postwar American National Security Policy*. New York NY/London, Oxford University Press, 1982. Still probably the standard account of US efforts to fight the Cold War by creating a national-level center for policy coordination, planning, and operational control of national strategy after World War II.

Ganley, Gladys D., and Ganley, Oswald H. *Global Political Fallout: The First Decade of the VCR 1976-1985*. Cambridge MA, Harvard University Center for Information Policy Research, 1987. An early but carefully researched study of a major new medium for international political communication. The authors conclude that video-cassettes "will have an important, perhaps critical, global political impact." Chapter 9, "Varieties of Global Political Acts Involving VCRs and Videocassettes," and Appendix B, "Penetration Figures: Broadcast Signal and VCR Distribution for All Countries as of December 31, 1983," will be useful to students of political warfare technology, not only for the information presented but also as examples of the kind of ongoing research needed by commanders for planning.

Gardiner, Patrick. *The Nature of Historical Explanation*. Oxford/London/New York NY, Oxford University Press, 1980 (1952). A brief, clearly written investigation of the logical character of explanations usually provided by historians. The author argues, "To understand history and the writing of it the scientific conception of knowledge must be discarded, and a distinct type of knowledge must be recognized: this type of knowledge has been variously named—it is termed sometimes 'insight', sometimes 'intuition' or 'empathy' and sometimes 'recreating past experience.' . . . This form of knowledge is appropriate to history and it is the only appropriate form of knowledge. . . . History is about what happened on particular occasions. It is not about what usually happened or what always happens under certain circumstances; for this we go to science. . . . The historian [thus], like the general or the statesman, tends to assess rather than to conclude." Useful for anyone involved in political warfare with Marxist-Leninists and other totalitarian ideologists whose propaganda positions depend upon exaggerated claims to scientifically grounded historical analysis.

Garlinski, Josef. *Poland, SOE and the Allies*. London, Allen Unwin, 1969. Describes the changing political background against which the operations of SOE and Section VI of the Polish General Staff (in London) were carried out in trying to support the AK (Home Army) operations in Poland against the foreign occupation. Gives a realistic and dispassionate view of the UK-US decision at Tehran in 1943 to surrender the fate of Poland to the Soviets, but concludes that the English and American leaders got the worst of the trade-off between their choice of military expediency over longer-term political aims.

George, Alexander L. *Propaganda Analysis: A Study of Inferences Made from Nazi Propaganda in World War II*. Evanston IL, Row, Peterson and Co., 1959. This rigorous study—launched after World War II—involved a comparison of captured German documents with the assessments reached by Allied intelligence analysts reading Nazi propaganda output during the war for clues to underlying German intentions. It was intended to help clarify some of the conceptual issues facing Western foreign policy analysts seeking to assess Soviet intentions from the monitoring of Soviet open sources. Still useful for its systematic approach to the problems and opportunities inherent in the use of propaganda analysis for intelligence assessment.

Goebbels, Joseph. *The Goebbels Diaries*, edited by Louis Lochner. New York NY, Doubleday, 1948.

——————————————. *The Goebbels Diaries 1939-1941*, edited by Fred Taylor. New York NY, 1982.

——————————————. *Final Entries 1945: The Diaries of Joseph Goebbels*, edited by Hugh Trevor-Roper. New York NY, Putnam, 1978. Taken together, these personal records of Hitler's propaganda minister offer a unique insight into the mind of a man who conducted strategic propaganda operations of a hitherto unknown scale and intensity, using the vast technical and cultural wealth of a highly developed industrial power, and enjoying an unprecedented degree of authority in commanding resources. The cumulative effect of these pages on a student of propaganda is appalling, but instructive.

Gross, Babette. *Willi Muenzenberg: A Political Biography*, translated by Marian Jackson. East Lansing MI, Michigan State University Press, 1974. A partisan but valuable account by his widow of one of the most innovative and skillful propagandists in modern history. Muenzenberg was murdered, probably on Stalin's orders, in World War II after serving for over a decade as Chief of the Comintern's West European agitprop operations. His skill in the formation and deployment of political fronts merits study by any serious operator.

Hansen, Allen. *US Information Agency: Public Diplomacy in the Computer Age*. New York NY, Praeger, 1984. An account, by an experienced USIA officer, of the official, publicly acknowledged arm of US information and cultural programming, with a discussion of current problems and opportunities.

Henderson, John W. *The United States Information Agency*. New York, Praeger, 1969. The standard history of America's overt, official oversea information and cultural arm. Now dated, but still useful for documentation and description of USIA's first twenty years.

Hollander, Paul. *Political Pilgrims: Travels of Western Intellectuals to the Soviet Union, China, and Cuba 1928-78*. London/New York NY, Oxford University Press, 1981. Case studies by an American sociologist of a political warfare tactic developed and long used to good effect by the International Departments of most ruling communist parties.

Howe, Ellic. *The Black Game*. London, Michael Joseph, 1982. Serves as a companion volume to the Delmer book, recounting British use of print media, produced during World War II in London but purporting to come from resistance elements within German-occupied Europe. A valuable source on technical and organizational problems inherent in the clandestine use of print media, even though modern printing techniques are now quite different, at least in developed industrial societies. Howe headed the operation.

Hyde, H. Montgomery. *Secret Intelligence Agent*. London, Constable, 1982. Of several biographies and accounts covering the operations of the British Security Co-ordination Office in New York during early World War II, this is probably the most authoritative. Particularly useful as an account by a key participant of inter-Allied public diplomacy and counter-propaganda operations against hostile third powers in an Anglo-Saxon wartime setting. Includes an appendix by Hyde's chief, Sir William Stephenson, on British involvement in the creation of the US Office of Strategic Services.

Jaeckel, Eberhard. *Hitler in History*. Hanover VT, University of Brandeis Press, 1984. A lucid and concise exploration by a modern German historian of Hitler's mind. Helpful to students of propaganda for its comparison of Hitler's personal vision—which he never altered—with his frequent shifts in propaganda posture.

Johnson, Paul. *Modern Times: The World from the Twenties to the Eighties*. New York NY/London, Harper & Row, 1983. *Zeitgeist*, or Spirit of the Times, is an elusive but critical element for any commander seeking to assess the context within which he may have to conduct, or defend himself against, political warfare. This book is probably as good—and readable—an appraisal as we are likely to find on the seminal ideas that have shaped the *Zeitgeist* of our own times.

Johnson, Paul. *Elizabeth I.* New York NY, Holt Rinehart & Winston, 1974. A recent, highly readable biography of an outstanding practitioner of the art of political war. Recommended reading for anyone inclined to think that propaganda is foreign to the best traditions of English-speaking peoples, or doubtful that political warfare is a powerful instrument of strategy.

Kitrinos, Robert W. "International Department of the CPSU." *Problems of Communism* (Washington DC), September-October 1984. One of the few accounts available in English of an organization that still represents the Sovietized version of the global political warfare aspirations of the old Communist International—a subject much in need of further study by those interested in political war, particularly in light of CPSU General Secretary Gorbachev's foreign policy innovations.

Kris, Ernst, and Speier, Hans. *German Radio Propaganda: Report on Home Broadcasts During the War.* London, Oxford University Press, 1944. A composite of research papers produced by the Research Project on Totalitarian Communication at the New York-based New School for Social Research during World War II. Using the BBC "Daily Digest of Foreign Broadcasts" for the period to the end of 1943, the work offers a valuable example of systematic propaganda analysis under wartime conditions. Kris had worked for BBC Radio Monitoring, and Speier subsequently became Chief German Analyst of the US Foreign Broadcast Intelligence Service.

Lamphere, Robert J., and Schachtman, Tom. *The FBI-KGB War: A Special Agent's Story.* New York NY, Random House, 1986. Recounts, from a counterintelligence viewpoint, the US government's efforts to identify, apprehend, and convict Soviet agents of influence operating in Washington after World War II. Particularly valuable for its sober description of the problems faced by a democracy in addressing this particular aspect of political warfare.

Lasswell, Harold; Casey, Ralph; and Smith, Bruce Lannes, eds. *Propaganda and Promotional Activities: An Annotated Bibliography.* Chicago IL and London, University of Chicago Press, 1969. A standard reference, now dated but useful for its coverage of the literature of the time.

Leary, William M., ed. *The Central Intelligence Agency: History and Documents.* Montgomery AL, University of Alabama Press, 1984. Probably the most reliable summary in the public domain. Includes a brief but well-documented history written by Ann Karalekas in 1974 for the Church Committee of the US Senate, plus a selection of official documents dating from OSS days to 1981. Has a short but quite useful bibliography, index, and list of acronyms. Particularly helpful for the evidence it offers of semantic usage in both the Legislative and Executive Branches.

Le Bon, Gustave. *The Crowd: A Study of the Popular Mind*, translation and introduction by R. K. Merton. New York NY, Viking Press, 1960. First published in 1895, this study by an early French sociologist drew on the author's observation of European popular attitudes toward the charismatic personalities of the Bonapartes, Napoleon I and his nephew Napoleon III. The book had a strong influence on European totalitarian leaders of a later generation, notably Lenin, Hitler, and Goebbels.

Leites, Nathan. *A Study of Bolshevism*. Glencoe IL, Free Press, 1953. One of the early attempts by American scholars to describe in intellectually rigorous terms the essence of Soviet communist attitudes and outlook. The longevity and tenure of many of the Soviet officials responsible for political warfare, such as Mikhail Suslov, Boris Ponomarev, and their surviving senior associates such as Vadim Zagladin, make the work still well worth reading.

Lenin, V. I. *Selected Works*, 12 vols. New York NY, International Publishers, 1937. Incomplete, but the most readily available source in English. There are five editions of the complete works, in Russian, published in Moscow, of which the second and fourth have appeared in other languages, including English. Several editions are indexed, none very reliably. For a selection of Lenin's writings on propaganda, see V. Viktorov and B. Zaslavskiy, eds., *V. I. Lenin: O Propaganda i Agitatsii*, Moscow, Gospolitizdat, 1962, second edition. Some familiarity with Lenin's style of slash-and-burn polemics is essential for any student of Soviet propaganda, including the most recent versions.

Lerner, Daniel. *Psychological Warfare Against Nazi Germany: The Sykewar Campaign, D-Day to VE-Day*. Cambridge MA, MIT Press, 1949/1971. An analysis, in retrospect, by an American social scientist who served with the Psywar Detachment of SHAPE operating against the Axis powers in Europe. Useful for its description of the conceptual framework within which programming was generated, and for its discussion of the limitations imposed by the Allied political leaders in their unbending insistence upon a policy of unconditional surrender.

Liddell Hart, B. H. *Strategy*, second revised edition. New York NY, Praeger/Signet Reprint, 1974. A classic statement of the English, or "indirect," school of strategic thought. It includes (characteristically) a continual and careful account of the psychological dimensions in both strategy and tactics. Students of political war may find this approach a useful contrast to the German, or "direct," school of strategy attributed to Clausewitz.

Lloyd George, David. *War Memoirs*, 2 vols. London, Odhams Press Limited, 1942 (1936). Noteworthy for the insights into the political style and attitudes of one of the few democratic leaders in modern times who oversaw and pushed through a successful campaign of strategic political warfare. The specific passages relating to the campaign are in volume 2, pp. 1873-74.

Mansell, Gerrard. *Let Truth Be Told: 50 Years of BBC External Broadcasting*. London, Weidenfeld and Nicolson, 1982. An officially inspired but nonetheless frank account by a long-time BBC staffer. The account of Britain's creation, almost from scratch, of a highly effective, world-class international broadcasting capability under the pressure of war and military disaster is a useful lesson which the English-speaking world has reason to admire but should not be compelled to repeat.

May, Arthur J. *The Passing of the Hapsburg Monarchy 1914-1918*, 2 vols. Philadelphia PA, University of Pennsylvania Press, 1968. A study in depth, based on Austro-Hungarian state archives and contemporary newspapers, and diplomatic archives of Germany and the Allies. Particularly useful for its integration of domestic and international politics with military operations including propaganda.

Marx, Karl, and Engels, Friedrich. *The Communist Manifesto*, Introduction and notes by A. J. P. Taylor. Harmondsworth/Baltimore, 1967. First published, in German, in 1848 as the alleged proclamation of a then non-existent political movement. Worthy of attention by students of political warfare today for its significance as one of the touchstones of modern radical politics, and for its spirit of intransigent class hatred. The extended introduction by Taylor is one of the best brief critiques available in English.

Mayer, S. L., ed. *Signal: Hitler's Wartime Picture Magazine*. Englewood Cliffs NJ, Prentice-Hall, 1976. Selected reprints from a large-format, glossy, up-scale product of German World War II propaganda in occupied Europe, published fortnightly in 20 languages, with a peak circulation of three million copies. A noteworthy example of the level of technical proficiency and political sophistication that a totalitarian propaganda operation can achieve, and a useful corrective for the mistaken view that all Nazi propaganda was uniformly crude and simplistic.

Meyer, Cord. *Facing Reality: From World Federalism to the CIA*. New York NY, Harper & Row, 1980. Memoirs, necessarily less than complete, but nonetheless authentic, of the senior CIA official responsible for building one of the most effective covert information media in modern times. The assessment, in retrospect, of Radio Free Europe's role in the Polish and Hungarian uprisings of 1956 is relatively candid, balanced, and authoritative.

Mickelson, Sig. *America's Other Voice: The Story of Radio Free Europe and Radio Liberty*. New York NY, Praeger, 1983. The only reasonably complete account in print of the two radios, covering both their early covert phase and their operations since 1972 as openly funded assets of the US government. The author was a senior executive of CBS before he became President of RFE/RL, Inc., the American corporate parent organization.

Mihalka, Michael. *German Strategic Deception in the 1930s*. Santa Monica CA, Rand Corporation Note N-1557-NA, July 1980. Provides useful background on the strategic goals and political style that shaped German foreign propaganda operations prior to the outbreak of general war in 1939.

Milton, John. *Areopagitica*, in K. M. Burton, ed., *Prose Writings by John Milton*. London/New York NY, Everyman, 1958. A seminal statement, first published in 1644 by the English poet and diplomatist who counseled Oliver Cromwell on the uses of propaganda in statecraft. Milton insisted, in the face of contrary advice from Puritan fanatics, on establishing freedom of thought and a free press as essential features of the English-speaking style in political conflict. His principles still inform Western practice on this issue.

Nowak, Jan. *Courier From Warsaw*. Detroit MI, Wayne State University Press, 1982. One of the best accounts from the body of World War II resistance memoirs of life and death in an underground military and propaganda operation against an occupation army. The author, who served throughout the war as an officer in the Polish Home Army, began his resistance as a civilian producing and disseminating clandestine patriotic media. After the war he served for several decades as chief of the Polish Broadcast Service of Radio Free Europe.

O'Brien, William V. *The Conduct of a Just and Limited War*. New York NY, Praeger, 1983. A solidly researched study, in historical perspective, presenting a broad conceptual framework for the philosophical and moral issues raised by war. Propaganda—or the psychological instrument, to use O'Brien's term—is discussed in the context of limited war on pp. 232 and 236-37.

Oxford Companion to Classical Literature. London/New York NY, Oxford University Press, 1984. Contains a number of stimulating entries, including general articles, on such topics as Rhetoric, Oratory,

Satire, Theater, Education, and Army. Entries on Alexander, Alcibiades, Aristotle, Plato, and Caesar offer food for thought to anyone inclined to think that the arts of political warfare were invented by twentieth-century social scientists.

Pipes, Richard. *US-Soviet Relations in the Era of Detente*. Boulder CO, Westview, 1986. A compressed but carefully documented summation of the constants in Soviet foreign policy and strategic thought, based upon the author's historical studies and his contributions to US intelligence assessments. Useful for its citations of both Soviet and US sources. The author was Director of the Russian Research Center at Harvard University from 1968 to 1973 and has served in various consulting capacities with the US government, including chairing the group that produced the "Team B" report submitted to then CIA Director George Bush in 1976. (See "Team B: The Reality Behind the Myth," *Commentary* (New York NY), October 1986, pp. 25-40.)

Peters, J. *The Communist Party: A Manual on Organization*. New York NY, Workers Library/Bookmailer Reprint, no date. A bibliographic rarity, first published in the 1930s as a handbook for CPUSA organizers by a senior Comintern representative. Useful for its uncharacteristically explicit account of the need for both overt and covert party organizations, and for its statement of party organizational principles in an American context.

Read, Conyers. *Mr. Secretary Walsingham and the Policy of Queen Elizabeth*, 3 vols. Oxford, Clarendon Press, 1925. Reprint, New York NY, AMS Press, 1978.

——————————. *Lord Burghley and Queen Elizabeth*. London, Jonathan Cape, 1960.

——————————. *Mr. Secretary Cecil and Queen Elizabeth*. London, Jonathan Cape, 1955. The three-volume biography of Walsingham, with the two-volume companion biography of William Cecil (later Lord Burghley), is the classic source on statecraft and diplomacy practiced by Elizabeth's senior foreign policy staff. Both works focus on diplomacy, but also take account of intelligence collection, political influence operations, and some of the propaganda initiated and supervised by Burghley and Walsingham in their capacities as principal secretaries to the Privy Council (in effect, the Cabinet) of Elizabeth. The author was a University of Pennsylvania academic who served during World War II in the Office of Research and Analysis of the US Office of Strategic Services.

Rose, Clive. *Campaigns Against Western Defence: NATO's Adversaries and Critics*. London, Macmillan/Royal United Services Institute, 1985. Offers a useful overview of current Soviet political warfare operations throughout Western Europe, and a concise historical summary of the activities of several key instrumentalities, such as the international Front Organizations. The author was UK Ambassador to NATO 1979-82.

Selznik, Philip. *The Organizational Weapon: A Study of Bolshevik Strategy and Tactics*. New York NY, Arno Press, 1979. A reprint of a classic study derived from a Rand Corporation report of 1952 and first published by Free Press in 1960. The work is essential for an understanding of Soviet political warfare practices under Lenin and Stalin, but is also useful for the clarity and rigor of the conceptual framework and definitions.

Shultz, Richard H., and Godson, Roy. *Dezinformatsia: Active Measures in Soviet Strategy*. Washington DC, Pergamon-Brassey's, 1984. One of the best descriptions available in English of Moscow's conduct of political war in the early 1980s. Needs revision and expansion to account for recent changes in Soviet political leadership and foreign policy style, particularly for organizations like the CPSU International Department.

Speer, Albert. *Inside the Third Reich*, translated by Richard and Clara Winston. New York NY, Macmillan, 1979. Memoirs by Hitler's architect, who later took over major responsibilities for Germany's wartime industrial economy. Offers the student a useful reminder of the role played by architecture in the mobilization of a totalitarian society and the creation of an international image of relentless imperial power.

Staar, Richard F., ed. *Public Diplomacy: USA vs USSR*. Stanford CA, Hoover Institution Press, 1986. Offers a variety of perspectives, from both academics and operators, on some of the features of US and Soviet operations in the mid-1980s. For a useful discussion of the distinction between public diplomacy (aimed abroad) and public relations (for domestic consumption), see the exchange among Malone, Tuch, Lord, and Habib in chapter 7.

Steenberg, Sven. *Vlasov*. New York NY, Alfred A. Knopf, 1979. A revealing and dispassionate account by a German intelligence officer of the relations between the German authorities and a senior Soviet general officer who led the large numbers of former Soviet citizens fighting in alliance with the Wehrmacht during World War II. An interesting case study of how one totalitarian power managed—and

disastrously misused—emigre military formations from another totalitarian state.

Stuart, Sir Campbell. *Secrets of Crewe House: The Story of a Famous
Campaign*, second edition. London, Hodder and Stoughton, 1920.
An overly enthusiastic but nonetheless informative account by the
Deputy Chief of British propaganda operations against enemy areas
during World War I. One of the few insider accounts of a successful
strategic propaganda operation. Translated into German, Japanese,
and other languages, the book had a significant—and excessive—
influence abroad in the 1930s.

Sworakowski, Witold S. *The Communist International and Its Front
Organizations: A Research Guide and Checklist of Holdings in
American and European Libraries*. Stanford CA, Hoover Institution, 1965. A rich mine of valuable information, and a basic research
tool for all students of the period.

Taylor, A. J. P. *Beaverbrook*. New York NY, Simon and Schuster, 1972.
Full-dress biography of a Canadian financier who became one of
Britain's leading press lords, serving as Minister of Information in
World War I. Pages 144-48 provide a useful description of Beav-
erbrook's influence on the main fronts—home front, allied coun-
tries, and hostile nations—in Britain's political warfare. Many of
Beaverbrook's concepts and organizational solutions still inform
Anglo-American political warfare methods.

Treverton, Gregory F. *Covert Action: The Limits of Intervention in the
Postwar World*. New York, Basic Books, 1987. A skeptical, but not
totally negative, analysis from the American perspective of three
main categories of covert action: propaganda, political action, and
paramilitary operations. The author is a Fellow at Harvard University's Kennedy School of Government, who has drawn upon his
experience as a staff member in the 1970s of the congressional
committees of the US Congress investigating CIA operations.

Troy, Donald F. *Donovan and the CIA: A History of the Establishment
of the Central Intelligence Agency*. Frederick MD, University Publications of America, 1981. An official history completed by the
CIA in 1975 and released—with deletions—in 1981. Contains more
documentation than the Ford book, but lacks a sense of the international context.

US Central Intelligence Agency. *Soviet Covert Action and Propaganda*.
A study presented to the Oversight Subcommittee, Permanent Select
Committee on Intelligence, House of Representatives, February 6,
1980, by the Deputy Director of Operations, CIA. Appendix I to
Hearings before the Subcommittee, Ninety-sixth Congress, Second

Session. Washington DC, USGPO, 1980. The most recent in a series of such reports, offering a considered US estimate of the scope, funding, and achievements of Soviet strategic political warfare operations outside the continental United States.

US Department of the Army. *The Art and Science of Psychological Operations: Case Studies of Military Application*, 2 vols. Washington DC, USGPO, 1976. An extended collection of essays and reprinted articles from other sources, produced on contract by a civilian research organization. Contains a number of valuable first-hand accounts.

US Department of Defense. *Dictionary of Military and Associated Terms*, Joint Chiefs of Staff Publication 1. Washington DC, June 1979. Provides the authoritative definitions, used throughout the US Armed Forces (and, where indicated, NATO forces), of military terms, including those applicable in psychological warfare.

US Department of State. *Soviet International Fronts*, Publication No. 9360. Washington DC, US Department of State, 1983. A listing, showing organizational relationships and key personnel, compiled mainly from the voluminous publications of the Fronts. Helpful and reliable as a handy open-source reference.

Valiani, Leo. *The End of Austria-Hungary*. New York NY, Knopf, 1973. Standard work by a well-known Italian historian. Unusual among modern historical and foreign policy studies for the attention paid to the role of propaganda in wartime.

Vickers, Brian. *In Defence of Rhetoric*. Oxford, Clarendon Press, 1988. A recent, cogently argued presentation of the case for classical rhetoric as an enduring and positive aspect of the human condition. Argues that the human will is best directed to the good by means of rhetoric—the art of persuasive communication and the systematization of natural eloquence—and that the channel through which persuasion works is the power to feel (*affectus*, or passion) which the orator, painter, poet, or musician arouses in himself before transmitting it to his audience. A useful reminder of the need to consider both training and talent in recruitment.

Volkogonov, D. A. *Psikhologicheskaya voina: Podrivnie deistviya imperializma v oblasti obshchestnennovo soznaniya* (Psychological War: Subversive Activity of Imperialism in the Field of Social Consciousness.) Moscow, Voenizdat, 1983. A textbook for Soviet officer training courses, giving the official Red Army view of NATO psychological warfare. The author is one of the Deputy Chiefs of the Main Political Administration in the USSR Ministry of Defense.

Walzer, Michael. *Exodus and Revolution*. New York NY, Basic Books, 1984. An insightful and scholarly view in historical perspective, by a Harvard-based political scientist, of one of the main roots of Western radical thought.

Weeks, Albert, and Bodie, William, eds. *War and Peace: Soviet Russia Speaks*. New York NY/Washington DC, National Strategy Information Center, 1983. A useful collection of statements revealing the extent to which a xenophobic and self-righteous view of the world and the Soviet Union's place in it still pervades Soviet official discourse.

Weinstein, Alan. *Perjury: The Hiss-Chambers Case*. New York NY, Vintage/Random House, 1978. A richly-documented reprise, with benefit of many new sources, of the question, "Was Hiss really guilty?" (He was.) The book offers valuable evidence of the ways in which otherwise subtle and well-informed minds can be misled into a betrayal of trust by intellectual arrogance and misplaced idealism.

Williams, John. *The Other Battleground: The Home Fronts: Britain, France and Germany 1914-1918*. Chicago IL, Regnery, 1972. A well-documented study with a useful bibliography. One of the few dispassionate attempts to look at civilian morale among belligerents on a comparative basis, weighing the relative significance of various forms of radicalism. The attention accorded mass media as a new ingredient in morale is noteworthy.

Winkler, Alan M. *The Politics of Propaganda: The Office of War Information 1942-1945*. New Haven CT, Yale University Press, 1978. A full-scale scholarly study of OWI revealing, in its account of the domestic political pressures, ideological differences and differing policy perceptions bearing upon American operators of the day.

Zagladin, V. V. *Mezhdunarodnoye Kommunisticheskoye Dvizheniye: Ocherk Strategii i Taktiki*, (The International Communist Movement: Outline of Strategy and Tactics), 2 vols., second edition, revised and supplemented. Moscow, Politizdat, 1972. A definitive statement of the Soviet party line, and a text for use in party schools, written by a senior official, trained under Suslov and Ponomarev, of the CPSU International Department.

Zeman, Z. A. B. *Nazi Propaganda*. London/New York NY, Oxford University Press, 1964. One of the best analytical studies in print of the propaganda operations carried out by a major totalitarian power in both peace and war. A closely reasoned, solidly researched study.

INDEX

THE AUTHOR

Paul A. Smith, Jr, was a Senior Research Fellow at the US National Defense University in Washington DC in 1986-87. He has previously served with the US Information Agency as Chief Editor of the journal *Problems of Communism*, and as Chief of Soviet Area Research; with the US Census Bureau; and with the US Department of State, including assignments in Moscow, Washington, Paris, Munich, Trieste, and Bucharest. He holds degrees from Georgetown and Harvard Universities.

ON
POLITICAL
WAR

Text composed in Times Roman
Book design by Thomas Gill
Cover mechanical prepared by Alex Contreras
Display lines composed in Belwe Bold and Medium

Editorial clerk, Jim Zackrison
NDU Press editor, Thomas Gill